A Secular Bible Study

By Christy Knockleby

Houseful of Chaos Press
Sudbury, Ontario

Copyright © 2020

Houseful of Chaos Press

All Rights Reserved. No copying or reproduction of any portion of this book is permitted without the express written consent of the publisher.

Houseful of Chaos Press

996 Beverly Drive,

Sudbury, Ontario

P3E 4B5

email: msknockleby@gmail.com

ISBN: 978-1-7771685-0-6

Acknowledgements

I want to thank my awesome husband James for all his help on this book. Thank you to my parents for your encouragement and corrections. Thank you to my kids for listening to me talk about the Bible day in and day out. As well, I need to thank Eleen Kamas for her valuable input and my online students for all their inspiring questions during classes.

Thank you to Amanda Durkin for helping with the front cover. The picture on the front cover is from a 1591 woodcut by Georg Straub Konstanz. The illustration shows the gathering of manna in the wilderness with a horned Moses watching over. Picture is from: https://commons.wikimedia.org/wiki/Category:Manna#/media/File:Manna_1591.jpg

Thank you to Viktoriia Riabova for the map on page 7.

Contents

Introduction	1
Getting Familiar with the Bible	3
The Big Picture of the Bible	5
Stories of the Patriarchs	9
Stories of the Patriarchs Continued	12
The Exodus	14
Conquest of Canaan	17
Different Names for God	20
Ancient Heroes	22
Samuel	25
The Request for a King	28
David's Rise to Power	31
The Kingdom of David	34
An Aside – The Psalms	38
From One Kingdom to Two	39
The Omride's Gain Power	41
King Ahab is Doomed	43
Elijah and Elisha	45
Multiple Rulers are Overthrown	48
Vassals, Tributes and the Assyrian Crisis	51
An Aside - Reading 2 Kings	53
Hezekiah's Reforms and the Assyrians' Perspective	54
Josiah's Reforms	57
The Fall of Jerusalem	59
The Returnees and those that Remained Behind	62
Review	65
Ruth	67
Priestly Code and the Holiness Code	69
Jonah	72
An Aside - Proverbs	74
Job and the Problem of Evil	76
Job, God, and the Advocate	80
Two Stories of Creation	83
Noah to the Tower of Babel	86
Maccabees to Herod the Great	89
Daniel	92
Entering the "Common Era"	96
The New Testament & Jesus' Birth	98
Mark	102
The Pharisees and Sadducees	106
Matthew's Sermon on the Mount	107
Parables from Luke	110
Crucifixion	113
Implications of a Crucified Messiah	115
Jerusalem Community	117
Mission to the Gentiles	119
Letters from Paul	121
Paul and the Problems He Helped Cause	124
Revelations	128
A Few Last Thoughts	131
Index	132
Selective Bibliography	133
Vocabulary Review	134
Memory Match Cards	135

Introduction

This book is born of love for the Bible. It is a love that does not require the Bible to be historically accurate or literally true. On the contrary, it requires me to confront the historical origins and modern scholarship, which exposes the lack of concern the Biblical authors had for historical accuracy as we know it. Nor does my love for the Bible involve a belief in the existence of any deity. I am fascinated with the texts and the stories of old, with their searching for meaning and stability, without embracing the same answers they do.

This book is written from a secular, agnostic perspective. That means I'm not taking a position on whether there is a god or not. Nor am I concerned with what a hypothetical god might want. Instead I want to understand what one particular group of ancient people wrote about their god and how their image of their god changed over time. Their writings have been passed down to us in a book called the Bible. However, to understand their beliefs we have to examine the Bible carefully, taking into consideration the works of modern Biblical scholars. Stories, rituals and such should be seen in their Ancient Near Eastern context. The stories of the patriarchs, Moses, and the conquest of Canaan are all legends and that we begin to touch on historical fact only as we move into the middle of the monarchical period. Even then, we must allow for the fact that the text is not fact as written. When the Assyrians diverted a river to flood Babylon, the Babylonians described the flood as the action of their god Marduk. So too, did the ancient Hebrews understand the events that took place from within their own theological framework.

We must be careful not to project later theological ideas back into earlier texts. Early Biblical writers had no concept of heaven and hell. The early writers in the Bible likely considered other gods to be as real as their own god. They said be loyal to one god not because the other gods weren't real, but because they believed their own god was a jealous god. Only slowly did monolatry (the belief that one should worship only one god) give way to monotheism (the belief that only one god exists).

This book is intended for both the absolute beginner who has never read anything in the Bible before and for the person who, familiar with the Biblical stories, wishes to know more about their historical contexts. We can look at the Biblical stories themselves for clues about their history, but we have to remember that they weren't recording history as modern historians would. So scholars look elsewhere too. They look at the archaeology of the places that the Biblical writers wrote about. They look at the texts of other ancient civilizations. They compare different sections of the Bible with one another. The different Biblical scholars doing this work all come up with different ideas. This book cannot possibly share all the different interpretations, but it can give you a familiarity with some of the major Bible stories and introduce you to a few of the major theories and controversies.

This book is a resource for families either as a read-aloud or handed off to a teenager for independent study. Most chapters of this book are followed by one or more activities you can do to explore the topics more fully. A few chapters do not have separate activities, but instead have instructions for looking up Bible verses and reflecting on them while you are in the process of reading the chapter.

Many Bible stories are paraphrased here, meaning they are rewritten in my words. To make it easy for you to find the original stories, I'm putting the story's location in parenthesis. Seeing the verse numbers can help you be a Bible detective. You can learn which books of the Bible a paraphrased story comes from. You can see how long the story was in the Bible by looking at how many verses it covers. That may give you a clue to the story's importance to the Biblical writers. If you're reading the book aloud, you don't need to read the verse numbers all the time.

If I am quoting directly from the Bible, I will include the abbreviation for which version of the Bible I am quoting from. Most of the time this will be NIV which stands for *New International Version*.

In English we capitalize proper nouns (names) and we do not capitalize common nouns. Most people capitalize the word "God" when it is referring to the divine being worshipped in the Judeo-Christian faith. This makes sense, in that the word "God" has become the name for that divine being. However, the word "god" can also be used as a common noun to refer to gods like the Greek god Zeus or or the Egyptian god Ra. We do not capitalize the word "gods" in the sentence: "The Greeks believed their gods lived on Mount Olympus." Yet when we use the same sentence structure to refer to the divine being worshipped by the Judeo-Christian culture, most people capitalize it: "The Hebrews believed their God freed them from Egypt." This creates the belief that the Hebrew's deity was somehow completely different in nature than the other gods. One of the arguments in this book is that in the beginning their god was not significantly different than the other deities of their region. Only over time did their warrior god become seen as a divine creator. With that in mind, I will capitalize the word "God" when I am using it as a name and I will leave it in lower case when I am not using it as a name.

This is comparable to how you capitalize the word Mom when you are using it as a name for your mom, but you leave it uncapitalized when you are talking about your mom.

The exception to this is when I am quoting a Bible passage. In that case I will use the capitalization from the translation I am quoting.

Activities

Most of the chapters in this book have follow-up activities to do after you have finished the chapter, but the following ideas are ones you can do at any point as you move through the book.

1. Bible stories can be retold in different ways, just a people retell myths or fairy-tales. Try retelling the stories in any of the following ways:

   a. Tell the story from a minor character's point of view.
   b. Write the story in the form of a letter from one scribe to another, telling about the events in your kingdom.
   c. Rewrite the story in a different setting, such as the kingdom of cats or as a science-fiction story.
   d. Summarize the story in as boring a sentence as possible. The story of Jacob told on page 9 - 10 on this book could be summarized as "Man robs brother and is exploited by uncle."

2. Play memory match with the cards on the last page. Spread all cards out face down in a mixed up order. Take turns drawing two cards. If you match the character with the description, keep the cards. If not, return the face down on table.

3. Visit an art gallery, either in person or online. See how many pictures you can find that illustrate Biblical stories. With each Biblical themed painting, look for whether the artist attempted to represent the story in his own time period or whether he attempted to portray the stories in a historic context.

Getting Familiar with the Bible

The Bible is a huge book. You can imagine it a bit like a binder into which many different stories, poems and other pieces of writing were collected. Different parts were written by different people. Some of the different writers disagreed with each other. Some of the different writers edited the work of earlier writers.

The Bible has been printed in hundreds of different languages. It has been printed as very big books with large print and very small books with thin, delicate pages and tiny type. Since it has been printed so many times and in so many different ways, if ten different people with ten different Bibles were all told to turn to page sixty-five and read off what they find there, they'd all read something totally different! The story that is on page sixty-five of one Bible might be on page seventy of another Bible or on page fifty-two of a third Bible. We have a different system for talking about the Bible. Instead of talking about what page a Bible story is on, we talk about books, chapters, and verses.

When we want to refer to a section of the Bible we list the book name first, then the chapter, and then the verses. We put the verse numbers after a colon. For example, try to find Judges 5:3. Look for the book of Judges. Then look for the chapter five, and then within that look for verse three. It should go something like this:

"Hear this, you kings! Listen, you rulers!
I, even I, will sing to the Lord;
I will praise the LORD,
the God of Israel, in song." (Judges 5:3 NIV)

If you were to read the verses Judges 5:3 – 5, that means you would turn to the fifth chapter of Judges, and read the third, fourth and fifth verses. If you were asked to read Judges 5 – 6:10 that would mean you were supposed to start at the fifth chapter of Judges and read all the way to the tenth verse of the sixth chapter.

Occasionally you'll see letters after the verse number. The letters "a" or "b" will be used to signify a portion of the verse. If you wanted to reference to the second half of Judges 5:3 you would write Judges 5:3b. If you wanted to reference to the first half you would use Judges 5:3a. Your Bible won't show you where to divide the portions, but the context tends to make it visible.

> Your Bible may translate Judges 5:3 a little bit differently. Translators must make difficult choices in translating. Sometimes one word can mean multiple things, and the translator must decide which word he or she thinks matches the writer's intent in each situation. Then there are some words where no one knows what the word means. There are some words that people used to think meant one thing, but then archaeologists found other texts that includes that same word, and those other samples of that word show that it can mean something totally different. In most Bible verses the variation between different versions is minor and unimportant, but for some verses it is worth looking up how different Bibles translate them. Sometimes the meaning changes.

Sometimes there is a number before the name of the book, like 2 Kings. Sometimes that is because some books were so large they were split in two books of the same name, and the number before the book name tells you if you are supposed to read the first or second part. Other books of the Bible are in the form of letters to communities. They take their name from the community, and if there are two letters to the same community we'll distinguish which letter is being referred to by the number before the community name. For example, 1 Corinthians and 2 Corinthians are both letters from a man named Paul to people in the city of Corinth.

The text of the Christian Bible can be divided up into two parts, each consisting of many books. The first part is known as the Old Testament or the Hebrew Scriptures. This section is used by Jewish people as well as Christians, though there are differences in the order of the books and some differences in which books are included. The second part of the Christian Bible is called the New Testament or Christian Scriptures.

Follow-up Activities

1. If you have a Bible, open up your Bible and check if it has a table of contents listing the books of the Bible in order. If your Bible does not have such a list, you may wish to find a copy online to print out and tuck into your Bible. Use the list to answer the following questions to help you get familiar with the Biblical books:

    a. Which book comes first in the Bible?
    b. Which books have a number in front of their name?
    c. What are the first four books of the New Testament?
    d. What is the last book of the Bible?

2. Play a game with a friend. Take turns opening the Bible to a random page, choose a random verse and write down the book, chapter and verse number. Then the other player must find that verse.

> Ancient Romans used to use the practice of *Sortes Virgilianae* where they would open a text such as the *Illiad* or *Aeneid* to a random page and pick a random passage to try to apply to their lives. After the advent of the printing press and the translation of the Bible into many languages, people started applying this same practice to it. The practice is known as Bibliomancy.

The Big Picture of the Bible

The Bible tells the stories of a group of people that live in an area we now call Israel. Over the years the land had many names – Canaan, Palestine, the Levant, the Holy Lands. There were also names for smaller parts of it, such as the Kingdom of Israel, Judea, Judah, Samaria, Galilee.

For many centuries Canaan was ruled by many small kingdoms. These small kingdoms paid tribute to the pharaoh of Egypt, and in times of need they could call upon him to assist them. Many of the letters the Canaanite kings wrote to the pharaohs were preserved at the abandoned city of Amarna, particularly those written from the middle of the 14th century BCE (approximately 1360 – 1330s BCE). These help shed light on the history of the land the Bible took place in.

The people who wrote the Bible were very adamant that they were not Canaanites. They said that their god gave them the land as the fulfillment of a promise he made to their ancestors. There were various names for these people who wrote the Bible. They were called Israelites, Hebrews, Judeans, and Jewish people. All of these terms have slightly different meanings and implications.

In subsequent chapters you will learn about how the Hebrews claimed to have captured the land of Canaan and some different theories for what might have really happened. You'll read about how they fought off attacks from neighbouring tribes and how they eventually established a kingdom. A few generations later the kingdom split into a northern kingdom called Israel and a southern kingdom called Judah. Several hundred years later, the northern kingdom fell to the Assyrians. Later, the Southern kingdom fell to the Babylonians. The Babylonians fell to the Persians, and the Persians allowed the Hebrew elite to govern the southern area (Judea) as a province of Persia. The northern kingdom became the province of Samaria. The Persians eventually fell to the Greeks, and the Greeks to the Romans.

When later groups tried to claim independence from foreign rule they

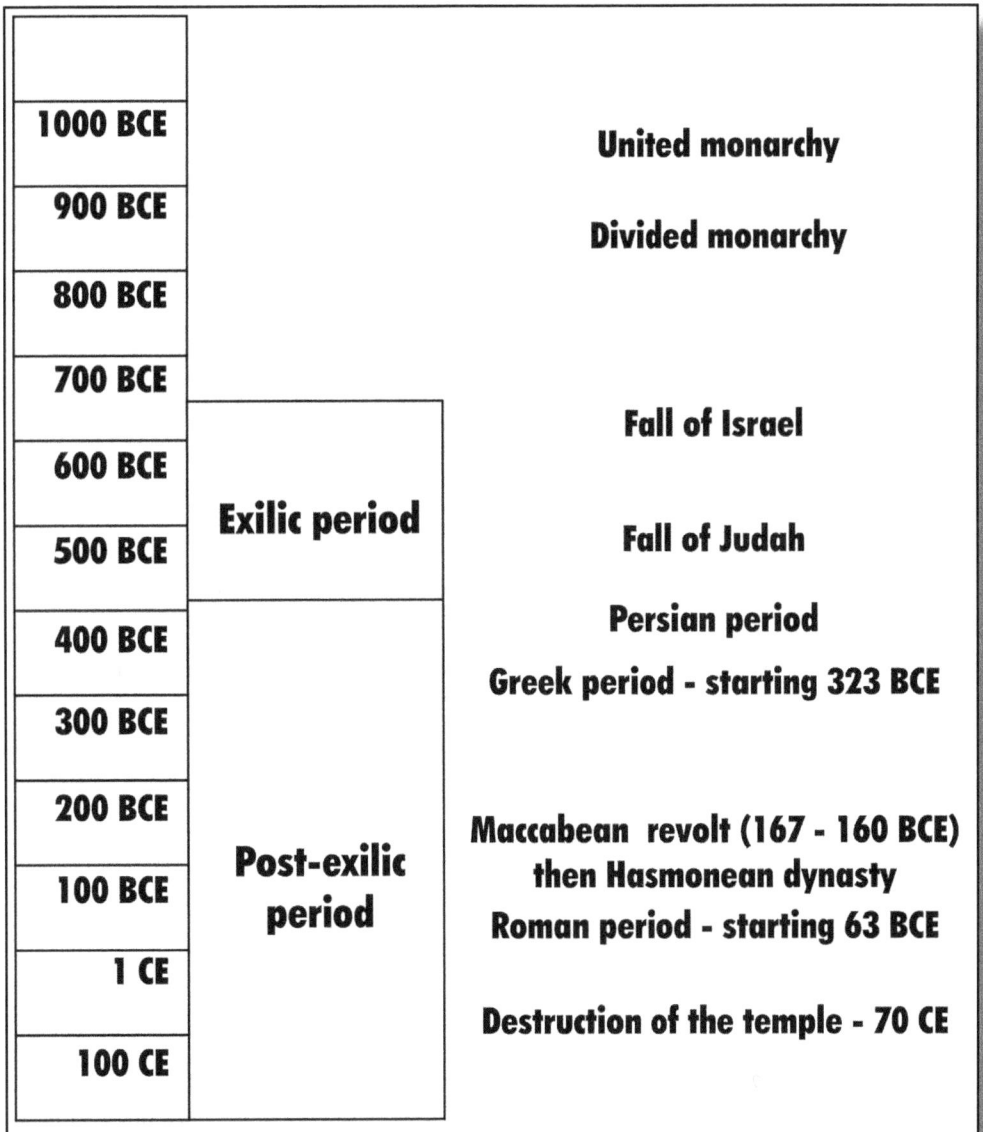

claimed the memory of a united kingdom ruled from Jerusalem and applied the name Israel to it. So the name Israelites was often applied to the whole people, right back to the landless people believed to have captured Canaan, instead of using the term just for those of the northern kingdom, as the term probably applied during the divided kingdom. The term Jewish, related to the words Judah and Judean, was also applied to the whole people throughout history, though religious beliefs of the ancient Jewish person and those of a modern Jewish person are not the same. Religions and identities evolve over time.

The Hebrew people wrote different stories at different times. Sometimes they would write about what was happening in their own lifetime but often they would write about things that happened years earlier, even hundreds of years earlier. Some of the historical inaccuracies in the Bible likely came about when writers were writing from later periods about the earlier periods. It is easy to make mistakes when writing about an earlier time period.

One major section of the Bible is known as the Deuteronomic histories. It consists of the book of Joshua, Judges, 1st and 2nd Samuel, 1st and 2nd Kings. Though it might have been written by several different people or compiled from several sources, the different books share a similar belief system. They tell the story of the Canaanite period to the beginning of the exilic period, and deal with the question of why god let the kingdoms of Israel and Judah be taken over.

Other parts of the Bible were written during the exile and Persian period. People continued to struggle with why the destruction had been allowed to happen, but also with questions of how they could worship their god in a different land. Their religious beliefs continued to change as they rebuilt the temple and reformed their community under Persian rule. If being Jewish wasn't being part of a particular kingdom, was there a way for someone to become Jewish? Could someone stop being Jewish?

Understanding the big timeline of the Bible is important for understanding the individual stories, so the first part of this book will be devoted to explaining the big picture, at least up to the Persian period. After you have a sense of what those major events are, we'll look in more detail at some of the individual stories. Finally we'll move onto the New Testament and how people understood their current events in light of the earlier scriptures.

Follow-up Activities

1. Study the map of Israel. What is the major river running to the Dead Sea? Where is Jerusalem? Which areas were plains and which areas were filled with mountains?

2. Visit the website biblehub.com. On this webpage you can look up individual Bible verses and see different translations. Look up Numbers 34:2. Look first at the different translations for the verse. Which two translations seem most different from one another to you? What makes them different? Then scroll down to the section labeled "Lexicon" which presents the Hebrew text and its translations. What is the second word in the verse, and how do the different English Bibles translate it?

Stories of the Patriarchs

The Bible was not written in the order that it has been assembled. We're going to start with a passage that might be one of the oldest parts. The passage tells a founding myth – the idea that the Hebrew people came from elsewhere and were given the land.

> *When you have entered the land the Lord your God is giving you as an inheritance and have taken possession of it and settled in it, ² take some of the firstfruits of all that you produce from the soil of the land the Lord your God is giving you and put them in a basket. Then go to the place the Lord your God will choose as a dwelling for his Name ³ and say to the priest in office at the time, "I declare today to the Lord your God that I have come to the land the Lord swore to our ancestors to give us." ⁴ The priest shall take the basket from your hands and set it down in front of the altar of the Lord your God. ⁵ Then you shall declare before the Lord your God: "My father was a wandering Aramean, and he went down into Egypt with a few people and lived there and became a great nation, powerful and numerous. ⁶ But the Egyptians mistreated us and made us suffer, subjecting us to harsh labor. ⁷ Then we cried out to the Lord, the God of our ancestors, and the Lord heard our voice and saw our misery, toil and oppression. ⁸ So the Lord brought us out of Egypt with a mighty hand and an outstretched arm, with great terror and with signs and wonders. ⁹ He brought us to this place and gave us this land, a land flowing with milk and honey; ¹⁰ and now I bring the firstfruits of the soil that you, Lord, have given me." Place the basket before the Lord your God and bow down before him. ¹¹ Then you and the Levites and the foreigners residing among you shall rejoice in all the good things the Lord your God has given to you and your household. (Deuteronomy 26:1-11 NIV)*

Arameans were the people who lived to the north of Israel, in what is now Syria. Some translations of the Bible say "desperate Syrian" instead of "wandering Aramean." The word used to describe the person does imply a level of desperation. It wouldn't be unreasonable to translate this as: "My father was a Syrian refugee."

If people started reciting the story of how their father was a wandering Aramean at the time when the Hittite empire was collapsing, they might have been describing a journey down into the Egyptian controlled Canaan. The rescue from Egyptian oppression might have been describing the feeling of relief when the Egyptians pulled back their borders and people moved into the countryside to start farming on their own. However, most people assume that going down into Egypt meant someone traveled all the way to the Nile.

There could have been a family that started telling about their Aramean ancestor's journey down into and how he came out of there and settled in Canaan. Perhaps the story was true for a few people, but then it was shared with others until a larger and larger group recited the creed as though it was true for them. Over time they might have embellished the story, making it larger and larger. They gave names to the ancestors, saying that it was Jacob who went down into Egypt. They made up stories about Jacob's father and grandfather. Those stories are called the stories of the patriarchs.

According to the Bible, Jacob's grandfather was a man named Abram. According to the Bible, God gave Abram a new name - Abraham - and promised him that his descendants would be given the land of Canaan. Abraham and his wife Sarah didn't have any children, so he wondered how that could happen. However, he went with his wife, his nephew Lot and all of their servants and slaves to Canaan. They lived as shepherds amongst the Canaanites. (Genesis 12 - 18:15)

There's a Bible story where Abraham tried to split the land with Lot, encouraging Lot to take half. Perhaps Abraham though since he had no sons his nephew Lot should inherit the promise of land. However, the story says Lot choses to move into a different area instead. (Genesis 13) Lot's descendants become the Moabites and the Ammonites, two tribes nearby. Perhaps the story of Lot and Abraham was meant partly to explain the relationship between the Hebrew people and one of their neighbours. It describes the neighbours as related to them, but not a part of the promise that their god made to them.

In another of the stories Lot is living in near the city of Sodom and is captured by raiders when the city is attacked. Abraham takes three hundred and eighteen people to go rescue Lot. Lot returns to Sodom. Both Sodom and the neighbouring city of Gomorrah are destroyed by Abraham's god, but just before their destruction an angel leads Lot and his family out of the city. The angel tells Lot and his family not to turn around, but Lot's wife does, and she becomes a pillar of salt. (Genesis 19:15 – 29

Since Abraham and his wife went for a long time not having any children, they began to think she couldn't have children. Sarah told Abraham to have a baby with her maid servant, Hagar, so that the baby could inherit

> I've been saying "In the Bible" or "in the story" quite a bit. I'm going to stop saying that as often, but I want you to remember that I still mean the story that way. I'm not meaning that the events took place the way the story says they did.
>
> If you were telling a parent about Harry Potter and you said, "Harry Potter was friend with Ron Weasley" your parent would still know that you were talking about things that took place in the story, even if you didn't say "in the Harry Potter stories…"
>
> In the same way, this book will be talking about things that happen in the Bible. If we start talking about things we know happened outside of the Bible, I'll mention that specifically.

the land God promised to Abraham. (Genesis 16) When Sarah did give birth to a baby of her own, she wanted her baby, Isaac, to inherit and not Hagar's son Ishmael. She had Abraham send Hagar and Ishmael away. They went out into the desert and when their water skin was empty Hagar prepared to die. However, God talked to her and promised her safety. (Genesis 21:1 – 20) In the Bible it was very unusual for God to speak directly to a woman, so Hagar's story is special for describing that.

The Bible tells several other stories about Abraham. In one story Abraham is told that he should sacrifice his son Isaac. (Genesis 22:1-19) He climbs up a mountain with Isaac and builds an altar. Then he ties the boy up and is ready to kill him as a gift to his god when he hears a voice tell him to sacrifice a nearby ram instead of the boy. This story can be quite disturbing. What kind of god would test someone by asking them to kill their child? Like other Bible stories, the question is not "did this really happen?" but "what were the writers trying to tell when they wrote this story?" Some people argue that the story was meant to show how incredibly loyal and faithful Abraham was that he would give up the thing most valued to him. Other people have theorized it might have been written at a time when the neighbouring cults required child sacrifice and this story is saying that their god doesn't want that. However, there is great dispute on whether there was any other child sacrifice in the area at the time.

The Bible says that once Isaac was an adult, his parents sent a servant to find Isaac a wife from the city of Ur, where they had come from. The servant selected a relative of Abraham's, a woman named Rebecca. (Genesis 24) Whomever wrote the stories really wanted to stress that the family were not Canaanites and did not marry into the Canaanite community. It was important to them that they were from elsewhere.

Isaac and Rebecca had twin children. (Genesis 25:21 – 27) Before they were born Rebecca heard God say to her that inside her womb were two nations, that would be divided. He also said that the elder would serve the younger.

When Isaac grew old and blind he wanted to bless his eldest son Esau. However, Rebecca told the younger son, Jacob, what was happening and helped disguise him as Esau to steal Esau's blessing. Esau became angry, so Jacob had to flee. He went to stay with his mother's brother, Laban. (Genesis 27)

Laban had two daughters. Jacob, the younger of two sons, fell in love with the younger daughter, Rachel. He agreed to work seven years for Laban in exchange for permission to marry Rachel. However, after working those seven years, Laban tricked him into marrying the older daughter, Leah, instead! Presumably the wedding took place with the bride veiled, since it says Jacob didn't notice the different woman until the next morning. Jacob still wanted to marry Rachel so he agreed to work another seven years in exchange for being able to marry Rachel. (Genesis 29)

After Jacob had earned his wives by working the full fourteen years, he agreed to work longer in exchange for all the spotted and speckled lambs and baby goats born to Laban's flocks. Laban tried to prevent Jacob from getting many animals by sending all his spotted, speckled and black adult animals far away from the rest of the flock. He thought this would ensure that all the baby animals would turn out white and Jacob would get none. However, Jacob took spotted sticks and set them up in front of the water holes as a magic way of ensuring that the strongest of the white animals would give birth to spotted babies. So many of the babies turned out speckled that Jacob's flock grew to be larger than Laban's flock. (Genesis 30:25 – 43)

In many ways Jacob was a trickster character, but he was also portrayed as the ancestor of all the Israelite people. They said he had twelve sons by four different women – his two wives, plus his two wives' maidservants. The favourite of his sons was said to be Joseph, but his story is for another lesson.

The important part is that the Bible claims God had made a promise that went through Abraham, Isaac and Jacob. The other men – Lot, Ishmael, and Esau – were seen as excluded from that promise, but fathers of their own great groups of people. Esau was described as the father of the Edomites. Lot was described as the father of the Moabites and Ammonites. Ishmael was father a great nation and later people attributed him as the father of the Muslim people. The original storyline could have been partly written to describe a connection with the neighboring tribes.

Follow-up Activities

1. Check the map for where the kingdoms of the Moabites and Edomites were. You should also look up the kingdom of Aram, where the Arameans were from.

2. Draw out a family tree including the following people: Sarah, Abraham, Lot, Isaac, Ishmael, Rebecca, Esau, Jacob, Laban, Rachel, Leah.

3. Wilfred Owen was a soldier in WWI. He wrote a poem against the war using the image of Abraham and Isaac. Look up the poem "The Parable of the Old Man and the Young" online and compare it with the Bible story. How do they differ?

The Bible does not say what Rachel did when Jacob married Leah. However, the *Midrash on Lamentations*, a Jewish commentary on the book of Lamentations, shares a story about Rachel helping with the deception to spare her sister. In the *Midrash on Lamentations* the patriarchs are called from their grave to plead with God to spare Israel from destruction. Then Rachel pleads with God, saying that she knew her father was planning on tricking Jacob and so she taught him special signs to recognize if it was her. Then she had compassion for her sister, and she taught her sister those signs, so that Leah could successfully fool Jacob and be spared from shame. If Rachel, a mere mortal, could overcome her envy and not shame her sister, why could God be jealous and punish his people? The *Midrash* says God listened to her pleading.

Stories of the Patriarchs Continued

The Hebrew people lived in Israel and identified themselves as newcomers to the land. They claimed that their god had promised the land to them through their ancestors. According to the stories of the patriarchs, told in the book of Genesis, this promise went from Abraham to his son Isaac, then to Isaac's son Jacob, and then to Jacob's sons. Jacob had two wives – Leah and Rachel. Leah was his first wife, but Rachel was his favourite. Jacob also had children by each of his wives' maids. The result was a family of twelve sons and one daughter.

Jacob's favourite son was named . Joseph had dreams that someday people would bow down before him. The other brothers got jealous, so they faked his death by selling him as a slave and smearing his coat with some goat's blood. Then they told Jacob that Joseph had died. (Genesis 37)

Meanwhile Joseph was taken to Egypt and sold. In Egypt he earned his master's trust by hard work. However, his master's wife got angry at him and lied that he had tried to kiss her. He was thrown into jail. There he interpreted dreams for two other prisoners. He said the dream of the pharaoh's cupbearer meant that the cupbearer's head would be "lifted up" and he would be able to work for the pharaoh again. He said the dream of the pharaoh's baker meant that the Pharaoh's head would be "lifted off" and the baker killed. Both of the predictions came true. (Genesis 39 – 40)

Later the pharaoh had a strange dream that none of his magicians could interpret, and the cupbearer suggested he contact the prisoner Joseph. Joseph was brought before the pharaoh and interpreted the dream. He said there would be seven years of plenty followed by seven years of famine. (Genesis 41:1 - 36)

The pharaoh made Joseph into his second-in-command and gave him the job of preparing for the famine. For the seven years of plenty, the extra food was gathered up into storage. Then during the time of the famine it was sold to the people. (Genesis 41:37 – 57)

The Bible tells about the people of Egypt having to give up first their money, then their animals, and then their land to the pharaoh in exchange for the food necessary to survive the famine. What do you think of that? Should people lose all their belongings in exchange for help surviving a natural disaster? The story says that after that they were allowed to farm their land with seed the pharaoh gave them, but they had to pay a fifth of their harvest to pharaoh. (Genesis 47:13 – 26)

The famine did not just affect Egypt. Joseph's father and brothers still lived in Canaan, but when the famine hit the father sent his brothers to Egypt to get food. Jacob recognized them, and he tested them to see if they were trustworthy. Then he invited them to fetch their families and live in Egypt so that he could look after them. (Genesis 42 - 47:12)

> Having to sell all one owns and even one's family members to buy food during times of famine was relatively common in the ancient times. One Canaanite king wrote during the 14th century BCE that "our sons and daughters and furnishings of our houses are gone, being sold in the land of Yarimuta [a Canaanite kingdom] for our provisions to keep us alive."

At the end of the story of Joseph, Joseph's father Jacob blessed Joseph's two children. Joseph brought his two children to Jacob, and put his older next to Joseph's right hand and his younger by his left hand. There was more prestige in the right hand than the left. However, Jacob crossed his arms, so that his right hand reached over and rested on the top of the younger grandson's head, while his left hand was on the older grandson's head. Joseph rebukes him for that, and Jacob responds that the younger son will be greater than the older. This is a common theme within the stories of the patriarchs. Which other stories of the patriarchs involved younger sons being favoured over the older ones? (Genesis 47:27 – 48:22)

After the blessing for Joseph's sons, the Bible has a long poem about Jacob's other sons (Genesis 49). To understand the significance of the poem we have to think about the people telling the stories of the patriarchs. The Hebrew people were the people living in the hill country of Israel, remember? They identified as outsiders – not Canaanites. They saw themselves as having a special relationship with their god. But they weren't unified. They belonged to different tribes. Sometimes they worked separately and sometimes when they were attacked the tribes came to one another's aid. Each tribe was identified with a descendant of Jacob.

The Bible says that Jacob's sons had descendants which formed tribes. More likely what happened is that the tribes existed, and then stories were written to tie the tribes together, giving them Jacob as their common ancestor. The tribes were not equal though. Some became more powerful than others. The poem in Genesis 49 has Jacob blessing his sons by telling them hints of what would happen to their tribes. He says to one son that "The scepter will not depart from Judah, nor the ruler's staff from between his feet, until he to whom it belongs shall come and the obedience of the nations shall be his." (Genesis 49:10 NIV) A scepter is a special staff a king carries, so this is a reference to the kingdom of Judah, which you will read about later.

Ten of the tribes were supposed to belong to ten of Jacob's sons. Joseph didn't get a tribe but his sons each had one. If there were twelve sons, and twelve tribes, but two of the tribes claimed to have descended from Joseph then what about the twelfth son? Did he get a tribe? His name was said to be Levi, and his people – the Levites – were said to have been given a special role in society as religious figures. They didn't get land of their own but lived within the other tribes.

The stories explain the political situations of the time much later. The story of Abraham, Lot, Isaac, Ishmael, Jacob and Esau explained the Hebrew people's connections to the neighbouring tribes, but the story of Joseph and his sons explained the relative power of the different tribes that together comprised the Hebrew people.

Follow-up Activities

1. Choose one part of the story above and look up the Biblical passages pertaining to it. How does the passage compare with my summary?

2. One way to review the story of Joseph is to watch the musical by Tim Rice and Andrew Lloyd Webber. The musical is called *Joseph and the Technicolor Dreamcoat* and there was a video adaptation made.

The Exodus

The Bible describes Jacob and his twelve sons going down into Egypt, and then generations later a man named Moses leading Jacob's descendants out. Their journey out of Egypt is called the Exodus, and the second book in the Bible is named Exodus.

The book of Exodus says that a later pharaoh did not know who Joseph was or how Joseph had helped Egypt. This pharaoh became scared of the Hebrew people and took means to oppress them. He made them work building with brick and toiling in the fields. Then he gave orders for the baby boys to be killed. (Exodus 1)

One woman hid her baby boy for three months. Then she put him in a basket and floated the basket down the Nile. The boy's sister followed the basket and watched as the daughter of the Pharaoh drew the baby out of the river. The Pharaoh's daughter decided to keep the child, and the boy's sister offered to go and fetch a nurse – the baby's mother – to breastfeed the baby until he was old enough for the child to be given to the Pharaoh's daughter to raise. The baby was named Moses. (Exodus 2:1 – 10)

As an adult, Moses saw an Egyptian beating a Hebrew, and he killed the Egyptian. The next day he realized that others had seen him. He could be in serious trouble. He was scared and ran away. (Exodus 2:11 – 14)

Moses found shelter with a nomadic group called the Midianites. When he encountered them, seven sisters were trying to water their father's flock when some shepherd thugs arrived at the same well. The thugs tried to water their flock from the troughs the women had filled. Moses intervened to help the women. The women's father, a priest of Midian, was grateful when he heard what Moses had done. He invited Moses to stay with his family. (Exodus 2:15 – 20)

Moses married the priest's daughter, Zipporah, and he lived as a shepherd with the Midianites for many years. Then the Lord appeared to him in the form of a burning bush. He went to investigate the bush and heard a voice telling him that he was supposed to remove his shoes, for he was standing on holy ground. Then God spoke to him and explained that he was to go back to Egypt to rescue his people. Moses expressed fear over doing so, and God agreed to send Moses' brother Aaron to help him. (Exodus 2:20 – 4:17)

Moses' and Aaron's first attempt to convince the pharaoh to let the Hebrew people leave Egypt did not go well, and instead of releasing them the pharaoh decided to increase the Hebrew's workload. He demand that instead of just making bricks with straw the Egyptians gave them, the Hebrew people would have to gather the straw for the bricks too. (Exodus 5)

The story continues with God bringing ten disasters down upon the Egyptians. These include swarms of insects, diseases for the livestock, hail, frogs, and finally the death of the firstborn children of all the Egyptian families. This death of the oldest children is brought about by the angel of death, said to come and visit the land. The angel of death passed over the houses of the Hebrews because they marked their door posts with lambs' blood. After this last plague the Egyptians released the Hebrews and sent them on their way. (Exodus 6:28 – 13)

> Exodus 34:29 says that Moses came down from Mt. Sinai with a radiant face, but an early Latin translated the word for radiant as "horned." Poems, sculptures and paintings have all memorialized this mistranslation.
>
> The cover illustration of people gathering manna features the horned Moses.

The pharaoh changed his mind – again – and chased after the departing Hebrews. He followed them till they were trapped between the Red Sea and the Egyptian army. Moses raised his staff, and God split the sea in two. The Hebrews walk through to safety. When the Egyptians tried to follow,

> Some people attempt to explain how this story could be the Sea of Reeds and not the Red Sea, and that Moses led the people over a safe walking path but the chariots were heavy and got stuck in the mud. Some say that if it were a different location really strong winds could have pushed the water. Those methods of thought are about as productive as trying to figure out how the ancient stories of Zeus or Hera could have been true. The story of Moses is a story about one god proving he's stronger than another people's gods. It can be appreciated as a story.
>
> At the same time, we can recognize that for some people it is not a story. Many people do take these stories as true. Whether you are someone who believes them to be a story or the truth, it is important to learn in life how to respectfully disagree on things, standing firm when necessary but without being insulting.

> Even while we don't know exactly who wrote the Bible, we do know that the Bible refers to the patriarchs and the people being led out of oppression over and over. Someone believed strongly that their god did not want them to be oppressed.

the water returned to normal and the Egyptians drowned. Or at least, that's how the story goes. (Exodus 14)

Moses lead the people to Mount Sinai where they acquired a new set of laws and instructions from their god. (Exodus 19-32) The Bible has several different sections devoted to laws delivered by Moses, probably written at different points in history. The most famous of these is the Ten Commandments, found in Exodus 20:1 - 17.

Despite the religious experience at Mount Sinai, the people were unable to trust Moses and his god fully. They were scared to enter their promised land, so they were condemned to wander in the desert for forty years. During the forty years of wandering their god provided them with food in the form of manna, a mysterious substance they could gather from the ground.

After forty years have past and those who left Egypt had died, a man named Joshua led the next generation into the promised land. Joshua helped oversee the dividing up of the land between the different tribes. (Numbers 13 – 14)

There is no archaeological evidence to support the believe that either the stories of the patriarchs or the story of the Exodus took place. There are no references to them in the contemporary scribal records of the other kingdoms. Yet the stories have become the basis of faith for many people.

The stories helped elaborate on the Hebrew people's belief that they were outsiders brought into the land by their god. We don't know exactly when these stories were written. It is possible that the stories of Abraham and Isaac come from one group of people and the stories of Jacob and Joseph come from another group. It is possible that the story of Moses resisting the Pharaoh's building project might have originated when a man named Jeroboam rebelled against King Solomon and then Solomon's son Rehoboam, with the story being projected hundreds of years into the past.

The story of the Exodus stretches over four books of the Bible: Exodus, Leviticus, Numbers and Deuteronomy. Many theories have been put forward about the origins of these different books and the way the different writers and editors changed the story as time went along. For example, it is likely that Deuteronomy was written by a group who say possession of the land of Canaan as the most important gift promised to the Hebrew people, even though Moses and his people didn't enter the land! Several Biblical scholars have suggested that the text of Exodus and Leviticus would have been written after the people had lost control of the land, and so they shift the focus of the Moses story, making the argument that the big gift was not the promise of the land but the instructions and laws given at the Mount Sinai. The book of Numbers might have been an attempt to bridge the theological gap between the beliefs of Deuteronomy and the beliefs of Exodus-Leviticus. You will read more about this later.

Follow-up Activities

1. Look up Sandro Botticelli's fresco "The Youth of Moses. It was made around 1481 – 1482 in the Sistine Chapel, Rome. How many scenes can you recognize?

2. Chapter 15 of Exodus is a long poem. As you read the poem try to picture what it describes. What does their god look like, according to the poem? In the early parts of the Bible God is described as a warrior god, a bit like people might picture the Greek God Zeus or the Babylonian God Marduk.

3. Read the Ten Commandments in Exodus 20:1 – 17. How many of them deal with correct worship? How many deal with correct behaviour towards others?

Around 300 BCE an Egyptian named Manetho wrote a story about a king collecting those with physical ailments and taking them away from Egypt. The original of his story was lost but the Jewish historian Josephus, writing in the 1st century CE, wrote that Manetho was trying to slander the Jewish people by saying they left together with lepers and others being banished from Egypt. One of the reasons Manetho's story, as told by Josephus, cannot be taken as independent confirmation that the story of Moses is true is that the story was not necessarily independent. There were significant Jewish communities in Egypt at the time when Manetho wrote his story, and he was purposely twisting their founding myth to slander them.

Conquest of Canaan

The Hebrew people believed their god had promised Abraham that his descendants would one day possess the land of Canaan and that this promise was fulfilled by twelve tribes entering Canaan, a generation after the Exodus. However, in most of the second millennium BCE the land of Canaan was controlled by Canaanite kings who were vassals of the Egyptian pharaoh. So how did the Hebrews gain control of the land? We will look at how the Bible claims the conquest of Canaan happened and then we'll discuss the modern theories.

In one key story the Hebrew leader Joshua sends spies into the city of Jericho. There the spies meet a woman named Rehab, who tells them that she knows God has promised the city to them. She offers to help them if they in turn will guarantee her safety during the upcoming attack. They tell her that when the attack comes, she is to gather her family into her house and hang a red string in the window to mark the house. Then she lowers the spies out of the city from her window, and they return to Joshua to make their report. (Joshua 2)

> In between the story of Joshua sending the spies and Joshua leading the people around Jericho, the Bible tells that the people engaged in ritual actions tying their story to Abraham and Moses by crossing the Jordan as Moses had crossed the Red Sea. Whomever edited the text to include these details wanted to demonstrate that the conquest of Jericho was fulfillment of earlier promises made.

Jericho was a walled city. When people attack a walled city, they can try to tunnel under the walls, climb over them or try to break the walls. Alternatively, they can lead a siege, which means camping for a long time around the city and waiting till the city runs out of food and surrenders. The Bible story about the attack on Jericho says that Joshua didn't do any of those. Instead he had everyone march around the city once each day for seven days. They brought with them the ark of the covenant, a gold-plated wooden box that was sacred to the group and believed to carry the stone tablets God had given Moses. Their priests blew trumpets. On the seventh day they circled the city seven times and the walls of the city came tumbling down and the Hebrew people attacked. In this way the Bible describes the Hebrew's god as winning the battle for them. (Joshua 6)

After the attack of Jericho, the Bible describes other attacks on different Canaanite cities. Did the Hebrew people conquer the area by violence? Was the story of Jericho true in any way – even without the magical tumbling of the walls?

Many scholars have looked at the archaeology of the area and have proposed other possibilities. One theory is that the people of the cities decided to leave the cities, and they moved out into the hill area. Certain hilly areas in Canaan that had not been settled because the lack of water and uneven terrain makes them difficult habitats. Perhaps social unrest and technological advances made it so that people were, at this point, willing and able to dig cisterns to gather rainwater and terraces to farm the slopes. This theory is called the "deurbanization theory" or "social revolt theory."

In the Amarna letters, the Canaanite rulers used the term *Habriu* to describe troublemakers, migrants, and deserters. Sometimes the *Habriu* were hired as mercenaries by the Canaanite kings. Scholars proposed that these were the early Hebrews. They may have included both landless Canaanites and foreigners. The *Habriu* could have adopted the newcomers stories of coming from elsewhere (such as the wandering Aramean creed) and the newcomer's god. Some people argue that the stories of the *Habriu* causing trouble could be the real records of the conquest of Canaan.

Biblical Scholar Nadav Na'aman argues against this. He says that the *Habriu* of the Amarna letters were likely an earlier, separate group of people. Think of it this way – there are many groups of refugees. If several groups of people were called refugees in text dating from several hundred years apart, we don't automatically assume they are descendants of the same group. The early group, Na'aman says, didn't cause significant changes to Canaanite society. Though they annoyed the Canaanite kings, they didn't threaten Egyptian control over the territory. They did not conquer Canaan.

Nadav Na'aman does suggest that in the older parts of the Bible, the Biblical term for Hebrew was originally applied in the same way *Habriu* was, to refer to migrants and troublemakers or to mock people by implying they are those things. Na'aman suggests it wasn't until much later that the term was used to refer to the whole of the Hebrew community. When you read the Bible you can watch for the word and ask yourself if the sentence would make sense if the meaning was not an ethnic or religious group (like the modern term "Hebrew" means) but a reference for people on the margins of society.

Other scholars believe that the Hebrew people came peacefully from other places and settled in those hilly areas where no one else was living. This theory is called the "immigration theory." This theory differs from the deurbanization theory in that it envisions the Canaanite cities continuing untouched in the valleys, and it accepts the Biblical insistence that the Hebrews did not descend from Canaanites.

We know that in the late thirteenth century BCE and part of the twelfth century BCE a massive famine devastated much of the Middle East. To the north of Canaan, rulers of the Hittite Empire were no longer able to maintain control or to resist invaders known as the Sea People. Waves of migrants flooded down into Canaan in search of food. Meanwhile to the south-west of Canaan, the kingdom of Egypt was also facing problems. Egypt could no longer defend its Canaanite vassals and instead withdrew its soldiers and assistance.

New immigrants to the land might have felt like invaders to the Canaanites, but their actions could not have followed the same steps laid out in the Biblical description of the conquest of Canaan. The descriptions of violent conquests were likely written hundreds of years after the events were supposed to have taken place and may have been inspired by later events. Parts of the stories of the conquest might have been based on how the Assyrians acted when they invaded the country around 700 BCE. Those writing after the Assyrian invasion could assume that their own ancestors did the same thing upon arriving in the country. For example, the Assyrians impaled the enemy leaders on poles as Joshua was said to do in Joshua 10:26. The choice of which cities to describe the Hebrews invading may also have reflected the cities the Assyrians invaded.

If the Hebrew people did not invade and capture Jericho and other cities, why would people write stories saying they did? Stories are binding forces between groups of people. Even if the events they describe didn't happen, they provide insight into the way people thought of themselves. The Hebrew people believed themselves to be separate, different, than the Canaanites. They believed that they had entered the land not through their own military might but because it was a gift of their god to them. The events described in Joshua 3 – 5 link the conquering of the land with other parts of the religious mythology they developed.

The stories of the conquest explain a problem that came up much later in the Biblical history. Later you will read about how the Hebrews formed a kingdom. After a few generations the kingdom split into two. A while later the northern half of the kingdom was defeated by the Assyrians. The survivors tried to understand how and why this happened. These events will be covered in more detail in later chapters, but for now what is important to note is that the stories of the conquest blames the people, but particularly the northern tribes, for making peace with the Canaanites and not eliminating them completely.

> *The angel of the Lord went up from Gilgal to Bokim and said, "I brought you up out of Egypt and led you into the land I swore to give to your ancestors. I said, 'I will never break my covenant with*

you, ² and you shall not make a covenant with the people of this land, but you shall break down their altars.' Yet you have disobeyed me. Why have you done this? ³ And I have also said, 'I will not drive them out before you; they will become traps for you, and their gods will become snares to you.'"
⁴ When the angel of the Lord had spoken these things to all the Israelites, the people wept aloud, ⁵ and they called that place Bokim. There they offered sacrifices to the Lord.(NIV)

The Biblical writers suggest that an incomplete conquest left the Hebrew people vulnerable to idol worship. They could learn the Canaanite ways and worship the Canaanite gods. This could cause them to break their commitment to their one single god and justify his deciding to punish them by allowing them to be conquered by the Assyrians.

One other thing important to note about the conquest literature is that it portrays the relationship between the people and their god as being similar to the covenants made between vassals and their lord. Like vassals, they have been put in charge of the land by a greater power, and they owe their claim to the land to him.

The description of the covenant found in the book of Joshua is very similar to the covenants the Hittites had with their vassals. The Hittite covenants started with a preamble naming who the superior was in the relationship. Then they would follow with a history of the relationship and all the things the superior had done to help the vassal. Next would come the list of obligations of the vassal, followed by a list of divine beings were called upon to witness the covenant. This would be followed by the curses that would fall on the vassals if they broke the agreement, and the blessings if they kept the agreement. Sometimes there would be a statement then about a special stone or stele that was placed in recognition of the treaty.

Follow-up Activity

1. Read Joshua 24. Review the parts of the Hittite treaty listed above and find the corresponding parts within this Bible chapter. Since no other gods can be evoked who will be the witnesses? This example does not clearly outline the curses and blessings, but instead focuses on the history of their relationship. The curse is listed in verse 20 and the implied blessing is the continued relationship between the people and their god.

Some people take the belief that Abraham's god promised his descendants the land of Canaan very literally. This idea grew in popularity in the 19th and 20th centuries, particularly among Christians who believed that restoring the land to Jewish people was a part of bringing about the end times and among Jewish people seeking refuge from persecution. One slogan was "a land without a people for a people without a land," a statement that ignores the fact that the land was never empty.

In March 2002 Senator James Inhofe gave a speech about America's policies on Israel in which he said:

> "I believe very strongly that we ought to support Israel; that it has a right to the land. This is the most important reason: Because God said so. As I said a minute ago, look it up in the book of Genesis. It is right up there on the desk... this is not a political battle at all. It is a contest over whether or not the word of God is true."

Other Christians have viewed the promises to Abraham as having passed to the Christians after the birth of Jesus and see it as fulfilled by people of faith - spiritual ancestors of Abraham - having spread all over the Earth. This can be a very big problem when people act like their God has chosen them rejected others, but people today are still basing their actions on how they understand the story of God making a promise to Abraham.

Different Names for God

As I said in the introduction, in English the word "god" can refer to any divine being, but capitalized it serves as the name of the Judeo-Christian deity. The word "lord" also has varied meanings. It can be a title for a knight, like Lord Byron, or we can use it to refer to "the Lord" as in God. We can also refer to "lords and ladies" in the plural.

> Semitic languages are a group of languages that are all related. Hebrew is one of them. Akkadian is another. Akkadian used to be the main language for international diplomacy in the ancient middle east, and the Amarna letters mentioned earlier in this book were written in Akkadian. Arabic is another Semitic language.

The ancient Semitic words for their gods were just as complicated as our modern words. In ancient Canaan the word "El" could refer to either the head of the pantheon (the Canaanite equivalent of Zeus) or to any divine being. Elohim, a variation of the word "El," was also used in the singular for the supreme being and in the plural for lesser deities.

The Canaanite god El was the father of the gods. He had many children including a daughter named Anat, and sons named Baal, Dagon and Yamm. Baal was the god of the storms. Dagon was the god of the harvest and Yam the god of the sea. Another of his sons, Mot, was the god of death. In Canaanite mythology these gods fought one another.

Baal was another word with multiple meanings. It could mean any lord (like a master or a god) or it could mean one particular storm-god. There is the possibility that worshipers of the storm-god Hadad called him "lord," which in their language was "baal". Eventually they forgot his earlier name Hadad, and just called him Baal, and they started to think of it as being another name for that god, which they decided was the son of El. In any case, the two words – Baal and Hadad – both became linked to a storm god, even though the word Baal could also mean "lord."

The Hebrew people referred to their god as El. They might have used that term because it was the generic term for god, or they might have started out worshiping the Canaanite god El. James S. Anderson proposed that some of the Canaanites started to see El's son Baal or Baal-Hadad as being more powerful than El, while other Canaanites believed they should stay loyal to El. He suggests that the early Hebrews were among the Canaanites who stuck to El. Anderson argues that many of the stories in the Bible are meant to show how things that people said about Baal were actually true of El instead.

> In modern Jewish tradition the name YHWH is too sacred to say, so the word Adonai, which means lord, is substituted instead.

The Hebrew people used another name too. That other name is sometimes written as YWHW or Yahweh. One part of the Bible suggests that Abraham and his descendants knew God as El until God revealed himself as Yahweh to Moses. Biblical scholars have proposed a number of other possibilities. El and Yahweh may have originated as separate gods, or they might have always been two names for the same god.

Whatever the history is, at some point El and Yahweh were both being used to refer to the same god of the Hebrews. The Hebrew people saw him as having rescued them from slavery in Egypt and given them the land of Canaan.

It wasn't unusual for a group of people to believe they had one god protecting them. Many ancient cities had a god associated with it. Athena was the protector of Athens. The Sumerian god Nanna was associate with the cities of Ur and Harran. Aššur was associated with the Assyrians. Why wouldn't the Hebrew people have their own god, Yahweh?

The Biblical writers portray their god as having entered into a covenant with Abraham to give his descendants the land. This covenant was renewed with Moses. The covenant included the promise that they would worship only their god and no other gods. The Biblical writers admit that they routinely failed at doing this and therefore were punished by God. But if Abraham and Moses were both part of mythology, and not real, then when did the people start worshiping one god? Some believe it was earlier and others believed it was later. It is possible that some stories were written originally about other gods were later shifted to be about the one god.

> The word Israel has the name El in it. So do many other names in the Bible: Michael, Gabriel, Nathaniel, Rachel. Other Biblical names are connected with the name Yahweh. These include Josiah, Joshua, Jesus. The name Elijah combines reference to both El and Yahweh.

The move towards monotheism was likely a slow process. Before becoming monotheists there was likely a time of being monolatrists. Monolatrists are people who believe that there are many gods, but only one of which they should worship. They described their god as a jealous god, demanding they worship him alone. Over time, and particularly after the destruction of their temple, they moved further towards monotheism.

The Bible mentions women leaving cakes out for the "Queen of Heaven." (Jeremiah 44:15 – 19) It also talks about people having household gods. (Genesis 31:34) At times it talks about them worshiping Dagon and Baal. Often this was portrayed as a temporary intrusion of another religion into their community, but it is just as likely that these were old, long-standing traditions which were being rejected by people wanting to rewrite their religious past.

Follow-up Activities

1. Look up Judges 4:11 on Biblehub.com and in your Bible. Which name of God is used in that verse? How is it translated? Then look up Psalm 68:35 on Biblehub.com and in your Bible. Which words are used for God in that verse? How are they translated?

2. Look up one of the Canaanite gods mentioned in this chapter and write a paragraph about him or her.

> The Canaanite god El had a wife Asherah. When Baal became seen as the more powerful god, Asherah was portrayed as his wife. In the Bible, Asherah poles - sacred objects connected with the goddess - are frequently associated with the worship of Baal.
>
> However, there is also archaeological evidence to suggest that Yahweh too was associated with Asherah. A late 8th century BCE inscription says "Blessed is Uriyahu to Yahweh, who delivered him from his enemies for Asherah." It is possible people prayed to Asherah to intervene with Yahweh on their behalf.

> Some people believe that the two different names of God reflected different traditions that were later merged together. Through much of the twentieth century scholars proposed variations on what is called the documentary hypothesis. The theory was that the first five books of the Bible could be divided up into recognized sources based on which name they used for God. Some of the older parts referring to their god as Yahweh were seen to have come from a source called the Yahwist (abbreviated as "J"). The older parts referring to god as El could have come from the Elohist (abbreviated as "E"). These two sources were believed to be edited together by a Priestly source and combined with the work of the Deuteronomist. Different people advocated that these were individuals or groups of writers sharing common views, and different scholars posited additional possibilities such as an early editor combining the Yahwist and Elohist material ("JE") before the Priestly source was added. Over time this whole theory has been drawn into question and people have recognized that the different sources for the Bible stories are not necessarily easily identified by which name of God they use.

Ancient Heroes

The book of Joshua – telling the tales of the conquest of Canaan – is followed by the book of Judges. The book of Judges tells stories set after the conquest but before the Hebrew people developed a monarchy. Sometimes this is called the premonarchical period or the tribal period. It is also called the period of the judges. The judges served as temporary leaders of the community in times of crisis, rallying people together to fight against their enemies.

Some of these stories may have had a long oral tradition before being edited into this context. Judges 5 is composed of a poem telling about a battle against "kings of Canaan." It includes mention of a woman named Deborah singing songs to rally people into action, and a leader named Barak. It lists from which areas the people came to join the battle and it offers a curse to a community that did not join the battle. Then it offers a blessing to a woman, Jael, into whose tent the Canaanite king went. Jael is said to give the king milk and curds and then:

> *"Her hand reached for the tent peg,*
> *her right hand for the workman's hammer.*
> *She struck Sisera, she crushed his head,*
> *she shattered and pierced his temple." (Judges 5:26 NIV)*

Hebrew poetry – like the poetry of others in the area – relies strongly on repetition. Ideas are repeated over and over. We do not have to interpret the mention of the tent peg and the workman's hammer as a sign that Jael held one item in one hand and one in the other. The demands of poetry required repetition, so the actions were described multiple times with variations. The definition of the second item held is not entirely clear. The point is that she grabbed some tool and struck him.

At some later date a story was written, based off of the poem. This is found in Judges 4. The author of it expands on the characters mentioned in the poem, and then attributes the poem to Deborah. Yet there are slight variations in how the two stories are written. The prose writer seems to have taken the poetry very literally, assuming that Jael took a peg and a hammer (using a different word for the second item than was in the song) and drove the peg in. For a multi-handed action like hammering a peg into someone's head the victim would need to be very still, so the prose writer said the man had fallen asleep first. We have an example here of how stories get expanded and altered.

Another story takes place when the Hebrews are being threatened by the nomatic Midianites. In that story a man named Gideon is told by God that he will free the people from their enemy, but that he must tear down the altar of Baal and a sacred pole of the goddess Asherah. The story assumes that worship of these other gods was happening close by and likely by the Hebrew people. People get angry at him for destroying their sacred space and go to his father to complain, but his father says that Baal can deal with Gideon himself and doesn't need the people to defend him. (Judges 6:1 - 35)

Meanwhile Gideon gathers an army from several of the tribes. He's still scared though and composes a number of tests for the god that has called on him. He puts out a piece of wool on the threshing floor and asks that it be wet with the floor dry in the morning. Then he asks that the following morning the floor be wet but the wool dry. Gideon's god passes his tests. (Judges 6:36 – 40)

> In Canaanite mythology Baal commands the rain and his three daughters represent the dew. Gideon's tests are challenging his god to do things traditionally ascribed to Baal.

Gideon's god told him to dismiss most of the army so that everyone can see it is their god that has brought them victory, and not the size of their army. Those who were scared were sent home first, but the army was still too big. It was large enough it might be able to defeat the enemy on their own power, rather than requiring their god's assistance. So then the soldiers were told to drink at a river and then separated based on how they drank the water. Did they lift the water up with their hands or put their head into the water? Perhaps Gideon wanted to take only the soldiers willing to get dirty. Perhaps he wanted only those who stayed most alert? They attacked at night with torches hidden in jars until they were close to their target. The stories of Gideon combine military heroics of a nighttime attack by an elite group with the idea that they should trust in one god and cease worshiping the others. (Judges 7)

Another set of stories are about a man named Samson. The stories tell how before he was born it was predicted that he would save the people from the Philistines, but that he must neither cut his hair or drink alcohol. As long as he doesn't do those things, he has super-strength. (Judges 13)

> Around 1180 BCE. the Egyptians described a flood of newcomers they called the "People of the Sea." Some believe that the People of the Sea were the Philistines.
>
> The word "philistine" has became an English word meaning uneducated and unsophisticated.

Samson is strong because he is kept separate, dedicated to god through those special rules. The Bible calls him a Nazirite, which refers to one consecrated to one's god and kept separate. Cutting the hair would make him less separate and take away his strength. Being involved with a woman makes him less separate, and each time he becomes involved with one he gets in trouble! The Biblical writers might have been both telling stories about their own fictional hero but they might have also been trying to argue that their strength as a people comes from being separate from their neighbours, dedicated towards their god.

The Samson stories tell of his involvement with the Philistines. In one story he marries a Philistine woman and poses a riddle for the wedding guests. If they guess the answer, he will give them all a new garment. If they can't, they have to give him one. The riddle goes "Out of the eater came something to eat. Out of the strong came something sweet." The wedding guests can't figure it out themselves so they pressure his wife to tell them, and she pressures him to tell her. Samson admits to his wife that the answer is honey coming out of the carcass of a lion he had killed with his bare hands. His wife tells the wedding guests the answer, and Samson loses the bet. When he finds he's been tricked he's angry, so he kills a bunch of Philistines and steals their clothes to pay his debt. Then he storms off angry. (Judges 14)

Samson's new in-laws assume he's abandoned his wife and his wife marries someone else. When Samson returns to discover this, he gets really angry again. He ties three hundred foxes together and ties torches to their tails so they burn the fields. (Judges 15)

In a second story he is in love with a different woman. The Philistines pressure her to tell them how to take away his power. She in turn pressures Samson. At first Samson tells her a false explanation. He says if he's tied with fresh bowstrings he'll be as weak as any other man. She ties him up and calls the Philistines, but he breaks the binds and goes free.

Samson's girlfriend pouts that he lied to her and begs to know the truth. He says if he's tied with fresh ropes he'll be weak, and she tries again. Again, he breaks free, and again she pouts about him lying. Next he tells her that if his hair is woven into a web and fastened with a pin he'll be weak, but again this doesn't work.

Again she pouts, and this time he tells her the truth. If he's shaved, he'll be weak. She shaves his head and turns him over to the Philistines. They blind and imprison him. As his hair grows back, so does his strength and in the end when they bring him out to where they are worshiping the god Dagon, he pushes against the columns of the building and collapses it down killing hundreds of people. (Judges 16)

Obviously, a story involving super strength and tying hundreds of foxes together is a sort of tall tale, like an ancient version of Paul Bunyan or a Hebrew Hercules, but it also deals with the issue of keeping separate.

We see in the book of Judges songs were transformed into story. Myths or folktales were rephrased as history. The stories tell of people who are protected by their god, and yet are still vulnerable because they are small separate tribes who must be rallied in times of need.

The book of Judges also tells of an early attempt to establish a monarch. The potential king, Abimelech, features briefly in the Bible. The parable speaks to the difficulty of getting a worthy king.

Follow-up Activities

1. Look up the story of Hercules and compare it with Samson. In what ways are they similar? In what ways are they different?

2. The name Samson could be connected to the Hebrew word for sun and/or to the ancient sun-god Shamash. How would the story change if it were of a deified sun?

3. Stephen M. Wilson suggests that the story of Samson fits into the tradition of folktales in which a boy fails to transition into adult society but instead remains a boy. Reread the story of Samson and look for clues that might support that.

4. Read the parable of the trees in Judges 9:7 – 15. Translations of the Bible differ on exactly which plant agrees to be the king of the trees in Judges 9:7 - 15. In some versions it is a bramble, a low plant that cannot actually offer shade to the mighty trees. In some version it is translated as mistletoe, a parasitic plant that lives by drawing energy from other plants. In what way could a king be seen as a parasite?

5. Write a proposal as to how a small tribe or collection of tribes could choose a monarchy. What would it take to ensure that the person is qualified?

Samuel

The judges had to rally people together in times of crisis, encouraging different tribes to come to one another's defense. One way to rally people together in a time of crisis is to bring forward religious artifacts. Religious artifacts can be a symbol of unity, reminding the different tribes of what they have in common with one another. However, the religious artifacts were also believed to help bring the power of the god himself to the tribe's defense.

Do you remember the ark of the covenant? It was the religious artifact carried around the city of Jericho before the walls fell down and it was said to contain the tablets their god gave Moses. 1 Samuel 4:1b – 7:2 tells of the ark of the covenant being brought from the shrine at Shiloh to aid the troops fighting against the Philistines.

According to the story the ark had been kept at the shrine at Shiloh. There the priest, Eli, lived with his two sons, Hophni and Phinehas. Both sons were also priests and when they were told the troops wanted the ark brought to them, they took the ark to the troops.

The Philistines saw the ark. They recognized the ark as bringing the power of the god that had rescued the Hebrews from the Egyptians and they feared that god. Yet they were determined not to be captured and they fought bravely. They fought bravely, and they won! Despite the presence of the ark, no god had come to the Hebrews defense. They captured the ark itself and they killed the two priests.

A messenger ran to Shiloh to deliver the news of the defeat to the old priest Eli. Eli was sitting on a seat by the gate. When he heard the ark had been captured, his people defeated and his sons dead, he tumbled over backwards and died!

The ark, meanwhile, went on a strange journey. It was taken by the Philistines to the temple of Dagon. Presumably they thought this captured god would serve their own god. The next morning the statue of Dagon had fallen to the ground. The temple staff put the statue upright again. The morning after that, the statue was again on the ground, but this time the hands and head had broken off. The symbolism would have been disturbing. Had the captured god defeated theirs?

> In ancient Canaanite mythology when the goddess Anat fights against Dagon she cuts off his hands and head. The mention of the head and hands falling of Dagon could be related to the Canaanite myth or it could simply be a way of saying that the god can neither speak, think, nor act.

Next disease hit. The inhabitants of the city had enough. They wanted to get rid of the ark so it could bring them no more punishment. So they packed up the ark and shipped it to another Philistine city. When disease struck the next city, the people said they wanted the ark moved again. When the ark arrived at the third city the people asked "what are you doing bringing it here? Do you want to kill us all?"

The Philistines called for their priests and diviners and asked what they should do about these disasters that were befalling them. What should they do with the ark? The priests and diviners said the ark must be returned to the Hebrews but with extra gifts! Two cows were hitched to a cart, and the cart loaded up with the ark and some gold. Then the cows were sent on their way, and the Philistines watched as the cows plodded out of their land and towards the Hebrew's land.

The cows dragged the cart to the Hebrew community of Beth-shemesh. The people there took the ark off the cart, and then used the cart and cows as a burnt offering to their god. But one group of people within the community did not celebrate the ark's return. God punished them for that, killing off seventy men. Then the people of Beth-shemesh were scared of the ark, and they sent it away, to another community.

The story of the ark's capture and return is sandwiched in the Bible within another story. (1 Samuel 1 – 4 and 1 Samuel 7) The ark's capture is the filling of the story, but the "bread" is just as interesting. The "bread" tells more about the shrine at Shiloh.

The shrine was a place where people could go to offer sacrifices. A person wishing to butcher an animal could take it up to the shrine and have it offered in sacrifice. Part of the animal would be given to the god and most returned to the family for a feast. Similar, though probably smaller, shrines would have existed throughout the land so that everyone lived within distance of one. It is possible that all animal butchering took place in this type of religious context, and that the Hebrew people didn't have secular butchering rules until much later when religious reformers were trying to close all the small shrines and centralize worship in Jerusalem.

In the story a man brought his two wives for his annual sacrifice at Shiloh. The animal was butchered and the man gave portions to all his family members. To his favourite wife, Hannah, he gave two parts but Hannah wept and refused to eat. She was upset because she had no children, and even her husband's devotion did not help her resign herself to that.

After the meal Hannah went to pray. She made a vow that if she had a son, she would give the son back to god as a Nazirite. As she said her prayers and made the vow, she was so upset that she appeared drunk. Eli, the old priest, chided her for being drunk. She explained that she wasn't drunk, only upset, and he promised that her prayers would be granted.

Hannah's prayers were granted. She became a mother and named her son Samuel. When the boy was several years old and weaned, she brought him to Shiloh to become a servant to God. Each year his mother would make him a special robe and bring it to him when the family brought the sacrifice. She must have been pleased to see each year how much he had grown and how he was doing, and what he had learned at the shrine.

Samuel likely saw how Eli's sons would take more of the offerings than they were supposed to, even forcing people to break the proper rules about how to give the offerings so that they could get better parts than they were supposed to. Eli heard rumors about the evil his sons were doing, and he tried to talk to them, but they did not listen. A messenger of God came and told Eli that God was angry with what his sons were doing and that they would not be allowed to continue, but still Eli was unable to stop them from doing bad.

One night Samuel was lying in the room with the ark of the covenant and he heard a voice calling his name. He assumed it was Eli calling for him and ran into Eli's room.

Eli said no, he had not called, and sent Samuel back to bed.

Samuel heard his name called again. He raced back into Eli's room asking to find out what Eli wanted. Again, he was told that Eli hadn't called him, and he should go back to sleep.

The voice called a third time. Samuel rushed into Eli's room a third time. This time Eli realized what was going on. Eli told Samuel to go lie down again and when he hears his name again, he should say "Speak, Lord, your servant is listening."

Samuel's name was called for a fourth time. This time instead of running out he said what Eli had told him to say. The message that God gave was that the house of Eli would be punished and nothing anyone could do would stop it. What a message for the boy to have to tell his master!

When Eli heard the message, he was resigned and accepted it.

Here is where the story of the ark being taken out to the troops fits in. Eli's sons took it out and were killed.

Eli heard the news and he died. The ark's power resulted in it being brought back to God's people.

If the story of Samuel's childhood is the first piece of bread in a story-sandwich, and the story of the ark being captured is the filling, what is the second piece of bread? It is Samuel being established as judge of the land and him saying to all the people that:

> *So Samuel said to all the Israelites, "If you are returning to the Lord with all your hearts, then rid yourselves of the foreign gods and the Ashtoreths and commit yourselves to the Lord and serve him only, and he will deliver you out of the hand of the Philistines." 4 So the Israelites put away their Baals and Ashtoreths, and served the Lord only.*
> *(1 Samuel 7:3 – 4 NIV)*

> Note that Ashtoreths is another spelling of the name of the goddess Asherah.

Then Samuel invited everyone to go to one place to pray, and as they went the Philistines attacked. Samuel offered a sacrifice to God. God thundered in a mighty voice disrupting the Philistine's advance and the Philistines were defeated. Eli's sons bringing the ark to the battle had not brought victory, but Samuel's offering did.

As a judge, Samuel did not stay at Shiloh, but moved around between Bethel, Gilgal, Mizpah and his home of Ramah.

Why share the story with you out of order? Why did I not start with the story of Samuel's childhood, then tell of the ark being captured, and then of Samuel becoming judge in the order it is in the Bible? I wanted you to see the possibility that the story of the ark's capture and return could be one source independent of the second. It could be a story of the power of one god over another god. It could potentially be older than the story of Samuel that is made to frame it.

Without the discussion of Eli's son's sinfulness, the ark's capture and return could be a way of one god showing his power over Dagon. With the story of Eli's son's sinfulness, the story becomes one where the nation is punished because their priest and his children are not good. It becomes a story of the transfer of power between the house of Eli and Samuel. It a story about a transfer of power away from the shrine at Shiloh.

The first seven chapters of 1 Samuel form a carefully crafted piece of literature. It might have started out as a smaller story, later framed to change the meaning. Or it might have been written as one story. It ends with Samuel as a judge. The next chapter opens with the people approaching Samuel, but by then he has, like Eli, grown old. Like Eli, his sons are deemed unworthy. The people want a king to rule over them instead, and that is what we will discuss in the next chapter.

Follow-up Activities

1. Compare the stories of Samson and Samuel. What is one thing the same about them and several things different?

2. The story of Eli coming across Hannah as she prays for a son and the story of Samuel getting a message in the night are both good stories to practice retelling or rewriting. Choose one of the two and read the original in the Bible. Choose whose point of view you will retell it from. Then retell it in your own words, expanding and elaborating on it.

> Stephen Spielberg's 1981 action movie *Indiana Jones and the Raiders of the Lost Ark* has an archaeologist played by Harrison Ford working to prevent the Nazi's from locating the lost ark.

The Request for a King

The Biblical judges were said to arise at times when they were needed to defend the different tribes of Israel against attacks. They didn't build standing armies. They tended to have the loyalty of only a few tribes for a short period of time. Their ability to acquire resources from other tribes was limited. In short, they were not kings. Eventually the people wanted a king. When Samuel grew old, they asked that they be given a king "like other nations" had.

The Deuteronomic historians, compiling and rewriting the history hundreds of years after the first king of Israel had taken the throne, were not entirely in favour of the monarchy. It had united their people and at times promoted what they felt was the right away of worship. Yet they believed at other times the kings had led them astray, encouraging people to worship other gods and put them in danger of attack from larger empires. Their writing reflects this mixed appraisal of the monarchy.

Read Samuel 1:8 - 22. In it Samuel talked to his god, telling him that the people wanted a king. God responded to Samuel that the request wasn't a rejection of Samuel but a rejection of him (God) being the king. God says Samuel should warn them the problems that kings bring. (1 Samuel 8:7 – 8) Nevertheless, God agrees that the people shall have a king.

> Note the role of Samuel as go-between between people and their god. (1 Samuel 8:1 – 6) In many cultures ancient cultures it was the king who acted as the intermediate between the god and his people. As you read through the next few chapters watch for how the Hebrew scriptures limit this role.

The Bible tells three different stories of how Saul became the first king of Israel. In 1 Samuel 9 – 10:14 Saul is out searching for his father's lost donkeys. He is directed to "the seer Samuel" and when he finds Samuel, Samuel anoints him as king. Then Saul goes home, and his uncle asks him what the seer has said to him. Saul replies that the donkeys have been found, but he says nothing about being anointed king.

> Anointing someone means putting special oil on their head to mark them as specially chosen. What does it mean though for someone to be anointed king in secret? Can one be a secret king?

In 1 Samuel 10:17 – 10:27 the prophet Samuel summons all the different tribes together and draws lots, first to determine from which tribe the king would be, then to determine the family, and finally to identify which member of the chosen family would be king. We don't know exactly how they drew lots, but you could imagine it like putting a bunch of stones in a bag, with one of them specially marked. One person from each tribe draws a stone out and the tribe that drew the specially marked stone is chosen. All the stones go back in the bag. Then one member of each family from that tribe draw a stone until one person draws the special stone. Then all the stones go back in the bag and just the members of that family come forward and draw stones until one of them draws the special stone. It was Saul, from the tribe of Benjamin who was chosen. He was appointed king (again). Then he ran and hid. They found him hiding and had to bring him back. Then Samuel told everyone the rights and duties of the king, wrote it down and sent everyone home. Saul went home "and with him went warriors whose hearts God had touched."

Samuel 10:27b – 11:14 tells us about how one Hebrew tribe tried to make a peace agreement with the king of the Ammonites. The king of the Ammonites said he'll make peace only if every member of that tribe gouges their right eye out. Obviously, this was an unacceptable condition to a peace treaty. Saul heard the story and cut up his two oxen into pieces, sending the pieces with messages to all the different Hebrew tribes and threatening them that if they did not come and fight on behalf of those threatened by the Ammonites, he would cut up their oxen! It was through threats, not royal prerogative, that he forced people to come to fight. Enough people responded to his call that he could defeat the Ammonites. Then the people asked that Saul would be king over them.

Some people read those three stories as three things that all happened, one after another. They believe that Saul was anointed privately first, then anointed publicly, and then he stepped forward when needed to fight a war. Perhaps the intent was to show that he was reluctant rather than ambitious. Perhaps the intent was to show multiple proofs that he was suppose to be king. Asking for repeated omens was common throughout the ancient times.

Another possibility is that the stories were originally separate stories, from separate places. Or perhaps they were different arguments about how kingship should be. One argument is that kings should be appointed by a prophet. Another is that whomever can rally the people to defend the nation should be king. Perhaps the argument of the second story is that the king should be someone humble who doesn't want to be king.

The Bible tells of Saul fighting several different wars. When he was preparing for a war against the Philistines he made plans to meet with Samuel so Samuel could preside over a burnt offering to their god. Saul and his army arrived at the location and they waited for seven days for Samuel to arrive. People were getting restless and didn't want to wait longer, so Saul gave the burnt offering himself.

Then Samuel arrived and asked Saul what he had done. Samuel accused Saul of not keeping the commandments of their god and announced that Saul's kingdom would not continue indefinitely. Perhaps this was written by people who wanted to ensure that the kings would not try to be both king and religious leader, so that the kings would not be too powerful. Or perhaps they were simply trying to justify what happened later, when Saul's kingdom was taken over by a different king. (1 Samuel 13:1 – 15)

Another story tells of Saul demanding that all his army should fast – go without food - until after they have defeated their enemies. Saul said anyone who disobeyed would be put to death. Saul's son Jonathan had not heard the instructions, and so when he came upon some honeycomb, he ate it. When he was told that the king had ordered against anyone eating, he scoffed and said it was a bad order leading to weakened, hungry soldiers. (1 Samuel 14:24 — 30) Perhaps this is an example of how Saul again was trespassing on the role of the prophet, trying to implement religious restrictions?

Later Saul realized that someone had disobeyed him, and he drew lots to discover who the culprit was. Jonathan admitted it was him. Saul announced that Jonathan must die. The people said that Jonathan was their war hero they paid a ransom to have Jonathan spared. (1 Samuel 14:24 – 45)

Saul had already been told, privately that he had lost God's approval. In many ways Jonathan would have been the obvious replacement. He was Saul's son. He had lead a raid on the Philistines and he was popular with the soldiers. The story of him eating the honeycomb shows him disapproving of his father's decisions, distancing himself from his father and his father's errors. Yet he never became king.

In 1 Samuel 16, the prophet Samuel is sent by God to anoint an alternative king. Samuel is told which family the king will come from, and one by one the sons of that family are led before him. After all the older sons have been rejected, the youngest is summoned from where he was guarding the sheep. His name was David. The spirit of the Lord enters him. David's anointing resembles Saul's in several ways. Like the first anointing of Saul, David was caring for animals. Like the second anointing of Saul, there was a selection process - not lots, but similar. Like Saul, he returns to his normal life after. He was secretly anointed, but not publicly king.

Despite the similarities in the anointing stories, there's also a big difference between how Saul and David take power. Saul was described as becoming king because the nation had no king. He was filling a vacant role. David was anointed by Samuel while Saul was still alive. The role of king wasn't vacant. He became a threat to Saul. The Biblical writers were careful to try to frame the situation in one that legitimizes David's rule, claiming that their god chose for David to rule instead of permitting Saul's descendants to rule, but they tried to do it without discrediting the mechanisms that put Saul in power in the first place.

Follow-up Activities

1. In 1 Samuel 8, the Biblical authors say that the Hebrew people begged their prophet Samuel for a king. God responds that in doing so the people are not rejecting Samuel, but rather rejecting God. This implies that someone might have assumed a king would replace Samuel. In what way could a king replace a prophet? In what way could a king replace their god?

2. Samuel talked to God and God warned them what the problems of a king would be. Read chapter 8 and make a list of the problems.

3. When you think about a king, what do you picture? What makes someone a king? Is there any one thing where you can think "if this was taken away from a king, he would no longer be a king"? If the story of Saul happened with all three steps exactly the way they are described in the Bible, is there a particular moment where one can say "there – that is where he became the king"

David's Rise to Power

Perhaps you have already heard of the famous incident when Saul and his army were facing off against the Philistines. A Philistine giant named Goliath stepped forward and demanded that someone fight him in single combat. Everyone in Saul's army was too afraid to do so. The only one brave enough to fight was a young man named David, who wasn't in the army but had come to deliver supplies to his older brother. (1 Samuel 17)

David was a shepherd. It is easy these days to imagine that shepherds were peaceful young men tending to peaceful sheep, but being a shepherd was a hard and dangerous job. Shepherds were at risk not just of being attacked by wild animals but also by raids from other people. To the east of where the Hebrews lived, the Mesopotamians had stories about a shepherd god killed while watching his flock. It is not surprising that a shepherd would know how to fight, even if it is considered a miracle that he could defeat this particular gigantic soldier.

David killed Goliath using his sling, a cloth weapon that is whirled around until one strap is released, sending a stone towards the target. Then the Philistine army fled and Saul's troops gave chase.

After David killed Goliath, Saul made David into a military commander. A good commander can provide the king with military victories to keep him popular in the people's eyes. Alternatively, if the people rebel against a king, but the king maintains the support of his military, then the military can be turned against the people. The military, led by a good and loyal commander, can be a great asset to a king. Yet the military and its commander can also be a danger to the king. If an individual commander can draw more loyalty from the troops than the king himself does then the military can turn against the king.

> Nowadays the names David and Goliath are often applied to situations when someone small or powerless goes up against someone or something more powerful.

The Bible says that people sang, "Saul has slain his thousands, and David his ten thousands." (1 Samuel 18:7 and again in 21:11 NIV) David was becoming more popular than Saul. Saul became jealous of David and fearful that David's popularity would allow him to take over as king. David was forced to flee for his own life, and he was aided in this by Jonathan, the son of Saul. (1 Samuel 19 – 20)

David fled to the kingdom of Gath. The king of Gath was a Philistine and enemy of Saul. The king recognized David as the hero of Saul's kingdom. David pretended that he was insane so that the king would believe he wasn't a threat and throw him out of the city. (1 Samuel 21:10 – 15)

David began gathering crowds around him. "All those who were in distress or in debt or discontented gathered around him, and he became their commander. About four hundred men were with him." (1 Samuel 22:2 NIV)

It scared Saul that David gathered together the people who were unhappy with his rule. Saul traveled to the areas to meet the men. He accused the people of believing that David would be king, able to distribute fields and vineyards as a king does, and able to appoint them commanders of armies. He accuses them of being traitors. After a group of priests provide David with assistance, Saul had the priests killed. Likely the thought of priests joining David was particularly troubling to Saul as

> Note that one of the things that implies David was claiming kingship was promising to distribute land to his followers. The giving of land from a more powerful king to a less powerful king, or from a king to his followers, would have been part of kingship.
>
> One overall theme in the Deuteronomic histories is that their god is their real king, giver of the land to the people of Israel.

they could, if they chose, tell the people that God wanted David as king. (1 Samuel 22:1 – 23)

When a Hebrew city was attacked by the Philistines, David came to the city's defense. What did this mean for Saul? Perhaps he should have been happy that one of the cities was defended against their mutual enemies, but for someone other than the king to lead an army to the city's defense poses a threat to the king's authority. It meant the king was too weak to defend his people. It meant someone else was strong enough to do so. David had become an alternative power-base, an alternative king. (1 Samuel 23:1-14)

Saul pursued David into the wilderness. Read 1 Samuel 24, where David and Saul were (temporarily) reconciled. Think about the politics of this. What did Saul ask David to promise?

Then read 1 Samuel 25. Here David demanded that a wealthy man provide food for his men on the basis that David's men have been protecting the man's shepherds. When the man refused to pay such tribute, David prepared to attack him. The man's wife managed to sooth things over, offering generous tribute as well as praise to David, saying that David will become king. When the man died, David took the woman as one of his many wives.

David repeatedly rejected opportunities to kill Saul. (1 Samuel 26) The writers are trying to protect David from accusations that he attempted to steal power from Saul. Yet the events they are describing – gathering men, defending cities, forcing people to pay for his protection, even the taking of multiple wives – involve David behaving as a king while Saul is alive. The events themselves describe actions that threaten a king's power, no matter how many times the king's life is spared.

David left Saul's land, taking his men into the service of Saul's enemy, the Philistine King Achish of Gath. When David first went to Gath he was alone and vulnerable. Even his reputation could not protect him and had to resort to tricks to escape the city. When he returned to the city later he had followers and from them power. He could negotiate a relationship with the king.

From Gath, David and his men lead attacks on other tribes – the Geshurites, the Girzites, and the Amalekites – returning to the King Achish with the plunder. He pretended that he had attacked people in Saul's kingdom. To keep up this ruse he made sure to slaughter every last person of the villages they attacked, so there were no witnesses from the other tribes to accuse him of attacking them. (1 Samuel 27, 29)

The king of Gath saw the treasures that David brought back. He believed David's lie that they had come from villages in Saul's kingdom. He believed that David had so angered his own people by attacking them that David would never be let back into that kingdom, and that David would have no choice but to be loyal to him.

Yet, despite this, the other Philistines commanders didn't trust David. When they decided to attack Saul's kingdom, they urged that David be left behind. The king called David to ask about his loyalties, and David answered:

> "But what have I done?" asked David. "What have you found against your servant from the day I came to you until now? Why can't I go and fight against the enemies of my lord the king?""(1 Samuel 29:8 NIV)

Read that verse twice. While David acknowledged he was in the service of the Philistine King, the text leaves it open that "my lord, the king" could in fact be Saul. David had claimed to be leading raids against Saul's villages while secretly leading raids against Saul's enemies' villages instead. The vague answer allows the readers to see David as secretly loyal to his own people. The story continues that although the king believed David, he agreed to send David away from the battle, so David was spared having to fight against his own people. The text succeeded in doing two things. It explained how David could remain safe within the Philistine court while at the same time defending how this eventual king of Israel was loyal to his people.

The Philistines killed Jonathan and some of Saul's other sons. Saul did not want to risk being captured so he killed himself. A man found his body and cut off Saul's head, taking it to David in the hopes that David would reward him for killing Saul. Instead David punishes the one claiming responsibility for Saul's death and grieves.

After Saul's death, David returned to his home tribe of Judah and was anointed as king. Then for a while there are two kings – David, king of the tribe of Judah, and Saul's son Ishbaal. Ishbaal's general defected and joined David's army. Eventually Ishbaal was killed and David was recognized as king over all Israel. (1 Samuel 31 – 2 Samuel 2:7)

> Remember the prophecy that the patriarch Jacob was supposed to have made to his son Judah, about his tribe will bear the sceptre? David becoming king fulfils this prophecy.

David captured the city of Jerusalem, which until then had been held by a group called the Jebusites, and he made it his capital. He brought the religious artifacts that the tribes had rallied around previously into Jerusalem. However, his god told him not to build a temple for those artifacts, but to leave that for the next generation. (2 Samuel 5:6 - 6:19)

David did not forget that he loved Saul's son Jonathan. Jonathan had left behind a boy named Mephibosheth. Mephibosheth had a bad leg and could not walk properly, but he was still a potential heir to Saul should the people choose to rally around him. When he was called into David's presence, he assumed it was so that David could have him killed. Instead David accepted the boy into his household. (2 Samuel 9)

Follow-up Activities

1. Make a list of what a king's job entailed in the stories of Saul and David. How does this compare to modern royalty in the United Kingdom or in Saudi Arabia?

2. Review the story of Eli and Samuel. Do the stories of Eli and Samuel have similar themes or messages as the story of Saul and David?

The Kingdom of David

The Bible describes God as showing special favour to David and loving David. When the kingdom split in two, the surviving southern kingdom, which kept descendants of David as their king, used his kingship to claim to be the legitimate heirs of the earlier undivided monarchy. When both kingdoms were destroyed, the prophets could claim that God's promise to David that his line would last forever was their assurance that the kingdom would someday be restored. Praising David's relationship with God offered legitimacy, stability and hope to future generations.

> Psalmists wrote poems of praise to David. Some people believe David himself wrote many of the psalms, but this is less likely.

Yet, the Bible also describes David as doing something really bad. David fulfills some of the warnings that the Bible has about how kings steal from their people. He became interested in a woman named Bathsheba, even though she was married to another man. Then he sent that other man off to die in a war so that he could marry Bathsheba. After this a prophet named Nathan came to David and told him a story about a wealthy man and a poor man. In Nathan's story, the poor man had only one sheep that he hand-raised and cared for dearly. The wealthy man had lots of sheep, but when a traveler came to visit him the wealthy man decided to slaughter the poor man's sheep instead of his own. When David heard the story he felt anger at the wealthy man. To his surprise the prophet said to him that he was the wealthy man for taking another man's wife when he already has many wives of his own. (2 Samuel 11:1 – 12:23)

> The Bible says that David and Bathsheba's son died because of what David did in marrying another man's wife. Modern international law says that people should not be punished for crimes they themselves do not commit, but in ancient times not everyone held that belief. In Biblical times people believed that a child could be punished for the bad things the parents did.
>
> David and Bathsheba went on to have another child together.

David had other problems to face too, many related to his sons and to the fact that though the text works hard to legitimize his claim to the throne, he was an usurper. Later generations would praise his kingdom, but during his lifetime people were likely less certain about his claim to rule.

One of David's sons, Amnon, was abusive towards his half-sister Tamar. Tamar's brother Absalom killed Amnon, and then fled for fear of his father's wrath. (2 Samuel 13)

One of David's advisors arranged a scheme to reunite David and Absalom. He arranged for a widow to meet the king and tell the king a story. She said that one of her two sons killed the other and if anyone avenges that one son she'll lose the remaining one. A widow with no surviving children was very vulnerable. When David says that her remaining son must be spared for her sake, she turned the situation around on David and urged that he must bring back his own banished son. (2 Samuel 14:1 – 20)

David agreed to allow Absalom to return but refused to meet him. Absalom waited and waited. Two years passed, and Absalom still had not been able to see his David.

Frustrated by the wait, Absalom tried to summon his father's advisor to explain why he had been called back if he was not actually accepted back into the family, but the advisor refused to come to Absalom. (2 Samuel 14:21 – 29)

Absalom told his servants to set the advisor's fields on fire. This forced the advisor to come and speak to him, and Absalom was able to ask for the advisor to intercede with his father. He said if he was so guilty he could not see David then he should be killed, and if not guilty enough to deserve death then he should be permitted to see his father again. (2 Samuel 14:30 – 33)

David relented and forgave his son, but all was not well. Like David during Saul's rule, Absalom began to gather people about him. He sat at the city gates, like elders did in the time before the monarchy. He said, "If only I were appointed judge in the land! Then everyone who has a complaint or case could come to me and I would see that they receive justice." (2 Samuel 15:4 NIV) He encouraged people to imagine that he would be a better ruler than his father.

After four years, Absalom had won enough support from the people of Israel that he was willing to make a move. He told his father that he was going to Hebron to offer a sacrifice to God. There at Hebron he gathered his army. When David heard of the support Absalom had, he decided to flee from Jerusalem. (2 Samuel 15:7 – 23)

As David fled, he met a servant of Saul's grandson Mephibosheth. The servant told David him that Mephibosheth was staying in Jerusalem with the expectation that the people were going to give him back his grandfather's crown! It is unclear whether Absalom had any thought of helping Saul's family, but David met other people who threw rocks at him, saying that the revolt against him was revenge for what he had done to the house of Saul. The people had not forgotten that David had been an usurper to the throne. (2 Samuel 16:1 – 14)

Absalom had two advisors. One told him that he should send out a team to go and capture David quickly, without risking his own life in battle or waiting for all of Israel to rally behind him. The other was a spy for David and advised Absalom to wait and gather a larger army and then attack with Absalom leading the army. When Absalom chose to follow the spy's advice, the spy quickly sent word to David about what to expect. David had time to muster his own army and prepare them for battle. (2 Samuel 17)

Before the armies met for battle, David told his soldiers that he wanted his son's life spared. Yet, Absalom was not spared. While riding he caught his head on a branch and ended up suspended in the air alive. His father's advisors saw him and had him killed. (2 Samuel 18)

David grieved for his son. His grief was insulting to the army that had just fought to defend him against his son's uprising. His advisors spoke to him:
> "Today you have humiliated all your men, who have just saved your life and the lives of your sons and daughters and the lives of your wives and concubines. ⁶ You love those who hate you and hate those who love you. You have made it clear today that the commanders and their men mean nothing to you. I see that you would be pleased if Absalom were alive today and all of us were dead. ⁷ Now go out and encourage your men. I swear by the Lord that if you don't go out, not a man will be left with you by nightfall. This will be worse for you than all the calamities that have come on you from your youth till now." (2 Samuel 19:5b – 7 NIV)

David did as his advisors insisted. He stood before the army and said what they needed him to say. He negotiated the end to the rebellion, including making his peace with those who had been disloyal to him. He spoke with Mephibosheth. Mephibosheth claimed that the servant had lied and that he was still loyal to David. (2 Samuel 18 – 19:30)

After that revolt there was another revolt, and after that one can imagine the king being rather ill at ease. How can he ensure peace? How can he ensure prosperity?

There was a famine for three years. When David inquired from the Lord what caused the famine, he was told that there was blood guilt on the house of Saul. Long before then, Saul had tried to kill a Canaanite tribe. David attempted to make amends to the tribe, but was told that the only thing they would accept is the death of seven of Saul's descendants. The king spared Mephibosheth but sent seven of Saul's other descendants to their deaths. Afterwards the rain returned. From one point of view this could be David making an unfortunate sacrifice to fulfill a requirement that God requires in order to restore the natural order of things.

From another point of view, the story is one where Biblical writers were once again explaining away how David got rid of yet more potential contenders to his throne while at the same time shifting the blame away from David. (2 Samuel 21)

2 Samuel 24:1 – 17 tells that David had a census done, counting all the people. Then he felt guilty for doing this and said to the lord that he should be punished. Through a seer named Gad, David was told that he should choose one of three punishments. Either three years of famine should come to the land, or he should have to flee for three months before his foes, or the land would face three days of disease. David begged for mercy and said he didn't want to fall into human hands. Then for three days a plague went through the land, killing thousands of people. As the angel bringing the plague approached Jerusalem, God stopped him. At the same time, David saw all the destruction and said that he alone had done wrong, and begged that the punishment be against him and his father's house alone. David was told to go and build an altar in the place where the angel had stopped.

Why would David having a census done be problematic? It might have been that a census was a step towards either taxing people, demanding corvee labour, or drafting people to build an army. Or perhaps the writers thought only their god was supposed to know the number of people.

At the beginning of the text in 2 Samuel, it says that their god was the one who was angry at the kingdom and thus stirred David to take the census. Perhaps David was supposed to do bad so that the kingdom could be punished. Or perhaps the census itself was bad for the kingdom.

The Chronicler, writing sometime later, changed the story in several ways. The Chroniclers said it was not God but an adversary who stirred David to take the census. Then David's commander did not agree with the census so he did not do the census properly, and that, the Chronicler says, was the evil which was then punished.

> Who was the adversary who inspired David to take the census in the Chronicler's version of the account? You will read more about him in the chapter on Job. Originally the term - Satan - probably referred to any opponent or obstacle but eventually the term became a reference to one being, the Adversary.

The Biblical writers were willing to portray David as flawed in many ways. They were willing to show his fear, his grief, and at times his bad choices. But they were still determined to portray him as loyal to Saul, as God's anointed king, and to Jonathan, because of the promise of loyalty between them.

The stories of David portray an imperfect king with a kingdom that, at times, revolted against him, yet the stories are framed in such a way as to emphasis his loyalty and his appointment by God. In 2 Samuel 7:1 – 17 David decides to build a house for God. God sends a message through the prophet Nathan telling David that he should not build the temple but that his son will build it, and that their kingdom will be established forever. It warns that when David makes mistakes he will be punished, but that God will not pull his 'steadfast love' away from David as he did from Saul.

The text testifies to a belief that the kingdom was divinely established, would last forever, but would potentially face punishments. In times of political instability people could turn to the belief that their king and his lineage had been established by God, and that God's covenant would protect them.

Follow-up Activities

1. This chapter has included two times where David was told a story only to be told afterwards that he is the villain of the story. What would be the benefit of chastising someone in this way? Why might people be more willing to listen to correction in this way than if they were told up front that they were wrong?

2. How does David's relationship with Absalom compare with Saul's relationship with Jonathan. Read 1 Samuel 18 – 19 to learn more about Jonathan and Saul's relationship before answering this.

3. In the ancient world it was common to believe that gods had aided in establishing a kingship. The ancient Sumerians saw kingship as a gift of the gods. In The *Iliad* King Agamemnon's scepter had been given down to him by the gods. In many ancient cultures (Sumerian, Greek, Hebrew, etc) the king was a shepherd appointed by the gods to care for the people. Yet this divine appointment didn't necessarily mean they could do anything they wanted. The gods' authority was on loan to the king as long as he followed the god's will. In ancient literature a disaster befalling a community was often taken as a sign that the king was no longer following the will of the gods. Centuries later Europeans would develop concepts around the divine right of kingship where they believed that because God had presided over them inheriting their throne, whatever they did was justified, approved of by God. Look up the "divine right of kings" and compare it to the limits set on Saul.

4. Listen to the song "Hallelujah" by Leonard Cohen. Can you recognize the references to the story of David?

An Aside – The Psalms

The book of Psalms is not quite in the middle of the Bible, but if you open your Bible to half way through and thumb backwards through it a bit you should be able to find it. (The "P" at the beginning of Psalms is silent. The word is pronounced "salms.") The psalms are poems or songs, and for a long time many of them were attributed to David. Depending on what translation of the Bible you have, you might even see the phrase "of David" underneath the psalm numbers. Some of these songs touch on kingship, deliverance from enemies and other topics relevant to King David's life, and as he was said to have musical abilities, people attributed them to him. There's no historical evidence to support this.

Let's look at a few of the psalms. One of the most famous psalms is Psalm 23. This psalm is frequently attributed to King David because he had been a shepherd. However, the image of the king as a shepherd was a frequent one in ancient literature, dating back to at least the ancient Sumerians.

Some of the psalms might have been part of rituals. Psalm 2 might have been part of a coronation celebration. Read Psalm 2. The first scene of it is the rulers of the Earth plotting against God. Where does it switch from that setting to talking about God laughing at them? Verses 7 – 12 have God speaking. Who would God be speaking to, if the psalm was a coronation ritual?

Some psalms might have been recited as a means of giving courage and appealing for divine protection. Psalm 91 is an example of these, and a good one to see how the Biblical poetry relies on parallels and imagery instead of rhymes. Turn to Psalm 91 to see these at work. Read the psalm slowly taking note of the following:

- The first verse of this psalm has two parallel lines. Both lines say basically the same thing. The sentence structure of both is similar.

- Verse 91:2 we have the parallel of "my refuge and my fortress." The second verse has two verbs, each attached to a name of God. The sentence structures are different though. One starts with the verb and then the name of god, and the other starts with the name of god and ends with the verb. It may be that this psalm was one recited in hard times and the poet wanted to draw a connection between saying and trusting.

- In the next verses we have a series of images of vulnerability and protection. Watch for pairs like "a shield and a buckler" but also for opposites like "day" and "night."

- Verse seven is composed of three lines together, rather than two. Mention of "a thousand" and then "ten thousand" provides emphasis. Think of Saul killing his thousands and David his ten thousands. (1 Samuel 18:7 and again in 21:11) In this case both the thousand and ten thousand are contrasted with the person who remains protected and untouched by all the destruction.

- Verse nine has a word in it that can be translated as "if," "because" or "for." How would that change the meaning of the lines? Search this verse as well for words that hint back to verse one.

- In verses eleven to thirteen we have a description of messengers – angels, in most translations – carrying the singer over the rough terrain and protect him from the dangers on the journey. There are five different Hebrew words for lion and two different ones are used in the text.

- Verses fourteen to fifteen are written as though spoken by god. Look at the structure of verse fourteen. The first line describes other's actions then the god's actions. The second line describes god's actions and then other's actions. What is the structure of the four lines in verse 15 or the two lines in verse 16?

From One Kingdom to Two

The Bible portrays Saul as a reluctant king willing to step up and defend his nation, but also willing to return home to his farm. It portrays David as a more ambitious warrior who establishes a new capital. It portrays David's son, Solomon, as a wise man who amasses great wealth and power.

The Bible tells that Solomon built a temple in Jerusalem. (1 Kings 5 – 6, 8) In ancient times temples were houses for gods, where the gods could live. In some kingdoms and some cities the temples were homes to multiple gods, but in Jerusalem the temple was just for the one god. It was a place where grain, blood, and fat could be offered in sacrifice. Like most ancient temples, there were special rules that applied to the temple in Jerusalem to keep it a worthy home for their god.

At first Solomon pleased the Hebrew's god, but then as he grew older he took many foreign wives and joined them in worshiping their gods. The Bible tells of him worshiping the Sidonian goddess Astarte, the Moabite god Chemosh, the Ammonite god Molech and suggests he worshiped others too. Each of these other nearby kingdoms would have had their own myths and stories just as the ancient Hebrews did, but their stories have not been as well preserved as the Hebrew's stories. (1 Kings 11:1 – 13)

A servant of Solomon's decided to revolt against Solomon. 1 Kings 11:28 says, "Now Jeroboam was a man of standing, and when Solomon saw how well the young man did his work, he put him in charge of the whole labor force of the tribes of Joseph." (NIV) It then tells of a prophet ripping up a garment into twelve pieces and giving Jeroboam ten of the pieces. The ten pieces of cloth were to represent ten of the twelve tribes which Jeroboam was to rule over, not as servant to Solomon but as king. Somehow word got back to Solomon that Jeroboam was supposed to take ten tribes from him, so he tried to kill Jeroboam. Jeroboam went to Egypt and remained there until Solomon died. (1 Kings 11:26 – 40)

After Solomon died his son, Rehoboam, became king. Jeroboam returned from Egypt and met with an assembly of people. He said to Rehoboam, "Your father put a heavy yoke on us, but now lighten the harsh labor and the heavy yoke he put on us, and we will serve you." (1 Kings 12:4 NIV) The yoke is a wooden bar used to tie beasts of labour to their carts or worn over the neck to haul heavy loads. To say one must wear a heavy yoke is to say one is being made to work too hard.

Rehoboam asked for three days to think about the people's request. During that time, Rehoboam went first to the old men who served his father and asked their advice. They said that if he is gentle with the people they will serve him forever. (1 Kings 12:5 – 7)

Then Rehoboam went to the men his own age and asked them for advice. They said that he should show he is tougher and stronger than his father by making the people work even harder. (1 Kings 12:8 – 11)

When Rehoboam went back to the people, he told them that he was going to make them work harder. This angered the people and the people of ten tribes rejected Rehoboam and made Jeroboam their king instead. Their kingdom became known as the Kingdom of Israel, or the northern kingdom. Only the tribes of Judah and Benjamin stayed with Rehoboam, and their kingdom became known as the Kingdom of Judah or the southern kingdom. (1 Kings 12:12 – 19)

Does the story of Jeroboam sound familiar? There are echoes in it of the story of Moses. There is an initial slight action against the oppressors. In one story Moses kills an Egyptian and in the other story the initial action is the prophet predicting that Jeroboam will take ten tribes. Then in each story the hero flees. In one story the flight is away from Egypt; in the other story the flight is to Egypt. There is a return and confrontation with the oppressive power and finally a freeing of the people from the oppressor. It is possible that the story of Moses was based off of people's experience under Jeroboam. It is also possible that later writers telling of Jeroboam purposely shaped their story to resemble the one of Moses. The slight mention of Joseph's house and forced labour was likely included in the Jeroboam story to remind people of the story of Moses. However, it is more likely that there was a real Jeroboam than a real Moses, simply because there is no record of Moses in Egyptian stories and his story is filled with much more magic, while Jeroboam's story takes place closer to the time it was written down and relies less on supernatural events.

The Bible says that once Jeroboam was king, he needed to ensure that people wouldn't go down to Jerusalem to worship. So Jeroboam set up two calves made of gold, one in Dan and one in Bethel. The shrine at Bethel became more important than the shrine at Dan. (1 Kings 12:25 – 33) Later Biblical writers and editors would view these statues as proof that the northern kingdom was founded on idol worship and that they took on foreign ways. However, the ancient Canaanite god El was worshiped as a bull, so the calves might have seemed like a perfectly traditional way to worship and not as foreign or idolatrous to Jeroboam or his people.

There is a saying that "history is written by the victors." This means that the people who win a war tend to write about it as though they were the good side. The northern kingdom would eventually be defeated by the Assyrians and their history would be told by people of the southern kingdom who believed that the northern kingdom must have worshiped god wrong. So they describe the golden calves as idols and bad things. Perhaps if the southern kingdom had been destroyed before the northern one, the rest of the Hebrew scriptures might have been written to promote the worship of God in the form of golden calves!

Follow-up Activities

1. Read the story of Solomon's wisdom found in 1 Kings 3:16-28. Retell the story in your own words.

2. Read the descriptions of Solomon building the temple in 1 Kings 6 and the dedication in 1 Kings 8 and look up models of the temple of Solomon online. Can you build a model with card paper or Lego?

The Omride's Gain Power

After Jeroboam there were a few kings of Israel about which the Bible doesn't tell us much. The next really important king was one called Omri. Omri had been a general in the Israelite army when someone else - a man named Zimri - had the king killed. Omri led his army in battle against the Zimri. After the Zimri's death, Omri became king. Omri built a new capital for the northern kingdom and named the capital Samaria. That name stuck around so that even after the northern kingdom was no longer a kingdom on its own, but just a province of other empires, the province was called Samaria. (1 Kings 16:15 – 28)

It might seem from that little description that Omri wasn't very important but he started a ruling dynasty called the Omrides. Their power grew to the point where other kingdoms nearby had to pay tribute to them and at times they went to war to force the payment of tribute. They also made diplomatic marriages. Omri's son, Ahab, is described as marrying a Sidonian princess, Jezebel. Ahab and Jezebel were said to have worshiped Baal and put up an Asherah pole. You read earlier about a story of the warrior Gideon tearing down an Asherah pole and breaking an altar to Baal before going to fight to defend the Hebrew people. Now, you read about someone else setting ones up! (1 Kings 16:29 – 34)

The Deuteronomic historians who recorded these stories wanted to explain why the northern kingdom had been defeated by the Assyrian empire and why the southern kingdom was being defeated by the Babylonians. They believed that the defeat of the two kingdoms by their enemies were signs of God's displeasure. Since the northern kingdom fell first, it must have angered God first, and perhaps if the southern kingdom had been very careful to only worship God, then God would have protected it against the same end. All through the stories they wrote or edited, they put in little descriptions of how different kings either did good or did bad in the sight of God.

These historians were not fond of Jeroboam, because after all he had split the northern kingdom off from the south, and they were writing or editing from the southern kingdom. However, they were even less fond of the Omri family, and even less fond of Omri's son Ahab. They wrote "Ahab also made an Asherah pole and did more to arouse the anger of the Lord, the God of Israel, than did all the kings of Israel before him" (1 Kings 16:33 NIV)

Ahab's story is tied in with the story of the prophet Elijah. Elijah predicted that there would be a drought. During the drought, Elijah traveled from Samaria to the city of Zarephath, which was right in the middle of Baal's territory. There Elijah stayed with a widow. She had almost no food, but while Elijah stayed with her the little food she had did not get depleted. When her son became ill, Elijah prayed to his god to save the life of a little boy. Elijah waited there in Zarephath for three years before returning to Samaria to meet with Ahab. (1 Kings 17 – 18:19)

Ahab and Elijah arranged a meeting on the nearest mountain, together with all the Israelites and the prophets of Baal and Asherah. The Bible says there were 450 prophets of Baal and 400 of Asherah. Elijah challenged the prophets of Baal. He said that they should build an altar and sacrifice a bull to Baal. The prophets were to ask Baal to start a fire on the altar to consume the sacrifice and to bring rain to end the drought. Then Elijah would sacrifice a bull to his god and make the same request. (1 Kings 18:20 – 24)

The prophets accepted the challenge and made their request of their god, but there was no response from Baal. Elijah mocked them: "Shout louder! Surely he is a god! Perhaps he is deep in thought, or busy, or traveling. Maybe he is sleeping and must be awakened." (1 Kings 18:27 NIV) This references to one of the old myths about Baal. According to Canaanite mythology Baal, the god of storms and rainfall, was killed by Mot, god of death and barrenness, and had to be awakened.

When the prophets of Baal were unable to bring about either the requested fire or the rain, Elijah had his altar drenched in water. He filled a trench around the altar with water. Then he made his prayer, referencing to the God of Abraham, Isaac and Israel. Fire fell down and burnt the offering, the wood and stones of the altar and all the water in the trench. Then the rain came and ended the drought. Ahab had all the prophets of Baal killed. Jezebel, Ahab's wife, swore revenge upon Elijah, and Elijah had to flee. (1 Kings 18:30 – 19:10)

In the story of Elijah, Elijah's god is described in ways that take on the characteristics of the storm-god Baal. Healing people, making fire (lightening), and bringing rain were all things the ancient Canaanites believed Baal did.

The story could have ended right there, with the people celebrating Yahweh and recognizing his triumph instead of Baal. However, that isn't the way the story ends. The story has another section which repeats the idea from the books of Joshua and Judges that the Israelites were not to show mercy to the tribes around them.

The Arameans, who lived to the north of Israel, laid siege to Samaria and demanded tribute. Their king was named Ben-Hadad. The Israelites waited until Ben-Hadad was drunk and then they came out of their city and attacked the Arameans' camp. The Arameans ran away, and the Israelites chased after them. (1 Kings 20)

The Arameans told Ben-Hadad "Their gods are gods of the hills, so they were stronger than us in the hills, but let us fight against them in the plains and surely we'll be stronger than them." They gathered a big army and filled a whole valley, and the Israelites army looked tiny in comparison. (1 Kings 20:23 - 25)

The Israelites might have been scared, but a man of God came and assured Ahab that their god would prove that he was powerful. After seven days of waiting the battle began. The Arameans were defeated and fled once more. (1 Kings 20:26 – 30a)

Ben-Hadad decided to appeal to the mercy of Ahab. He put sackcloth - a rough uncomfortable material - around him instead of clothing and went to beg for mercy. Ahab agreed to spare him and made a treaty with him. (1 Kings 20:30b – 34)

This displeased some of the prophets. One prophet demanded another strike him. The second prophet refused, and the first said "ok, because you wouldn't obey, a lion will eat you." A lion ate the second prophet, and then the first prophet said to someone else "strike me." This prophet obeyed. (1 Kings 20:35 – 37)

> Hadad is another name for the god Baal, and the name Ben means "son." So Ben-Hadad means son of Baal.
>
> If there was no real King Ahab or Ben-Hadad, this could have been the Bible writer's way of saying their god is not only greater than Baal as a storm-god producing rain and fire, but also as a warrior god.

The prophet who had demanded that he be hit went to meet King Ahab. He told Ahab a story about someone who was entrusted to guard a prisoner but allowed the prisoner to escape. Ahab agreed that the man who let the prisoner go should have to pay a fine or lose his life. Then the prophet said to Ahab "you are the one who let the prisoner go! God trusted you to defeat Ben-Hadad and you let him free. Because of this you will lose your life and your people." (1 Kings 20:38 – 43)

Follow-up Activity

1. Think about the story of the prophet asking someone to strike him. How do you think that little story fits with the story of King Ahab and Ben-Hadad.

King Ahab is Doomed

King Ahab had built a palace for himself in the city of Jezreel. Near the palace was a vineyard, and he wanted the vineyard for himself. The owner of the vineyard was a man named Naboth, and he refused to sell the vineyard to the king. (1 Kings 21:1 – 4)

Why didn't Ahab just confiscate the vineyard? He was a king, after all. Perhaps he remembered the warnings that the prophet Samuel had given to the people of how a king would make them work too hard and take their good things from him? Or Ahab might have remembered how the ten tribes had split off from King Solomon's son and made Jeroboam their king when Solomon's son had threatened to be the type of king that Samuel had warned against. King Ahab might have believed he should be good and not oppress his people.

When Queen Jezebel heard that Ahab wanted the vineyard, she told him that, because he was the king, he should be able to take it. She was a Sidonian princess, and it is possible that the Sidonian kings had more power than the Israelites wanted their king to have. She wrote letters in Ahab's name to the elders and nobles of the city and had Naboth accused of cursing God and the king. She had Naboth taken out of the city and killed, so that Ahab could take the vineyard. (1 Kings 21:5 – 16)

When the prophet Elijah heard about how Naboth was killed and his vineyard taken, he went to Ahab and said, "In the place where dogs licked up the blood of Naboth, dogs will lick up your blood!" He also said that Jezebel would be punished and the kingdom taken from their family, just as Omri had taken the kingdom from the family of Jeroboam. (1 Kings 21:17 – 26)

Ahab tore his clothing and put on sackcloth and refused to eat. The Bible says "Then the word of the Lord came to Elijah the Tishibite: "Have you seen how Ahab has humbled himself before me? Because he has humbled himself before me, I will not bring the disaster in his days; but in his son's days I will bring the disaster on his house." (1 Kings 21:28 – 29)

Remember how Ahab had made an agreement with the Aramean King? After three years, the Ahab went to Jehoshaphat, king of Judah, to ask his help in attacking the Arameans. He said: "The Aramean king controls the land of Ramoth-Gilead, which should be paying tribute to us, not him! Will you come and fight for it with us?" (1 Kings 22:3 – 4a)

1 Kings 22 tells the story of how Jehoshaphat, king of Judah, inquired of some prophets as to whether he should go with the King of Israel to attack the Arameans or not. He summoned four hundred prophets and they all said to go ahead and fight the Arameans. Then Jehoshaphat asked if there were any other prophets they should check with too, and Ahab said yes, there was a prophet named Micaiah. Ahab didn't like Micaiah, because Micaiah always warned Ahab that bad things were going to happen. Nevertheless, he agreed to send a message to Micaiah to ask his opinion.

At first Micaiah said that yes, Ahab and Jehoshaphat should go and attack the Ramoth-Gilead.

Ahab must have been surprised. That was not what he expected from Micaiah. He chastised Micaiah, saying he must tell the truth and only the truth. Something about Micaiah's message must have made him doubt that Micaiah was being honest.

Micaiah replied, "I see all of Israel scattered on the mountains like sheep with no shepherd."

This is what Ahab had expected to hear from him. He told Jehoshaphat, "Didn't I warn you that Micaiah always predicts doom?"

Why had Micaiah first said to go and attack the Arameans and then predicted doom? Micaiah explained it saying he had seen a vision of God sitting with the "hosts of heaven." The hosts of heaven are other gods or angels. God said to the others "who will convince Ahab to go attack Ramoth-Gilead so that he can be destroyed?" One of the spirits said he would do it by becoming a lying spirit in the mouths of the prophets. So that is why the prophets, including Micaiah, lied.

Did Ahab like hearing this explanation? He decided to throw Micaiah into prison. Then he and the king of Judah went to fight at Ramoth-Gilead.

Jehoshaphat suggested that Ahab disguise himself and not ride out dressed as a king. Ahab did that, riding out in a chariot disguised as a normal person. At first their enemies ignored Ahab as they were looking to attack someone dressed as a king. However, one of the archers' arrows hit the king. Despite his injury, Ahab fought as bravely as he could until his death that evening. Then his body was brought back home and the chariot was brought to be cleaned. It was taken to where Naboth had died, and the dogs licked Ahab's blood from it. Part of Elijah's prophecy had come true. Would the second part come true? Would the kingdom be taken away from King Ahab's family?

Follow-up Activities

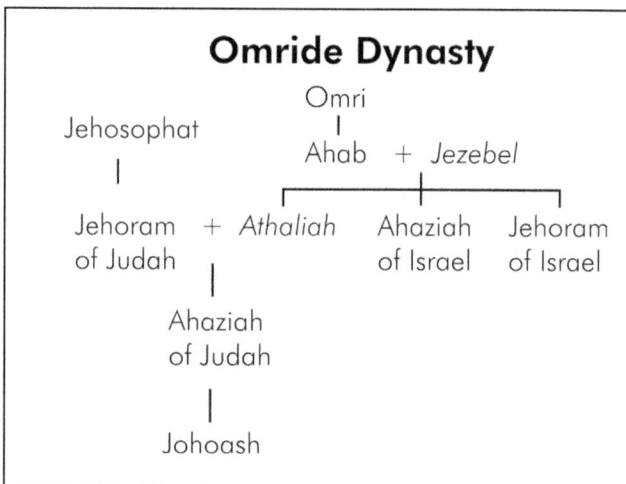

1. Read the story of Naboth's Vineyard in 1 Kings 21:1 – 16. Then reread it omitting verse 10. How would the story change if verse 10 was a later addition? With that verse the elders and nobles are involved in hiring the wicked me and they know that Naboth is innocent. With that verse, the elders are complicit. Without the verse could the elders have been set up, hosting the assembly without knowing that Naboth will be accused? Does the story make more sense with or without verse 10?

2. In 1 Kings 21:9 Jezebel tells the people to proclaim a fast. Fasts were sometimes done as an admission of collective guilt – a way of saying that they had all done something wrong, that was displeasing their god. How would asking them to fast help encourage them to kill Naboth?

Why did Ahab go to fight even after he heard the prophet tell him that God wanted him to be lured there to die? The Bible doesn't say. Perhaps the writers wanted to make it seem like Ahab didn't believe Micaiah and instead trusted all the prophets who had told him to go fight.

Or perhaps the writers wanted to show that Ahab was trying to do what he believed God wanted, even if that cost him his life. Maybe he went because he believed God wanted him lured there. Maybe he hoped obedience would change God's mind or perhaps make God not hold his mistakes against his children.

The writers of this story don't give a clear answer. There was a difficulty with prophecies of doom. If the person a prophet predicts doom for changes his mind and believes the prophet, then the doom won't happen and it will seem as though the prophet lied. A prophet's prediction of doom could only be proven true if the person disbelieved the prophet.

If Ahab had really changed his behaviour so greatly when Elijah told him that he was doomed, that God forgave him completely, then it would seem like Elijah's predictions were not true. Yet the writers wanted to believe God gave second chances to kings that changed their ways. How could they write stories where God gave second chances and yet have the prophecies be proven true? The story of King Ahab wrestles with this issue.

Elijah and Elisha

The story of the Omride's downfall is told through a series of overlapping stories. The stories emphasize that of all the gods worshiped in the area, it is Yahweh to whom the kings should turn to seek guidance and protection. They also emphasis that the prophets, not the kings, were the ones who spoke for Yahweh. The two most important of these prophets were Elijah and his successor Elisha.

After Ahab's death, his son Ahaziah became king of Israel. He reigned for two years, worshiping Baal. They tells us that he had an accident and fell through a lattice in an upper room in his palace in Samaria, and became injured. He sent messengers to inquire of Baal-zebub, the god of Ekron, as to whether he would heal properly. Elijah met the messengers and asked why messengers were being sent to Ekron's god, as though there was no god of Israel. Elijah told them that Ahaziah would never leave his bed. (2 Kings 1:1 – 4)

> Ekron was a Philistine city in the south-west of Canaan.

The messengers went back to Ahaziah and passed on Elijah's message. Ahaziah asked who had given them the message. They said it was a hairy man with a leather belt around his waist, and Ahaziah recognized the description of Elijah. So he sent fifty men plus their captain to go and get Elijah. (2 Kings 1:5 – 9)

Elijah told the captain, "If I am a man of God, let fire come down from heaven and consume you and your fifty men." Fire came down, and killed the fifty men. (2 Kings 1:10)

The king sent another captain with another fifty men to go and get Elijah. The same thing happened to them. (2 Kings 1:11-12)

The king sent a third captain with fifty men. This captain fell on his knees before Elijah and begged that he and his men be spared the same fate. So God told Elijah to go with the captain down to Ahaziah, and Elijah did that. (2 Kings 1:13 - 16)

Elijah told Ahaziah that because he sent messengers to the god of Ekron and not to the god of Israel, the king would never get up from his bed but instead die there. And he did. (2 Kings 1:17 – 18)

The folk-tale style of repetition continues in the next story. Elijah told his follower Elisha to stay behind while he was called from Gilgal to Bethel. Elisha said, "As long as the Lord lives, and you yourself live, I will not leave you." (2 Kings 2:1 – 3)

So they go to Bethel and meet a group of prophets there. The prophets warn Elisha that his master will be taken away from him that day, and Elisha replies that he knows. Then Elijah tells Elisha again to stay behind, and again, Elisha replies: "As long as the Lord lives, and you yourself live, I will not leave you." (2 Kings 2:3 – 4)

The same thing is repeated at Jericho. The prophets warn Elisha that his master will be taken away from him that day, and Elisha replies that he knows. Then Elijah tells Elisha again to stay behind, and again, Elisha replies: "As long as the Lord lives, and you yourself live, I will not leave you." (2 Kings 2:5 – 6)

> Note that the whirlwind and chariot of fire are both symbols of the god Baal, who was called the Rider of the Clouds. The Biblical writers were taking the symbols of Baal and making them symbols of their God, Yahweh/El.

Then they head to the Jordan, joined by fifty other prophets. There Elijah rolled his mantle up and struck the water with it. The water parted, and Elijah and Elisha walked on dry ground to the other side. There a chariot of fire pulled by horses of fire took Elijah up to heaven in a whirlwind. Then Elisha picked up Elijah's mantle, struck the water of the Jordan to part it, and returned to the prophets. The other prophets could see that Elijah's spirit rested on Elisha, but still they insisted on searching the far trees for Elijah's body. (2 Kings 2:7 – 18)

Elisha traveled back to Jericho, then Bethel, Mount Carmel, and then Samaria. At Bethel, some youth teased him for being bald. Elisha cursed them, so two bears came and mauled the boys. (2 Kings 2:19 – 25)

The story of Elijah and Ahaziah have parallels with the story of Elijah and Elisha. The two soldier-destroying fires can be seen as parallels of the two bears. Elijah was recognized for being hairy. Elisha was teased for being bald. The soldiers tell Elijah to come down. The young men teasing Elisha tell him to "go up." While the destruction of the soldiers is a rejection of the political and military power of the king, the mauling of the youth of Bethel may have been a slight towards the religious establishment there.

What does Elijah and Elisha's crossing the Jordan river remind you of? Does it remind you of Moses crossing the Red Sea or his successor Joshua crossing the Jordan river as he approached Jericho? Perhaps Elijah was the new Moses and Elisha was the new Joshua. If so, would Elisha conquer Canaan? From some perspectives the first conquest had been incomplete, with the Omrides bringing in worship of Canaanite gods and Canaanite practices. Yet Elisha is very different than Joshua. When Joshua left Jericho he made a curse against it. When Elisha went there he put a blessing on it, restoring its water. (2 Kings 2:19 – 22, Joshua 3 – 4, Joshua 6:26 - 27)

When King Ahab had been alive King Mesha of Moab paid tribute to Israel. Every year he gave lambs and wool to King Ahab. When King Ahab died, King Mesha revolted and said he would not pay the tribute to Ahab's sons. The oldest son, King Ahaziah, did not have time to try to punish King Mesha for this. When after Ahaziah's death King Jehoram took the throne, he decided to conquer King Mesha's land. He sent a messenger to the Jehoshaphat of Judah to ask if he would help. Jehoshaphat agreed. Another messenger went to the King of Edom, to ask for his assistance as well. (2 Kings 3:4 – 8)

> The name of Ahab's second son is written in the Bible as both Jehoram and Joram. He must not be confused with Ahab's son-in-law Jehoram of Judah.

So the three kings set out together to conquer Moab. On their way, they came to a wadi. A wadi is a stream bed which dries up when there has been no rain for a long time. The wadi was dry, and so they could offer their animals anything to drink. So Jehoshaphat, the king of Judah, suggested they call for a prophet. (2 Kings 3:9 – 12)

The prophet Elisha was summoned. Elisha said, "Why do you want to involve me? Go to the prophets of your father and the prophets of your mother." (2 Kings 3:13 NIV) Apparently Elisha didn't think that Jehoram worshiped the god Elisha served. However, Jehoram said it was that Elisha's god he worshiped, and that it was that same god which wanted them to attack Moab. (2 Kings 13) Note the contrast between this incident and when Jehoram's brother Ahaziah wanting to send for foreign prophet rather than Elijah. (2 Kings 1:3)

Elisha agreed to help and had a musician summoned to play music. While the musician was playing, Elisha spoke with his god. Then Elisha told the kings that though they would not see any rain or wind, the valley would fill with water and they would have victory over Moab. By the next morning water was flowing in from the direction of Edom, showing that Elisha's god had authority over that land too. (2 Kings 3:14 - 20)

In the early morning, the sunlight reflecting on the water looked to the Moabites like the river was flowing with blood. The Moabites believed that the people of Isreal, Judah and Edom had turned upon each other in war, and so they attacked believing they would have an easy victory. They found the

> Can you recall another Bible story of a river seeming to flow with blood?

battle harder than they had expected. The Israelites won, and were able to conquer one Moabite town after another. (2 Kings 3:20 - 24)

The king of Moab took refuge in his last walled city, and there he sacrificed his oldest child to his god. A fury or great wrath came against Israel and the people went home. The Biblical text is vague. The term used for fury or great wrath is one used elsewhere to refer to God's wrath against Israel, yet here it does not specify that it was God's wrath. Perhaps an early version of the story described the Moabite's god accepting the sacrifice and turning his wrath upon the sacrifice, but the other god was edited out to conform to the notion that only the god of Israel and Judah existed. Or perhaps the author of the text believed that the people of Israel and Judah had done something to justify their own god being angry at them at that moment. (2 Kings 3:24 – 27)

The Bible tells other stories of Elisha. It says that Elisha, like Elijah before him, went to help a widow. The widow had no money and owed a debt so great that her sons were going to be taken as slaves to pay the debt. Elisha told her to take the little jar of oil she had and borrow as many empty jars as she could. Then she poured oil from the small jar into the other jars and it filled one jar after another. She could then sell the oil, pay the debt, and keep her sons. (2 Kings 4:1 – 7)

Elisha also resurrected a dead child, as Elijah did. (2 Kings 4:8 – 37) He also fed a hundred men with very little bread, and he took a poisonous pot of stew and made it healthy to eat. (2 Kings 4:38 – 41) Just as Elijah had done miracles for people who lived outside the land of Israel, Elisha went and healed the commander of the army of the Arameans. (2 Kings 5)

Follow-up Activities

1. Read the rules of warfare in Deuteronomy 20 and compare them with what is described in 2 Kings 3:16-19. You will read about the likely origins of the Deuteronomy texts in a later chapter. For now, just know it was likely written long after the time Elijah and Elisha were believed to have lived. What practical purposes might these rules have? Which of these latter rules is broken according to the text in 2 Kings 3:19?

2. Read 2 Kings 3:13 - 27, paying special attention to what Elisha says will happen when his god hands Moab over to the three kings. Which of those things does not happen? People have made all different arguments about what happened here. Was God's promise left unfulfilled because of the Moabite king's sacrifice? Did Elisha give a false promise to lure the kings into battle as Micaiah did to King Ahab? Could the promise be conditional to something that the three kings failed at? Choose one possibility and write a paragraph arguing for or against it.

Multiple Rulers are Overthrown

Remember how King Ahaziah had not asked Elijah if he would recover from his injuries but sent messengers to inquire of a different god instead? The Bible says when the Aramean King Ben-Hadad was ill he sent for Elisha. In that instance, he was portrayed as being more loyal to God than the king of Israel had been! (2 Kings 8:7 – 9)

Elisha told the messenger that Ben-Hadad was going to die but to say that he will recover. (2 Kings 8:10) This mention of the prophet saying one would happen but to tell something different would remind careful listeners of the story of Micaiah telling Ahab to go attack Ramoth-Gilead even though he knew Ahab would die from it. (1 Kings 22: 13 – 28) Like a musical song that keeps returning to variations of the same theme, the Biblical text keeps returning to variations of other stories. The writers were clever and wanted one story to remind the listeners of the other.

Elisha, having told the messenger to say that Ben-Hadad would recover, started to weep. The messenger, a man named Hazael, asked Elisha why he cried. Elisha said it was because Hazael was going to do evil things to Elisha's people. (2 Kings 8:11 – 12)

Hazael replied "What is your servant, who is a mere dog, that he should do these tremendous things?" (2 Kings 8:13a)

Elisha replied that Hazael would become the next king of the Arameans. (2 Kings 8:13b)

Hazael left Elisha and went home. The next day he wet a blanket and used it to smother King Ben-Hadad. He became king. Elisha's prophecy had come true. (2 Kings 8:14 – 15)

> Do you remember when dogs were last mentioned in the story? They were last mentioned drinking Ahab's blood. The mention of dogs again should remind you of the prophecy about Ahab's family losing their throne.

The kings of Israel and Judah decided they would fight together against Hazael. They gathered their troops near Ramoth-Gilead. King Jehoram of Israel was wounded and had to retreat home to heal. King Ahaziah of Judah went to Jerusalem and then to meet Jehoram. (2 Kings 8:28 - 29)

When their armies had assembled, sent a prophet among the soldiers to find the commander of the Israelite forces, a man named Jehu. The prophet anointed Jehu as king of Israel, then Jehu was publicly declared king. Elisha's words had inspired Hazael to overthrow the king of the Arameans, and then through a fellow prophet he had encouraged Jehu to overthrow the king of Israel! (2 Kings 9:1 – 14)

Jehu left the army in Ramoth-Gilead and went to where Jehoram was waiting injured. When Jehoram heard that Jehu was approaching he sent a messenger to ask him, "Is it peace?" Could he have been asking if Jehu had made peace with the Arameans they had gone to fight? Or did he suspect that Jehu was preparing to overthrow him? (2 Kings 9:14 – 18)

Jehu replied to the messenger, "What have you to do with peace? Fall in behind me?" So, the messenger followed Jehu and did not return to Jehoram. The guard at the city told the king that the messenger had met Jehu but was not returning. (2 Kings 9:18)

A second messenger was sent to ask the same question, and everything happened the same as before, with the messenger falling in behind. Again, the guard at the city told Jehoram that the messengers had met Jehu but was not returning. (2 Kings 9:19 – 21)

Unable to get an answer from the messengers, the King Jehoram of Israel and the king of Judah went out to meet Jehu. They called out, "Is it peace?" (2 Kings 9:21 – 22)

Jehu answered, "How can there be peace as long as all the idolatry and witchcraft of your mother Jezebel abound?" (2 Kings 9:22 NIV)

Jehoram of Israel and the Ahaziah of Judah both got scared and tried to flee, but both kinds were shot by Jehu's archers. (2 Kings 9:23 – 27)

Jehu rode into the city to the palace where Jezebel was. She had been Ahab's wife and was the mother of King Jehoram. She looked out the window at Jehu and called out "Is it peace?" (2 Kings 9:30 – 31)

> Ahaziah of Judah's mother was Athaliah, a daughter of King Ahab of Israel and therefore Ahaziah was a grandson of King Ahab and potential heir to the northern kingdom as well as the southern kingdom. Jehu might have ordered Ahaziah's death to prevent Ahaziah from claiming the throne of Israel.

King Jehu called to her servants "Who is on my side?" The servants pushed the queen-mother out the window and she died. (2 Kings 9:32 – 37)

Then Jehu wrote to the people of the capital city, Samaria, and invited them to put whichever of Ahab's sons they thought best on the throne. The wording is such that he was not promising to obey whomever they put on the throne, and so the elders of the city answered back that they would not put anyone on the throne. Jehu replied that if they were willing to submit to him they should give to him the heads of Ahab's sons. (2 Kings 10:1 - 17)

Thus the prophecy that Elijah had made to Ahab that his family would lose the kingdom of Israel had come true. The kingdom passed into the hands of the commander of the army, Jehu.

Jehu made an announcement that "Ahab offered Baal small service, but now Jehu will offer much more." He summoned all the prophets of Baal making it sound like he was summoning them to something great. He said any prophets of Baal that did not come would not live. Then he had all the prophets killed. (2 Kings 10:18 – 31)

It is impossible to know exactly what brought the deaths of these kings about. The Biblical story is that the prophet Elisha set both Hazael and Jehu on the path to overthrowing their kings. The former was portrayed as something rather sad, for Hazael's rule of a nation at war with Israel would make him an enemy of Israel. The revolt by Jehu was portrayed as something good. The repeated stories of Jehu asking others if they were on his side creates a picture of a coup done with the consent of the people, rather than simply a military coup forcing an unwanted dictator on them. We are told the messengers, the palace servants, the people of Samaria all join him voluntarily.

In 1993 CE a stele was found at Tell Dan that has often been interpreted to say that King Hazael killed Jehoram and the king of Judah. This contradicts the Biblical account that Jehu ordered their deaths. Perhaps the story of Jehu killing the two kings was made up by Jehu's supporters to explain why he took the throne. Or perhaps it might have been that King Hazael encouraged Jehu to revolt, claimed Jehu as a vassal, and hence could claim responsibility for the deaths of those Jehu killed. That would explain why Jehu was able to leave the army where it waited to fight with Hazael's army and instead go and overthrow the king. If Jehu started out as a vassal of Hazael, he could not have been a particularly loyal vassal as the Biblical texts records that Hazael continued to attack Israel. It is also possible the translators have mistranslated the damaged stele.

Meanwhile, the kingdom of Judah also had to deal with the loss of its king. We do not know how many sons Ahaziah left behind, only that the queen mother seized control of the nation by ordering her own relatives killed. Ahaziah's sister was able to hide one of Ahaziah's sons, a tiny baby, from the massacre. (2 Kings 11:1 - 3)

When the child, whose name is listed as both Johoash and Joash, was seven years old a priest arranged with the guards for the child to be proclaimed king. The queen-mother was killed. Then the priest arranged for the priests of Baal to be killed as well, and the altars to Baal be removed (2 Kings 11:4 - 21.)

One would expect that King Johoash, put into power by a priest, would have a close relationship with the priests. The Bible records that he granted the priests the ability to collect certain taxes and offerings at the temple, but that he required that they do repairs on the temple. In the twenty-third year of his reign (when he was thirty), he saw that the priests had not kept up the repairs. A locked chest was placed in the temple with a slot in the lid, and the funds were to be put in that rather than given to the priests. Then when the chest was filled the king's secretary and high priest would together count the money and give it over to the workers responsible for maintaining the temple. The priests would, however, be allowed to keep two other types of offerings for themselves. (2 Kings 12:1 - 16)

King Hazael invaded further into Israel, conquering large sections of the land during Jehu's lifetime and more during the reign of Jehu's son. Eventually Hazael's power stretched far enough he could attack Judah as well as Israel. Eventually he threatened Jerusalem. Johoash bought him off, sending gold from the temple and palace to Hazael. (2 Kings 10:32 - 33, 12:17 - 21)

> King Johoash's own officers had him assassinated, putting Johoash's son on the throne instead. It would be interesting to know why they did this. Perhaps they did not approve of him sending their kingdom's gold to King Hazael.

After Hazael's death, his son Ben-Hadad continued to invade Israel. The Bible says that King Jehu's son Jehoahaz prayed to his god and:

> *The LORD provided a deliverer for Israel, and they escaped from the power of Aram. So the Israelites lived in their own homes as they had before. (2 Kings 13:5)*

Who was this new deliverer? The Bible does not specify but it might have been King Adad-Nirari III of Assyria, who invaded Aram around that time. King Adad-Nirari III recorded in his steles that both the king of Aram and the king of Israel paid him tribute. In return he may have ended their fighting and prevented Aram from taking over all the land of Israel. He may have been experienced as a saviour at the time and then, later, after the Assyrians destroyed Israel the identification was removed.

Remember that these stories come to us in the sections of the Bible known now as the Deuteronomic histories. The Deuteronomic historians said it was good that Jehu killed the descendants of Ahab and the prophets of Baal, but criticized Jehu for not destroying the golden calves that Jeroboam had built at Bethel and Dan. Thus, in their eyes, the northern kingdom was still worshiping wrong. With each ruler the Deuteronomic historians claim that the ruler either walked in the ways of the lord or did evil in the eyes of the lord, but they were not quite able to attribute the king's success or failure to that, as Jehu's son was said to be evil, yet their god sent him a deliverer.

In the southern kingdom, on a literary level, the restoration of the legitimate ruler after the rule of the queen-mother functions as a parallel to the restoration of the legitimate worship after the worship of foreign gods.

> Shalmaneser III of Assyria was the grandfather of Adad-Nirari III. The black obelisk of Shalmaneser may mention King Jehu of Israel. The translation of the text is uncertain but some people believe that the inscription reads: "The tribute of Jehu, son of Omri: I received from him silver, gold, a golden bowl, a golden vase with pointed bottom, golden tumblers, golden buckets, tin, a staff for a king [and] spears." The Bible says that Jehu was not the son of Omri but a general who claimed the throne from the Omri family! The Assyrians called the land of Israel the "House of Omri" without concern for whether there was still an Omride on the throne.

Vassals, Tributes and the Assyrian Crisis

Did you note in King Ahab's time the kingdoms of Israel and Judah were powerful enough they could go to war to force other nations to pay tribute to them? Kingdoms that had to pay tributes to larger kingdoms were called vassal states. If they rebelled, they risked being attacked. If they stayed loyal, then the more powerful kingdoms were supposed to come to their defense against other enemies. The kingdoms of Judah and Israel both had their own vassals for a while, but eventually they became vassals of other countries! When exactly they became vassals is unclear. Jehu might have paid tribute to both the Assyrians and the king of Aram. His son likely paid tribute to the Assyrians. King Jehoash of Judah paid tribute to Hazael of Aram and may also have paid the Assyrians.

The Assyrian empire had started growing in power around 900 BCE, but for quite a while their military adventures had to begin after the crops were planted and end when it was time to come home and harvest. Around 744 BC an Assyrian general seized the throne from King Adad-Nirari III's children, took on the name Tiglath-Pileser III, and reorganized the empire. He changed the tax system. He created a professional army that did not need to return home for harvest. He invaded Babylonia. Then he invaded the Medes, Persians, and Neo-Hittites.

Meanwhile, Israel had some trouble. The great-great grandson of Jehu reigned for only six months before being killed and overthrown by a captain in his army. The one who overthrew him was in turn overthrown by another military commander after only a month. This second commander was named Menahem, and he paid tribute to the Assyrians "to gain his support and strengthen his own hold on the kingdom.." (2 Kings 15: 8 – 22, quote from 2 Kings 15:19 NIV) One can wonder whether Menahem was supported by the Assyrians to begin with or whether the Assyrians approached Israel when the country was in chaos and Menahem simply submitted to them. In other words, was Menahem always a puppet of the Assyrians or did he ever have visions of ruling Israel independent of the Assyrians?

Menahem reigned for ten years. His son reigned for only two before being overthrown by his military commander, Pekah. In the late 700s BCE King Pekah of Israel decided to work with the King of the Arameans against the Assyrians, and together they attacked the king of Judah. Probably, their goal was to install a king in Judah who would help them to fight against the growing Assyrian empire. However, their siege didn't succeed and instead it inspired the king of Judah, a young man named Ahaz, to appeal to the Assyrian empire for protection. (2 Kings 16:5 – 7)

King Ahaz of Judah sent all his gold and silver to Assyria saying, "I am your servant and your son; come up and deliver me from the hand of the king of Aram and from the hand of the king of Israel, who are rising up against me." (2 Kings 16:7 NIV) He offered his nation to Assyria as a vassal kingdom. Tiglath-Pileser III agreed to defend Ahaz. Ahaz then had a model of the Assyrian altar built and placed in the temple in Jerusalem. (2 Kings 16:8 – 18)

Tiglath-Pileser III began his revenge for those who sought to unite against him. The Bible describes this in one verse:
> In the time of Pekah king of Israel, Tiglath-Pileser king of Assyria came and took Ijon, Abel Beth Maakah, Janoah, Kedesh and Hazor. He took Gilead and Galilee, including all the land of Naphtali, and deported the people to Assyria. (2 Kings 15:29 NIV)

Tiglath-Pileser III's records of his actions are badly damaged, but more colourful than the single Bible verse. He describes which the cities he placed provincial governors over. The city of Gaza was ruled by a man named Hanunu, but according to Tiglath-Pileser III "the terrifying splendor of (the god) Aššur, my lord overwhelmed him" and though he fled to Egypt, the Assyrian king reinstated him in Gaza as a puppet king.

King Pekah of Israel was killed, possibly by his own people hoping that doing away with him would allow them to make peace with the Assyrians, but potentially by the Assyrians. Tiglath-Pileser III claimed in his accounts that he put Pekah's successor, a man named Hoshea, on the throne and that he received from them gold and silver. The Biblical text describes the people overthrowing Hoshea and claims he became a vassal of the Assyrians after Tiglath-Pileser's successor, Shalmaneser V, attacked Israel.

> Tiglath-Pileser III's records, like those of other Assyrians rulers, refers to Israel as "House of Omri."
>
> You can read the relevant record of Tiglath-Pileser III here: http://oracc.org/rinap/Q003455/

Regardless of under whose rule Hoshea became a vassal, he definitely became one. Perhaps if he had accepted paying tribute, the kingdom of Israel would have survived longer than it did. However, after a few years he appealed to the king of Egypt for assistance. Could Egypt help defend them against the Assyrians? Trusting in Egyptians support, the king of Israel refused to pay tribute to Assyria. How do you think the Assyrians responded? (2 Kings 17:1 – 4)

The Assyrians attacked Israel. The Deuteronomists blamed this on the Israelites and their kings not worshiping God properly. We don't know exactly how many times the Assyrians attacked Israel. The Bible mentions both Shalmaneser V and Sargon II attacking, but it is possible that Sargon II was attacking as a general on behalf of Shalmaneser V. The two were likely brothers, and eventually Sargon II revolted against Shalmaneser V and claimed the throne of Assyria. (2 Kings 17:1 - 23)

Sargon II conquered Israel and took many of the Israelites away into exile. They took people from the other kingdoms they had captured and brought those people to the land of Israel. By mixing up the people like this, they could discourage anyone from revolting. (2 Kings 17:24 – 28)

The Deuteronomic historians said that these new people did not worship God, and so God sent lions to attack them. Someone told the king of Assyria this, and he said that priests of God should be sent to teach them how to worship. This, the Bible said, was done but everyone set up their own shrines as well, so that the gods of all different kingdoms were worshiped in the land that had once been Israel. (2 Kings 17:29 – 41)

Think back on the stories you've heard. Think how the people of Israel told themselves that they had been brought into that land by a god that rescued them from oppression. How would they feel being taken into exile? If their god is associated with that land, can he be with them elsewhere? Do the people brought into the land start to be part of his people? These were all questions people had to wrestle with.

Follow-up Activities

1. Read Isaiah 14:12 – 21. This text likely refers to Sargon II. Can you summarize it in your own words and figure out what happened to Sargon II? Depending on which Bible translation you use, you may see the word Lucifer. The word referred to the morning star or light-bringer. The image of Sargon II as the morning star falling from heaven became the inspiration for stories about an angel cast out of heaven.

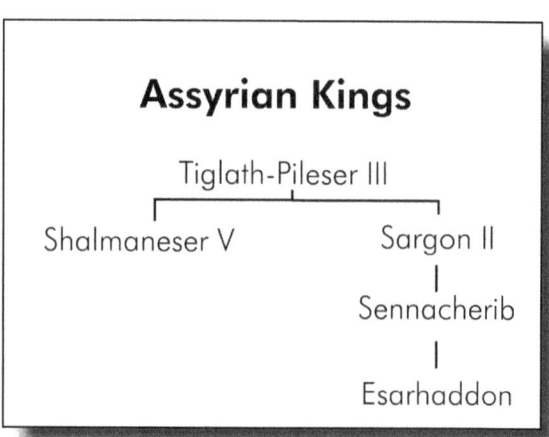

An Aside - Reading 2 Kings

Much of 2 Kings is structured so that it jumps back and forth between the stories of Israel and Judah. The events are dated according to how far into a particular king's reign the event takes place, and the reign of the king of Israel is used to date the beginning of the reign of the king of Judah, and vice versa. This makes the text somewhat challenging to read, as two king names will be presented in close secession. In many places the text will then say whether the king did good or evil in the eyes of the lord, and one will be left asking "which king are they talking about?" It is important to take the time to identify which king is being used for dating the other king's reign, and which king is the subject of the particular passage. Moreover, the text will loop back over time already described in a previous passage.

One example of this style of text is in 2 Kings 15 - 17:1. Use the following steps to help you parse the passage:

- Read 2 Kings 15:27 - 31. This passage is about Pekah of Israel. The text includes a list of locations, all of which were part of Israel. What does it say Tiglath-Pileser III of Assyria did during Pekah's reign?

- Read 2 Kings 15:32 - 38. This section jumps back in time, to before Pekah's death to talk about what was happening in Judah during the reign of Jotham. The most important verse is verse 37. What happens in that verse?

- Read 2 Kings 16:1 - 7. This describes events while Ahaz is king of Judah and Pekah is still king of Israel. The text has the standard accusations against kings believed to do wrong in the eyes of the lord. What does it say in verse 5? Who attacked Jerusalem? Verse 6 lists some victories on the part of one of Ahaz's enemies and verses 7 - 8 describe what Ahaz did in response. What is it Ahaz does? How does verse 9 tie in with verse 15:29?

- Read 2 Kings 16:8 - 20. What is the main theme of this section?

- Read 2 Kings 17:1. This verse brings us back to 2 Kings 15:30.

Do you see how the text spirals around in time, first giving a quick summary of King Pekah's life and death and then dealing with the other events that took place during his life before coming in verse 2 Kings 17:1 to the person who succeeded Pekah?

Many people have gone through the whole of 1st and 2nd Kings charting out the dates of the different kings. Doing so opens up some challenging questions. Ahaz is said to have taken the throne at age twenty and reigned for sixteen years. After that his twenty-five year old son Hezekiah takes the throne. If one does the calculation one may notice that this would mean Ahaz became a father at age eleven! It is best not to take the text too literally and not to assume that is free of errors, but it is possible that some of the confusion comes from the word "son" being applied to grandsons, brothers, and any male of a particular household, rather than just to a person's biological son.

Hezekiah's Reforms and the Assyrians' Perspective

The writings of Isaiah attempt to make sense of the fall of Israel and the danger faced by Judah. The book of Isaiah is a long one and many scholars believe that it was written by at least three different writers. These are often referred to as Isaiah, Deutero-Isaiah (meaning second Isaiah) and Trito-Isaiah (third Isaiah). It is the first Isaiah we will concern ourselves with here, but first, a review.

The Bible in its current form encourages readers to believe that monotheism has been the heart of the Hebrew religion from the time of Abraham onward. Biblical scholarship can call into question whether Abraham and his descendants really existed, or whether that was the mythos and identity created by a group of people who saw themselves as followers of the god YHWH. Worship of YHWH may have been a connecting identity that pulled separate tribes together to defend one another against the Philistines and other nearby tribes. It would have become the official belief system of their early monarchy. At different times kings were accused of worshiping foreign gods, but we have to stop and ask, "what was the problem with these foreign gods?"

Many people today assume the prophets and Biblical writers objected to the foreign gods because those gods were merely statues of gold or stone and not real ones like they believe the Judeo-Christian god is. The belief that there is only one real god is called monotheism. However, that might be a projection. Later monotheistic Biblical writers might have projected their understanding of monotheism back on the earlier writers.

The earlier writers might have been monolatrists, not monotheists. Monolatrists accepted the existence of other gods but believed in only worshiping one god. If some of the early Biblical writers were monolatrists, then they believed that YHWH was their state god, and that he demanded loyalty from them. He was a jealous god, upset when they gave attention to other gods. They might have understood the one god as competing against other gods.

The early stories would have made sense in a world where each kingdom had its own god. When Moses bested the Pharaoh's magicians and brought down plagues upon the Egyptians it showed their god's power as greater than the Egyptian's gods. When the statue of Dagon fell before the ark of the covenant, it showed their god's power compared to Dagon's. When Elijah healed a child in the territory of Baal it showed their god's superiority over Baal even outside the boundaries of Israel. The texts push the boundaries of a regional god's powers, suggesting he has power elsewhere too, but they didn't require one to believe that there was only one god in existence.

Then along comes Isaiah, and he describes Assyria as being the weapon with which God punishes those he is angry with .(Isaiah 10:5-6) Think about this for a moment. If their god was punishing them, then the defeat to the Assyrians wouldn't have to be seen as a sign of their god's weakness. It could still be a sign of their god's strength. Moreover, this would imply that Isaiah's god – YWHW/El/God – was not just a regional god concerned with one city, but one that could control other empires! If their god controlled everything, everywhere, then he could be the only god. He could be the creator of the whole universe.

Meanwhile in the kingdom of Judah, King Ahaz's son made some changes. His name was Hezekiah and he took down the sacred poles of Asherah and he closed the hill shrines where people worshiped. The Deuteronomic historians liked this because they believed that everyone should worship the one god, and that they should do so at Jerusalem and not in the hill shrines. It was too easy for people to worship other gods at those hill shrines, and the Deuteronomists believed the only way to protect the nation was to worship the one god alone.

The Deuteronomic historians were in favour of Hezekiah and his reforms, but they were critical of him for his foreign policy. Hezekiah of Judah joined with other kingdoms – small Canaanite and Phoenician kingdoms as well as the larger kingdoms of Babylon and Egypt – in rebelling against Assyria. The kingdoms withheld the tribute they owed to Assyria.

It may be that Hezekiah's reforms and his foreign policy were tightly connected. Centralizing the worship involved encouraging people to bring their sacrifices and tribute into Jerusalem. Hezekiah might have used the reforms as a way of preparing for war with Assyria. During Hezekiah's reign they were attacked a number of times, as revenge for their insubordination.

Assyria attacked Babylon and put a puppet king on the throne. It forced the smaller kingdoms to pay tribute. It defeated the Egyptians in battle. Then it laid siege to Jerusalem, but did not manage to capture the city. The story in the Bible is that the angel of the Lord struck the Assyrians in the night and killed them. The Assyrians writing their own description said that Hezekiah paid them tribute.

While the people of Judah were interpreting history as playing out according to the will of their god, their enemies were doing the same thing. The Assyrians were interpreting history as playing out the will of their gods. Sargon II may have attempted to expand the identity of the Assyrian god s by linking him with the earlier primordial god Anshar. Traditionally Aššur was a warrior god while Anshar was the father of the sky god, so linking the two would have helped re-conceive the Assyrian patron god as more powerful and omnipotent than he had been before. At the same time this Aššur/Anshar hybrid was written into the Babylonian creation myth to fill the role of Marduk, the Babylonian god. Yet the Assyrians couldn't completely deny the power of Marduk, the Babylonian god.

King Sennacherib of Assyria, son of Sargon II, decided to put his own son on the throne of Babylon to replace the puppet king he had placed there earlier. At the behest of the Babylonians, the neighbouring Elamites captured this son of Sennacherib and killed him, thus angering King Sennacherib. When the Assyrians invaded Babylon again, they destroyed the city. They even destroyed its temple and took captive the statue of Marduk. Then they diverted canals and flooded the city. The destruction was such that when Sennacherib died – murdered by another of his sons for choosing a different son as heir – people believed this was punishment by the Babylonian god Marduk for the destruction done to Babylon.

The death of Sennacherib is described in the Bible, in 2 Kings 19:36 – 37, but in the Biblical version his death appears to come immediately after his failure to capture Jerusalem. This skips over some twenty years of Sennacherib's reign, but it gently implicates the Hebrew god for his death rather than the Babylonian god!

Sennacherib's heir was Esarhaddon. Esarhaddon attempted to be reconciled with Babylon, but how could the Babylonians accept peace with those who destroyed their city? Texts that were likely circulated by the Assyrians promoted the idea that the destruction of Babylon had been the result of Marduk's anger at Babylon. Marduk and his divine wife had given their own city over to the Assyrians for punishment!

> *"Before my time, the great lord Marduk was enraged with the temple Esagil and Babylon, and he became angry. His people were answering each other 'Yes' (for) "No". They were speaking untruths. They laid their hands on property for the great lord Marduk and gave it to Elam as a bribe. Their deeds were offensive to Marduk and Zarpanitu, so they ordered their dispersal. They caused water to flow over the city and turned it into a wasteland. The gods and goddesses were terrified and went up to heaven. The site of the city was eradicated and its foundation could not be seen."* (Quote from "The 'Sin of Sargon' and Sennacherib's Last Will.")

Other texts from Esarhaddon's time rewrote the history to suggest that Sargon II's death was caused by failure to serve Marduk properly, and that Sennacherib had attempted to remedy this. Sennacherib, the one who invaded Babylon and destroyed Marduk's temple, was being praised as serving Marduk!

The important thing to note is that religious beliefs do not remain static. We have better records of the religious beliefs of the ancient Hebrews than we do of the Assyrians and Babylonians, but the Assyrians and Babylonians too were asking similar questions and their beliefs were shifting and changing. They were also interpreting their historic events in light of their religious beliefs, and shaping their religious beliefs in light of the historic events.

When Hezekiah of Judah died his twelve-year-old son Manasseh took the throne. Manessah tried to undo what his father had done. He put back the altars to Baal and the sacred poles to Asherah. He reopened the hill shrines. The Deuteronomist historians said he was so evil that God said:

> "I am going to bring such disaster on Jerusalem and Judah that the ears of everyone who hears of it will tingle. 13 I will stretch out over Jerusalem the measuring line used against Samaria and the plumb line used against the house of Ahab. I will wipe out Jerusalem as one wipes a dish, wiping it and turning it upside down. 14 I will forsake the remnant of my inheritance and give them into the hands of enemies. They will be looted and plundered by all their enemies; 15 they have done evil in my eyes and have aroused my anger from the day their ancestors came out of Egypt until this day." (2 Kings 21:12b – 15 NIV).

However, the Deuteronomic historians were writing after Manasseh had died and his kingdom destroyed. They were writers who believed strongly that YHWH should be the only god worshiped and condemned kings on the basis of whether they promoted YHWH alone or not. It is unclear whether the people saw Manasseh as evil during his era.

After Manasseh died, his son Amon ruled for twenty-two years. He followed in his father's footsteps. Some of the people close to him – servants or councilors – conspired against him and killed him. Likely those who killed Amon had plans to set their own candidate in power, but the Bible tell us that the people of the land rose up against them and put Amon's son Josiah in place instead. One Biblical scholar, Rainer Albertz, argued that it was likely land-owning farmers of Judah who put Josiah on the throne. They would not have wanted to risk any political instability that might lead to more civil war or draw the Assyrians to attack the nation. They would have wanted everything to be peaceful so they could farm.

Follow-up Activities

1. Look up the Annals of Sennacherib or Esarhaddon of Assyria's succession treaty.

2. Read 2 Kings 18:13-35. and write in your own words the arguments that the Assyrians used to try to persuade the people of Judah to surrender.

The Deuteronomic historians ran into a problem in their writing. According to their idea that God punishes the bad and rewards the good, the bad kings should have lived shorter lives than the good. This wasn't always true. So when a later writer or group of writers wrote the book of Chronicles, they tried to solve this problem. They altered the stories to suggest that those who lived a long life must have done some good, and those who lived a short life must have done some bad.

Josiah's Reforms

Josiah was eight years old when he became king. Since he was so young when he took the throne, it is very likely others would have helped guide him and tell him how things should be. The people who taught him and raised him would have great influence on who he became. The people who supported him wanted the nation to stop appealing to other nations – the Egyptians, the Babylonians or Assyrians – to save them and to trust in their God alone. Josiah and his supporters tried to reform Judah towards that goal.

The Bible says that when Josiah had ruled for eighteen years, Josiah sent Shaphan, the secretary, to the temple with instructions to the high priest Hilkiah to rebuild the temple. While the temple was being rebuilt, a book was found that was given to the high priest, who then gave it to Shaphan, who read it before the king and the king's servant Asaiah, Shaphan's son, and another man named Achbor. These people all took the book to the prophetess Huldah. (2 Kings 22)

The book was the covenant that God had made with the land, and the prophetess told them that if they read it and were humble, they could put off the disaster God planned for them. So, Josiah read the book to everyone and tried to implement its commands. (2 Kings 23:1 – 25)

Take a moment to think about this. Imagine that you are a young king. Your father had angered people, and they killed him. You know that you need to rule differently than he did. You also need to somehow keep your kingdom from being attacked by any of the empires nearby, and you want to try to bring some measure of peace and security to it. You and your advisors come up with a plan for how to change things. But how will you get everyone on board? Do you just announce, "this is what we're going to do now?"

> Take a moment and think about what kind of laws you would write if you were in Josiah's position?

Many scholars believe that the book from Josiah's story is a section of the fifth book in the Bible, now called Deuteronomy. The section claims to be the words that Moses spoke to the Hebrew people during the Exodus. It is more likely that the book was actually written by several of Josiah's advisors, perhaps Shaphan and the high priest Hilkiah. The other people named in the story are likely those who helped lend their support to the reform plan. With enough powerful people on board, the plan could be started.

The book of Deuteronomy tells that after Moses rescued the Hebrews from Egypt they were given the opportunity to enter the land God had promised them. However, they sent their spies in and their spies reported that the Canaanites were too strong and their cities were too fortified. Thus, everyone became too scared to enter the place God had promised, and God forced them to walk for forty years in the desert, so that only the next generation could enter. Through the stories of Moses, the writers of Deuteronomy argue that permission to be in the land is conditional to their obedience to God. If they do not obey, they do not get to be there. It makes possession of the land conditional.

> Scholars used to argue that the book of Deuteronomy and the Deuteronomic histories were written by the same person. Over time it became recognized that there were probably more than one person involved in the writing of the Deuteronomic histories and that there were subtle differences in the beliefs of the Deuteronomic historians and Deuteronomy. The Deuteronomic historians get their name from the book of Deuteronomy, and they have many similarities with the authors of Deuteronomy, but were probably different groups of writers.

In the chapter on the conquest of Canaan, you saw how the early Hebrew people portrayed themselves as having a covenant with their god similar to the Hittite kings had with their vassals. The Hittite treaties stressed the history of generosity on the part of the king towards his vassals. Likewise the Hebrews focused their covenant with their god on how God had led them out of Egypt. The Assyrian vassal treaties were focused more on curses than on blessings. There was an emphasis on punishment for disobedience. The writers of Deuteronomy and the writers of the Deuteronomic histories both took a more Assyrian view of the covenant between God and Israel than the earlier writers.

The goals of the reform were to try to make the kingdom of Judah a 'Holy People' separated off from all others, so that their god would protect them. Josiah's reforms included many of the same things his great-grandfather Hezekiah had tried to do. Josiah had the altars to Baal and the sacred poles of Asherah destroyed. He closed the high places where people worshiped. In the time since the Assyrians had conquered Israel, the borders of Judah had expanded so that Josiah could even tear down the shrine at Bethel attributed to Jeroboam when he separated the northern kingdom from the south.

Some of the reforms were also about making things fairer and more just. This fit with the concept of their god being one who led them out of oppression and bondage in Egypt. It also had some practical benefits. One risk during a siege is that unhappy people will throw open the gates and invite the enemy in. If they were to withstand outside attacks, they would need to make sure that everyone was cared for and no one might be tempted to betray them.

Follow-up Activities

1. Read the following passages and answer the questions:

   a. Deuteronomy 17:14 – 20 What are three ways this passage attempts to prevent the king from becoming too powerful?
   b. Deuteronomy 18:1 – 8. How are the to be different than other people?
   c. Deuteronomy 18:9 – 14. What types of things are banned here?
   d. Deuteronomy 19. How does this chapter promote justice?
   e. Deuteronomy 14:22 – 15:13 – What suggestions for economic justice does this contain?

The Fall of Jerusalem

For a while the Assyrians were the biggest threat around and other countries allied together to try to hold them off. Over time the Babylonians began to grow more powerful, until eventually the Assyrians and the Egyptians had to work together against the Babylonians. Around 609 BC Pharaoh Necho II of Egypt decided to go help the Assyrian king fight against the king of Babylon.

Necho II marched his troops up through Judah, and King Josiah went with his army to meet the pharaoh at Megiddo. There Josiah was killed. No one knows for sure what happened. 2 Kings 23:28 - 30 tells of Josiah's death without saying why Josiah went to meet the pharaoh. 2 Chronicles 35:20 - 27 claims that Josiah went to fight against Necho. It describes messages sent by envoys from Necho to Josiah, urging Josiah to leave Necho alone and claiming that it was against God's will for the two to fight. However, the text of Chronicles was written long after Josiah's death, and many scholars question whether it is accurate.

Consider the possibilities. Perhaps Josiah believed it was safer to side with Babylon against Egypt, for fear that the Babylonians would punish them for allowing Egyptian troops to move through their territory. Some have speculated that Josiah was a vassal of Egypt in the years preceding his death. Perhaps he chose that moment to rebel against Egyptian rule, fighting for independence on the battlefields. Or he may have been going to swear renew his vows of loyalty to Necho II and potentially even deliver supplies for the upcoming battle only to be attacked in some miscommunication. Some scholars believe that Josiah was not killed in battle but executed by the Egyptian king, perhaps for a failure to pay tribute on time. In any case, Josiah went and was killed by the Egyptians.

2 Kings 23:30 says that the people of the land then took Josiah's son Jehoahaz and made him king of Judah. Is this simply a fancy way of saying who came next, or does the mention of the people of the land putting him on the throne have political implications? It could suggest that Jehoahaz's power came from the people and not from a hereditary claim. Biblical scholar Rainer Albertz argues it meant that Jehoahaz was the younger son of the king but that the people chose to put him on the throne to continue his father's reforms. Or perhaps he was next in line, but the emphasis is in the people putting him there in contrast to the king of Egypt putting him on the throne. In any case, Jehoahaz did not reign long. The Egyptians captured him and put Josiah's other son, Eliakim on the throne, changing his name to Jehoiakim. Naturally, they demanded that Jehoiakim pay tribute to Egypt.

The Babylonians were growing in power though. They had a new king, Nebuchadnezzar. Nebuchadnezzar tried to force Jehoiakim to pay tribute to them too. When he did not, he was killed. Jehoiakim's son Jehoiachin took the throne.

Besides the Deuteronomic histories, we have other books of the Bible that speak of this period of time. One of these is the book of Jeremiah. Jeremiah was a prophet, claiming to speak for God. While he likely supported Josiah's reforms in the beginning, but over time he grew disillusioned with what was happening. He argued their god could not be worshiped without justice. He complained that the kings and the elites were not attempting to build a just kingdom but were instead trying to claim that just worshiping the right god was enough. He said the temple had become a den of thieves, because the people sought safety there despite robbing others through injustice. (Jeremiah 7)

Jeremiah said that Judah had turned its back on God and he predicted great disaster for them. He said the punishment was inevitable. At one point he put a yoke on his shoulders, like an ox would wear for pulling a wagon or hauling buckets of water, and he wore it saying that the Babylonians were like the yoke that Judah must bear as punishment for forsaking their god. They must accept being a vassal nation to Babylon.

Jehoiachin didn't listen to Jeremiah. He revolted against Babylon. The Babylonians attacked Jerusalem and took Jehoiachin and a group of his followers into exile. Jeremiah wrote to the exiles. He said "Thus says the Lord of hosts, The God of Israel, to all the exiles whom I have sent into exile from Jerusalem to Babylon: Build houses and live in them; plant gardens and eat what they produce. Take wives and have sons and daughters; take wives for your sons and give your daughters in marriage, that they may bear sons and daughters. Multiply, therefore, and do not decrease. But seek the welfare of the city where I have sent you into exile, and pray to the Lord on its behalf, for in its welfare you will find your welfare." (Jeremiah 29:4 – 7)

In other words, Jeremiah encouraged the exiles to build new lives in exile. He said they were in exile because God wanted them to be there, and that they should not hope or pray to get home quickly.

When the Babylonians took Jehoiachin into exile, they put one of Jehoiachin's uncles on the throne, changing the uncle's name to Zedekiah. Zedekiah ruled for eleven years, but in the ninth year of his reign he too rebelled against Babylon. When the Babylonians came to punish him for his rebellion, they blinded him and took him prisoner. They also broke down the walls of Jerusalem, so that the city could not be defended, and they broke the temple. They took more of the elites into exile with them in Babylon. Then the Babylonians appointed a man named Gedaliah to be governor over Judah.

After Zedekiah's rebellion and subsequent punishment Jeremiah bought land, saying that the god who had once led them out of Egypt would be able to make their lives good again. But Jeremiah also kept insisting that they should make peace with Babylon, and people took that as treason on his part, and imprisoned him for it. The Babylonians might have seen him as being on their side too, for when they installed Gedaliah as governor, the Babylonians offered to take care of Jeremiah, but he refused, wanting to stay with those left behind.

The book of Jeremiah says that after Gedaliah was murdered, many of the Hebrew people chose to leave Judah and go to Egypt. Jeremiah counseled against that, but he could not prevent people from going and they forced him to go with them.

Other authors wrote about the fall of Jerusalem too. A poet wrote a poem called Lamentations. It begins:
> *How deserted lies the city,*
>   *once so full of people!*
> *How like a widow is she,*
>   *who once was great among the nations!*

She who was queen among the provinces
   has now become a slave. (Lamentations 1:1 NIV)

Those who were left behind found life hard. Those who were taken away found life hard too. Jerusalem was not just their home city. It was Zion, the holy mountain where their god lived. Could their god be with them?

Follow-up Activities

1. Read Psalm 137. In the first three verses the psalm writer tells how their captors tried to force them to sing their religious songs. In the next three he asks how he could sing his religious songs in a foreign land and asks that he be cursed if he forgets his home. Then in the last three he sings songs of his god, but the songs are wishing evil upon those who have taken them captive. This Psalm has been part of the inspiration for the song "Rivers of Babylon" by Boney M.

2. One of the exiles was named Ezekiel. Before the exile he was a priest. In the book of Ezekiel it says that on the fifth year of the exile of King Jehoiachin, he started having visions. (This means that it would have been while Zedekiah was on the throne in Judah, before Jerusalem was destroyed.) You can read his

vision in Ezekiel 1:4 – 28. Can you picture the creatures he sees? Many artists have tried to paint his vision and you can find their pictures online.

3. The Judean city of Lachish fell to the Babylonians shortly before Jerusalem did. Several letters from the weeks before the invasion have survived. The letters reveal tension between the commanders. Look for copies of these letters online.

The Returnees and those that Remained Behind

No empire lasts forever. Eventually the Babylonian Empire was defeated by the Persian Empire. The Persian king, Cyrus the Great, wanted his empire to be run by small provinces, each paying taxes to him. He allowed descendants of those taken into exile in Babylon to return to Jerusalem to establish it as province and to rebuild the temple there. Thus the Hebrew people were allowed to restore the temple cult but not their monarchy.

> The term "cult" is not used here in a derogatory way, but to speak of a religion focused around the activities of the temple.

The Bible says Cyrus encouraged all the Hebrews in exile to donate gold, silver and animals for the rebuilding of the temple, so we can assume that over the years they had been in exile at least some of them had managed to create new lives and were living quite comfortably. Most of them did not return to Jerusalem, even if they sent goods to assist in the rebuilding.

Cyrus and his successor, Cambyses II, were preoccupied expanding Persia's borders. When Cambyses II died, his third cousin Darius I took the throne of Persia. As a distant relative to his predecessor, Darius I had to work hard to boost his own power within the empire. He asked all the provinces to put their legal traditions to writing. The Persians could then review the laws to ensure they weren't going to cause problems for the empire. Then Darius I could take credit as the lawgiver bestowing the laws, and whenever the laws were put in practice people could feel they were not only following their ancient traditions but that they were also obeying Darius and the Persians.

> The first five books of the Bible, collectively called the Torah, were likely edited and compiled during Darius' reign, in response to Darius' request for the codification of the laws. They may reflect a compromise between those who believed their god had promised them the land and those who believed his key gift were the teaching.

Darius I also provided funding for the temples, so he could have religious leaders beholden to the Persian empire. The temples would then teach a version of their own beliefs that was compatible with the Persian rule. The temple writings of the time had to promote an Israel focused around a priesthood and not an independent monarchy.

The books of Ezra and Nehemiah tell of some of the things that happened during Darius I's reign. Let's look closely at the book of Ezra. The book is written in two parts. The first part tells of the people returning and trying to rebuild their temple. They run into trouble with the neighbouring people.

> *Despite their fear of the peoples around them, they built the altar on its foundation and sacrificed burnt offerings on it to the Lord, both the morning and evening sacrifices. (Ezra 3:3 NIV)*

Who were those people around them that the returnees were dreading? If the text meant the people who lived in and around Jerusalem then the vast majority would have been Hebrew people descendant from those who were not taken into exile. Life was quite different for those people than the ones who were taken into exile.

Or perhaps the neighbouring people mentioned in Ezra refers to the neighbouring province. To the north of Judah, a second province was set up in Samaria. The new province of Samaria would have had both Hebrews and the descendants of those brought into the land by the Assyrians after the kingdom of Israel was destroyed. Ezra 4 describes the people of Samaria asking to be allowed to help build the temple in Jerusalem.

> *When the enemies of Judah and Benjamin heard that the exiles were building a temple for the Lord, the God of Israel, ² they came to Zerubbabel and to the heads of the families and said, "Let us help you build because, like you, we seek your God and have been sacrificing to him since the time of Esarhaddon king of Assyria, who brought us here. (Ezra 4:1 – 2 NIV)*

Judah and Benjamin were the two tribes that made up the southern kingdom when the other ten tribes became the northern kingdom. Note how the northern kingdom, the new province of Samaria, is described an enemies of the two southern tribes.

Those building the temple at Jerusalem said the others could not help them. So the others bribed Persian officials and accused the people of Jerusalem of disloyalty to the Persians to ensure that the temple could not be finished. The text includes a letter to a Persian king saying that the people of Jerusalem were rebuilding the city so they could revolt against Persia. This is followed by the letter back from the king saying that he will not let the Jewish people finish rebuilding Jerusalem. (Ezra 4 - 6)

The second part of the book of Ezra is written in first person and attributed to the priest, Ezra, after whom the book gets its name. Ezra was commissioned to go to Jerusalem and teach the Jewish people about God's laws.

According to the text, a group of officials approached Ezra and complained that the Jewish people had not properly separated themselves off:

> *"The people of Israel, including the priests and the Levites, have not kept themselves separate from the neighboring peoples with their detestable practices, like those of the Canaanites, Hittites, Perizzites, Jebusites, Ammonites, Moabites, Egyptians and Amorites. ² They have taken some of their daughters as wives for themselves and their sons, and have mingled the holy race with the peoples around them. And the leaders and officials have led the way in this unfaithfulness." (Ezra 9:1b - 2)*

> We will start using the term "Jewish" now, as the books of Ezra and Nehemiah use them to describe the people. Keep in mind though that this is still an early stage in the development of Judaism.

Note here that the 'foreigners' are not the Babylonians or Persians with whom the exiles may have intermarried but those who the people not taken on the exile may have married.

Ezra tore his clothing and pulled his hair out and was greatly disturbed by this. He wept and cried and refused to eat. Then the people became greatly disturbed and came to him and admitted that they had married foreign women and offered to give up their foreign wives and children. Chapters ten returns to talking about Ezra in third person. The book ends with the people sending away their wives and children, and it lists people by name.

It is likely that the banishing of 'foreign' wives was not as popular as Ezra wanted to make it sound. One possibility is that the testimony of Ezra was recorded as a defense against accusations made against him by those objecting to his policies. He might - and remember, this is speculation - have been summoned back to Persia to account for what he had done. The insistence that all he had done was cry, and the people voluntarily gave up their wives might have been part of this defense. The list of names at the end may have been people who supported him and his policies.

So, with the first part of the book of Ezra focused on the rebuilding of the temple and the second half on banishing foreign wives, what joins the two parts of the book of Ezra together? They are both about who gets to belong to the community and who does not get to belong! Both participating in the temple and being a marriage partner would be signs of belonging to the community. Being rejected from those would be signs of not belonging.

The book of Nehemiah is written in first person. Nehemiah was the cup-bearer to the Persian king before requesting permission to go to Judah to rebuild Jerusalem. When he got there he saw that the city walls were broken down, so he started the rebuilding. Then three foreigners – identified as Sanballat the Horonite, Tobiah the Ammonite official, and Geshem the Arab – asked, "What are you doing? Are you rebelling against the king?" (Nehemiah 2:19 NIV)

Building walls could be considered a form of rebellion since a walled city was able to defend itself. If you were a governor or a ruler and you wanted to rebel against the empire you paid tribute to, the first thing you'd want to do is make sure you had strong walls to defend yourself.

Nehemiah responded saying "The God of heaven will give us success. We, his servants, will start rebuilding, but as for you, you have no share in Jerusalem or any claim or historic right to it." (Nehemiah 2:20 NIV) Nehemiah did not outright deny the possibility of rebellion. He bypassed it by focusing on his allegiance to God. (Is God on the Persian king's side or not?) Then he focused on the idea that the men questioning him did not belong. The book of Nehemiah, like Ezra, is focused on boundaries and questions of belonging.

> Why would the text be so against foreign wives? Part of it could be a concern about keeping their religious beliefs clear. Foreign wives would potentially worship foreign gods and teach their children to worship those gods.
>
> There might have been an economic motivation to kick out foreign wives too. After the exile took place, the farmland would have been claimed by those who remain behind. When people return from Babylon and Persia to try to rebuild Jerusalem, they would have probably wanted access to farmland. The Hebrew scriptures restrict the selling of land, because that results in homeless people with no resources, so the returnees might have hoped to marry their daughters into families with land. Convincing people to divorce their wives would be a step towards that.
>
> Remember the stories of the patriarchs? In them Sarah doesn't want her son Isaac to marry a Canaanite woman and so they send a servant to go to Ur (a part of Babylon) to get a husband for Isaac. Sarah's grandson Jacob also marries women from Ur. Perhaps the legends of the patriarchs were written or edited by the post-exilic writers as part of their campaign against "foreign" wives. Perhaps the people who returned from Babylon to Jerusalem wanted their sons to marry members of the Babylonian exilic community, rather than marry the women who live in and around Jerusalem.

In the book of Nehemiah the people didn't just complain about the wall being built. Sanballat and his friends roused the army of Samaria to anger at the idea that the walls of Jerusalem were being rebuilt. If the wall repair was the preparations for rebellion, then its completion would endanger others by angering their overlords. (Nehemiah 4:1 - 8)

Nehemiah didn't stop with rebuilding the wall. Instead, Nehemiah armed the workers, so that if attacked they would be able to fight back, and people took turns guarding the city.

Another problem Nehemiah had to deal with was poverty. The text says people complained that they did not have enough food. Some said they had gone into debt during times of famine and others that they were going into debt to pay the king's taxes. If they could not pay their debt they would lose their fields and vineyards, and potentially have to sell their sons and daughters as slaves. Nehemiah became very angry when he heard those complaints. He urged the nobles and officials to stop charging interest on debts and to give people back their land. When he was appointed governor, he refused to take money from the job, so that paying him would not be a burden for the people. (Nehemiah 5)

The book of Ezra doesn't mention Nehemiah, but the book of Nehemiah does mention the priest Ezra and like the book of Ezra it ends with foreign wives being sent away.

Review

In the first part of this book we looked at how the Bible presents a story of the Israelite people. Let us do a quick review of the different time periods covered so far.

The Bible says the Israelites arose from one family, led by a man named Abraham to whom God made a promise. This promise was inherited by his son Isaac, who passed it on to his son Jacob. During a time of famine Jacob and his sons moved to Egypt, where the favourite son had become assistant to the Pharaoh. This collection of stories is referred to as the stories of the patriarchs and these stories are found in the book of Genesis.

Next we have the Exodus, where people exited Egypt. These are the stories of Moses and they include stories of Moses getting a set of laws from God to give to the Hebrew people. Over the years, different writers wrote their own sets of laws and attributed them to God and Moses. These stories start in Exodus and continue in the books of Leviticus, Numbers and Deuteronomy.

After Moses came Joshua, who lead the conquest of Canaan, at least according to the Bible. Do you remember the story of the fall of Jericho and the questions about whether the Israelites really conquered Canaan or whether they were peaceful immigrants or even Canaanites who moved out into the countryside and away from the cities? Whatever the true origin of the Israelites was, the Biblical story is written to portray them as winning their victories because of their god's assistance and in them failing to clear the land completely. This failure to remove other cultures from the land is portrayed as the cause of them continuing to worship other gods.

The next period of the Hebrew story is the time when the Hebrews lived without kings. In the Bible this is called the time of the Judges. Do you remember the stories of Deborah and Gideon, rallying the troops? What about the stories of Samson the strong man? The stories of this time preserve the memory (or belief) that the Hebrew people were once separate tribes that united for self-defense.

The period of the judges gives way to the time of the monarchy. The first three important kings were Saul, David and Solomon. At the time of Solomon's son ten of the tribes revolted, leaving a divided monarchy. The northern kingdom was called Israel. The southern kingdom was called Judah. This is the first part of the Bible for which we have some independent collaboration and the stories may have some basis in reality, though the writers were not concerned with historical accuracy but with explaining their history in relationship to their god.

Eventually the two kingdoms ended up being overthrown by larger kingdoms. Israel was conquered by the Assyrians. The Assyrians had a policy of mixing up the populations of their conquered kingdoms, relocating large numbers of people. At first Judah was able to expand up into the area once claimed by Israel, but eventually Judah was conquered by the Babylonians. The Babylonians took the elites of their conquered nations into exile to try to prevent further revolts.

The exile and post-exilic period really challenged people to think about who their god was. Was he a warrior god living in one temple, protecting one group of people? Could they worship him in a foreign land? Did he care about those people of the foreign land? Was he perhaps bigger and greater than they had imagined him being?

When the Babylonians were defeated by the Persians, some of the descendants of those who went into exile returned to Jerusalem to rule a province called Judea and build a new temple. People during this post-exilic period struggled with questions about who belonged to their religious community. The exiles had been away from Jerusalem a long time and their experiences and religious beliefs were different than those of the people who stayed behind.

The Persians encouraged the Jewish elites to write down and distribute their laws. They also encouraged the growth of the temple cult. The temple cult likely help rewrite the stories to emphasis that their god had given them laws and instructions to be a people together, even if they were under the rule of a foreign nation. Laws and not land become more important.

> Legend is that the first Greek translation of the Hebrew scriptures was done at the request of Ptolemy II Philadelphus who reigned between 283-246 BCE. The legend says that six men from each of the twelve tribes contributed to the translation.

Eventually the Persians were defeated by the Greek leader Alexander the Great. That is a very quick summary of the big picture story of the scriptures up to 323 BCE. Now that you know that story, we can start to talk about how the other parts of the Bible fit in.

Follow-up Activity

1. This book is attempting to talk about the history of the people who wrote the Bible, but also about the stories told in the Bible. What are some of the stories which are stories but not history? What are some stories that are likely based on real events? Which of the events are you unsure about whether it is based on history or purely story?

    Note that different people - including different scholars - have different ideas about which stories in the Bible are based on real events or not. Different people may come up with different answers. The important thing is to be able to think about why you put forward the answers you do. Those who believe that all of the Bible is true tend to be speaking from a place of faith and a belief that the Bible is revealed by God. Those who view the Bible as written by humans tend to look for which things have outside collaboration and fit our understanding of what is possible. Those who believe that very little of the Bible is based on real events are sometimes called Biblical minimalists, but even most Biblical minimalists will agree that some things, such as the destruction of the temple in Jerusalem by the Babylonians, are based on real life.

2. Using this review and the timeline on page five make a poster illustrating the major events discussed in the book so far that are history.

The books of Chronicles were likely written during the second half of the Persian period. It covers some of the same period of time that the Deuteronomic histories cover. 1 Chronicles starts with genealogies linking the first human to the twelve tribes of Israel. It goes quickly from mention of the exodus to David and focuses on David's role in bringing the ark to Jerusalem. 2 Chronicles starts with Solomon building the temple and continues to the fall of Jerusalem. The two books are a history focused on celebrating the temple.

While the Christian Bible puts Chronicles in the middle, the Jewish scriptures are arranged so that 2 Chronicles is the last book. 2 Chronicles ends with Cyrus the Great saying: "'The Lord, the God of heaven, has given me all the kingdoms of the earth and he has appointed me to build a temple for him at Jerusalem in Judah. Any of his people among you may go up, and may the Lord their God be with them.'" (2 Chronicles 36:23 NIV)

Think about how this ending for Chronicles serves as both an ending and a beginning. To the author of Chronicles, Cyrus the Great permitting people to return to rebuild the temple was fulfillment of the promises made earlier that David's kingdom would be restored.

Ruth

We saw in the books of Ezra and Nehemiah how during the post-exilic period people were urging that foreign wives and children be sent away. Not all the Biblical writers believed it was wrong to have foreign weives. The book of Ruth says that King David's great-grandmother was a Moabite woman. If the great-grandson of a foreign woman could become Israel's favourite king, why should the Hebrew men be told they cannot marry foreigners? While the text never references to the post-exilic era, it raises a question that was important during the post-exilic era. If Ruth can be a loyal member of the community despite being Moabite, why could other foreigners not be seen as loyal members of their community? The book is set long before the exile, but it could have been written after the exile.

In the story a Hebrew woman named Naomi goes into the kingdom of Moab with her husband and two sons. The two sons marry Moabite women. Then all the men in the family die, and the three women are left alone. Naomi tries to convince her daughters-in-law to go back to their families and from there find other people to marry. As a woman alone she cannot provide for them. One of the women agrees, but the other, Ruth, does not. (Ruth 1)

> But Ruth replied, "Don't urge me to leave you or to turn back from you. Where you go I will go, and where you stay I will stay. Your people will be my people and your God my God. *17* Where you die I will die, and there I will be buried. May the Lord deal with me, be it ever so severely, if even death separates you and me." (Ruth 1:16 - 17 NIV)

Here it is not birth or parentage that makes someone part of a people. Being loyal to the people and their god that makes someone belong.

Ruth and Naomi go together back to Naomi's hometown of Bethlehem. It is harvest time, and the reapers are gathering grain in the fields. Ruth is able to glean in the fields, picking up the grain that the harvesters have left behind. A kindly man named Boaz tells his workers to drop extra grain purposely for her. (Ruth 1:22 - 2:17)

Naomi encourages Ruth to visit Boaz at night. When Ruth does this she is taking the risk that she will be attacked or considered dishonourable for being out alone at night. Ruth takes a risk and is rewarded for it. Boaz agrees to marry her. (Ruth 2:18 - 3)

> One of the laws in the book of Deuteronomy was that:
>
> > "When you are harvesting in your field and you overlook a sheaf, do not go back to get it. Leave it for the foreigner, the fatherless and the widow, so that the Lord your God may bless you in all the work of your hands." (Deuteronomy 24:19 NIV)
>
> The book of Deuteronomy was written during King Josiah's reign, which was long after King David. However, Deuteronomy claims to have been written at the time of Moses, so a writer in the post-exilic period would have believed the law to be in affect at the time before King David.

Boaz says there is a little legal complication he has to take care of before he can marry Ruth. The legal complication involves a mix of two different Biblical laws, one involving allowing relatives to buy back land lost to debt so it stays in the family and the other requiring a man's nearest male relations to marry his widow so that she's not left without anyone to take care of her. These laws were probably all meant originally to help reduce poverty and desperation, though they sound strange to modern ears. The fact the laws are mixed up in the book of Ruth might suggest that the author of them was living at a time when neither law was being applied. Or perhaps the author purposely mixed the two laws to offer a solution to the problem Nehemiah had been hearing about of people losing their land because of debt. In any case, Boaz solves the legal complication by talking with another relative who is more closely related to Naomi. He offers the person the option to buy Naomi's land, and says that if the relative does that he must marry Ruth. When the relative declines to marry Ruth, Boaz says he will.

One of the beautiful details of the story of Ruth is that there are lines where someone will say something and then someone will respond with something that means something similar but yet different.

For example, there is this little exchange when Boaz is talking to Ruth:

> [12] *"May the Lord repay you for what you have done. May you be richly rewarded by the Lord, the God of Israel, under whose wings you have come to take refuge."*
> [13] *"May I continue to find favor in your eyes, my lord,"* she said. *"You have put me at ease by speaking kindly to your servant—though I do not have the standing of one of your servants."* (Ruth 2:12-13 NIV)

Boaz has said the Lord should reward her. Ruth says Boaz has rewarded her. Is this accidental or is this a theological statement on the part of the writers, shifting responsibility for helping one another away from God and onto people?

The book of Ruth is short, so you can and should read the whole thing from the Bible. In the Christian Bible it is placed between the stories of the Judges and the stories of Samuel, so that it fits chronologically according to the time the story is set. The Jewish scriptures places the story later with a collection of other short stories and poetry.

It is a carefully constructed story, with the second half meant to be a mirror image of the first half. It starts with a family tree. It ends with a family tree. Near the beginning the women of Bethlehem talk to Naomi and hear how unhappy she is. Near the end the women talk to her and hear how happy she is.

Follow-up Activities

1. Read the book of Ruth and make a timeline of the events that take place in the story of Ruth. One way to do this is to imagine that you were preparing to do a movie about Ruth. What settings do you need? Which characters are in which scene? Which settings are repeated? Which events mirror earlier events?

2. Look up Deuteronomy 25:5 – 10 and Leviticus 25:23 - 31. How does the story of Ruth incorporate a mix of these two sets of rules?

Priestly Code and the Holiness Code

You have seen how in the Deuteronomic histories God is portrayed like a mighty king to whom the people owe their loyalty, because he has given them the land as a vassal nation. Failure to follow him results in them being overthrown by other nations. The relationship between the people and God was influenced primarily by the king and the prophets.

The first sixteen chapters of the book of Leviticus provides an alternative image of the relationship between God and the people. These sixteen chapters are sometimes called the priestly code. They portray a relationship that centers not around the monarchy, but the priesthood. They describe a relationship between the people and God that could be regularly repaired through the offering of sacrifices.

Chapter one of Leviticus begins with a story about God summoning Moses to the tent used as a portable temple during the forty years in the wilderness. There God describes the different offerings that could be made on the altar. Burnt offerings could be made of beef, sheep, goat, or birds. These were said to create an odor pleasing to their god. When baked goods were to be offered, the priests would burn part of it and keep part for their own use. Certain parts of the animal were recognized as special, particularly the blood and the fat. Guidelines are laid out for offerings to be made when a person has done wrong. If one could afford it, a sheep was to be offered as a sin offering. If one could not afford a sheep, one was to offer two birds. If one could not afford birds, an amount of flour would be offered instead. (Leviticus 1 - 7)

The priestly code prioritizes classifications and divisions. Animals are either animals of the land, the air or the water. Animals of the land are divided with those that chew their cud and have cleft hooves in one category and those that do not in another category. Cud-chewers with cleft hooves can be eaten. All other land animals cannot. Animals of the sea are divided into those with fins and scales and those without. Only those with fins and scales can be eaten. Of the animals of the air, those that eat meat are forbidden, as are winged insects that lack a joint above their feet. The categories are clear-cut. The animals that people were forbidden to eat were not portrayed as evil or dirty when alive. Only when dead are they a problem. Touching the carcasses of the forbidden animals rendered a person ritually unclean. (Leviticus 11)

> Food that follows the dietary restrictions are called *Kosher* or *Kashrut*.

Ritual uncleanliness is a complicated topic. It did not mean that a person was bad or sinful, and no one could avoid ever being ritually unclean. Giving birth to a baby was a good thing, but it would make a woman ritually unclean for a while. Skin diseases made one ritually unclean. Sometimes the ritual uncleanliness overlapped with health concerns, where one could become ritually unclean by entering a house where a disease had broken out. However, even in those cases the solution to the house's ritually impure status was not just to scrape away the old plaster and replace it with new plaster - which may have health benefits - but also to take two birds, slaughter one and release the other. (Leviticus 14)

The priestly code outlines a way in which the priests could facilitate offerings to bring people into their god's favour, but there were dangers to it. Entering the presence of their God could only be done with great care. Moses was instructed to tell Aaron the proper ritual that must be followed to enter the holy place. Aaron would have to wash and put on special linen clothing. He would have to offer a bull as a sin offering for his household's sins. Then he would need to take two goats. One goat would be killed and the blood sprinkled around the sanctuary. Then he would stand with his hands over the other goat and confess

> Nowadays the term "scapegoat" is used for the person who takes all the blame.

> Rituals involving driving an animal into the desert have a long past. The ancient Hittites used to try to cure evil by wrapping a string around the hand and foot one afflicted and then tying that string to a mouse. The mouse would then be released into the mountains to take the evil back into the wild places where it belongs.
>
> The Elamites purified a space before a king's wedding by killing one goat and driving the other into the desert.

all the sins the community had done. The live goat would then be driven away into the wilderness. (Leviticus 16)

The passages describing the live goat are sometimes translated to say the goat is "for Azazel" and sometimes translated to say the goat is a "scapegoat." No one is sure what the original words mean. Azazel may have originally been a demon in the wilderness. Or the term may have marked the goat out as one the goat of departure, the one who escapes. The term in question appears in Leviticus 16:8, 16:10, and 16:26.

Since the text of Leviticus 1 - 17 is set in the time of Moses, people used to believe it was written by Moses. As Biblical scholarship progressed people began to assume it was written during the time of the Solomon's temple. After all, much of it was focused on temple rituals. More recent scholarship has questioned that and suggested that the text comes from the time of the exile or even afterwards. Why, during the exile when the temple is destroyed, would people be concerned about the proper ways of doing the temple offerings? At a time when people felt cut-off from their god, a text about restoring good relationships with their god might have been incredibly meaningful. The text also sets out certain restrictions that are to apply "in all your settlements" (Leviticus 3:17) rather than, as Deuteronomy specifies, "in the land that the Lord, the God of your ancestors, has given you." (Deuteronomy 12:1, with similar text at 6:1, 6:10, 7:1 and other locations)

It is also possible that the priestly code was written not during the exilic period itself but after, during the time of the second temple. It describes a hereditary priesthood descending from Aaron, the brother of Moses. The text may have helped elevate the priesthood during struggles for power during the Persian reign. The temple and priesthood were being re-established but the people were still scattered throughout the near east.

> There are parts of the Bible that say to love one's neighbour and parts of the Bible that say to love one's enemy. These two ideas probably come from the same place. Leviticus 19:18 (NIV) reads:
>
> > "Do not seek revenge or bear a grudge against anyone among your people, but love your neighbor as yourself. I am the Lord."
>
> One's enemy would not necessarily be a foreign power but the neighbour who has done one wrong.

Leviticus 18 - 26 contains a set of rules that scholars call the holiness code. It was likely written sometime after the priestly code, and has more rules for the community. Like the priestly code, it describes a relationship between God and his people that is not focused around the monarchy or the land. Unlike the priestly code, its focus is not on the priestly rituals but the ways in which all of the people can be holy. The heart of it is probably Leviticus 19:1 - 18. This section begins saying that the people shall be holy, for their God is holy. It then outlines calls for people to stay loyal to their god, to deal fairly with one another, to care for the poor and to practice justice.

The book of Numbers might have been written as a way of merging the theological ideas of the book of Leviticus (both the priestly and holiness codes) with the theology of Deuteronomy.

Where do ideas about ritual cleanliness come from? In many ancient near-eastern cultures there were purity codes associated with the temples. The home of one's god could only be approached by someone who took the right precautions. A sceptical person could say it was a way of keeping the temple space and priesthood special so that people would respect them, but a less sceptical person would argue that they may have genuinely feared their god's wrath or abandonment. Perhaps the taboos were built up as a way of dealing with times of abandonment.

One hint to the origins of cleanliness codes might be in the Assyrian divination prayers. Divination is an attempt to gain answers from one's god, and it was inherently fraught with difficulties. The Assyrian diviners would cut an animal open and examine its entrails, praying that their gods would "place in this the truth." In many ways to a modern person, this could be comparable to flipping a coin and expecting the coin to tell us the answer to some question posed to it. When a yes or no question is posed, there is a chance the answer is right and a chance it isn't, just by the luck of the coin toss or the way the entrails of the lamb happen to be shaped. The diviners evidently had hunches about why, at times, their divination did not work. Their prayers included requests for the gods to ignore or excuse certain imperfections that might, theoretically, be reasons why previous divination attempts failed. These clauses requested that the god being appealed to for guidance in the divination ignore their imperfections and still grant their request for guidance. Perhaps the cleanliness codes built slowly as people tried to figure out what would bring them the best results.

On the other hand, many ideas of ritual also reinforced their concepts about how the world was ordered. The priestly code divided space into sacred and common space, with the priest changing clothes as he moved between them. The actions reinforced their belief system. Maybe it was not a slow process of figuring out what pleased their god but an implementing of actions that would reinforce theological ideas.

Jonah

The book of Jonah tells a very short story about a prophet that didn't want to be a prophet. In it, God tells a man named Jonah to go to the city of Nineveh and tell the people there that God will destroy the city for its wickedness. Ancient readers would have known Nineveh as the capital of Assyria. While modern children's Bible writers often portray the city as having been wicked for not worshiping God, in ancient times it was probably seen as wicked for its political power. Assyria had ruled over other kingdoms and exacted devastating vengeance when those other kingdoms tried to withhold tribute. It had destroyed Israel, the northern kingdom. Depending on when the story was written, the first audience might have been hoping for Assyria's destruction or they might have known that it was destroyed by the Babylonians.

In the story, Jonah doesn't want to go and tell the people of Nineveh that they will be destroyed. Perhaps he fears that the people of Nineveh would punish or kill him for telling them that. Or perhaps he doesn't want to go because he likes the idea of Nineveh being destroyed, and he doesn't want to bring them a message that might in any way stop their destruction. The Bible story doesn't say what his motivation is at this point, but it does say that Jonah decides to flee from God instead and gets on a ship heading the opposite direction from where God has told him to go. (Jonah 1:1 – 3)

The ship gets caught in a storm and all the sailors pray to their different gods and throw goods overboard in order to lighten the ship. The captain of the ship finds Jonah asleep in the ship's hold and tells him to pray to his god too. The Bible doesn't tell us if he prayed then or if he didn't. He might not have wanted to draw God's attention to himself. (Jonah 1:4 – 6)

The sailors cast lots to find out who it is that has brought the storm down upon them. When the lots identify Jonah as the culprit, they ask him about himself and what they can do to calm the sea. Jonah says that he should be thrown overboard. The sailors are hesitant to do so and keep rowing to bring the ship to shore, but eventually they do throw him overboard, praying not to be held responsible for Jonah's life. The sea calms down, the sailors are spared, and they offer sacrifices to God. (Jonah 1:7 – 16)

Meanwhile a large fish swallows Jonah, and he spends three days and three nights in the belly of the fish. There he prays, saying a poem of thanksgiving. You can read it in Jonah 2. Different scholars disagree on whether the poem was originally a part of the story or a later addition. (Jonah 1:17 – 2)

After three days God tells the fish to spit Jonah up, and Jonah finds himself on dry land again. God again tells Jonah to go to Nineveh, and this time Jonah obeys. (Jonah 2:10)

Jonah tells the people that within forty days the city will be overthrown. The people believe God and put on sackcloth, an uncomfortable rough material that shows how sorrowful they were. When Jonah's message reaches the king, the king does the same as the people, and then more. He sits in ashes and proclaims that all humans and animals must fast and cry out to God. Fasting was going without food, and it was another way to show sorrow and guilt. By proclaiming a fast for humans and animals, the king of Nineveh was going to extreme lengths. The text is showing him being even more repentant than most kings of Israel. Jonah's message received an unbelievably good reception. (Jonah 3:1 – 9)

God relented and didn't destroy Nineveh. This made Jonah very angry. Finally the text tells us Jonah's motivation for fleeing. It wasn't because he was scared the people of Nineveh would punish him. He had fled because he knew that God was merciful and would spare the people of Nineveh. He didn't want that to happen. He wanted the evil empire destroyed. He became angry that people listened to his message and earned a reprieve. (Jonah 3:10 – 4:3)

Jonah went to sit and pout outside the city. God created a plant to grow over Jonah and give him shade. Then the next day, God appointed a worm to destroy the plant, and he made a warm east wind and had the sun beat down on Jonah's head. (Jonah 4:6 – 4:9)

Then, when Jonah was very miserable because of the heat, God asked him if it was fair for him to be angry about the destruction of the bush. God says, "You have been concerned about this plant, though you did not tend it or make it grow. It sprang up overnight and died overnight. [11] And should I not have concern for the great city of Nineveh, in which there are more than a hundred and twenty thousand people who cannot tell their right hand from their left—and also many animals?" (Jonah 4:10 – 11 NIV)

What do you make of that story? Stop and think about it. What kind of message do you think the writer was trying to convey?

Like any Bible story there are many different interpretations of the story of Jonah. Some people view it as a story of disobedience and second chances. God punishes Jonah for trying to flee, but also gives him a second chance. God threatens to punish Nineveh, but gives them a second chance. For many modern Christians this is a story about how God will give them a second chance if they repent. To a person in ancient times, the story might have meant quite a bit more.

For one, this story suggests God has power over Nineveh. His reach extends out into the Mediterranean Sea where Jonah tries to flee and west into Assyria. It credits God with caring about the city of Nineveh and the people there. It speaks of a god who is not just the tribal god of Israel.

Second, the story suggests that even the Assyrians could learn to worship God. If the story was written in post-exilic times, the story might be touching on the same politic issue the story of Ruth does. Can foreigners be included in the community of faith? Can they learn to worship God? When the Assyrians attacked the northern kingdom – Israel – they didn't just remove many of the people there into exile. They also were credited with taking other people from their other kingdoms and bringing those people in to repopulate the land. When Ezra and Nehemiah were trying to rebuild Jerusalem as a province of the Persians, they rejected cooperation with the people of the northern kingdom, whom they saw as foreigners brought in by the Assyrians. Could the story of Jonah be another attempt to argue for the inclusion of these people? If even Nineveh – the capital of Assyria – could be forgiven and cared for by God, could not the people the Assyrians brought into Israel be included in God's care too?

> One interesting detail to think about with the story of Jonah is how God's forgiveness could in some ways make their prophet look false. Jonah said the kingdom of Nineveh would be destroyed but it wasn't! The people could take that as a sign that their prayers to God worked and they were forgiven, but they could also have taken it as a sign that Jonah was wrong! The only proof that Jonah was a true prophet would have come about if people had doubted him!

Follow-up Activity

1. Choose a character from the story of Jonah – Jonah, God, one of the Ninevites, or a sailor – and write your own monologue for that character. Your monologue can be expressing a viewpoint expressed in the story or it can be expressing a contrary opinion. For example, you could write a monologue of a god who rejects the Ninevites repentance explaining why he will destroy them anyway. Or you could write a monologue of Jonah explaining why he made the decision to admit that the storm was because of him. There are infinite possibilities.

An Aside - Proverbs

In English the word "proverb" can refer to short pithy pieces of wisdom, such as "One bad apple spoils the whole bunch" or "he who laughs last, laughs loudest." Before you continue reading, take a moment to think of what other proverbs you know.

In ancient near eastern cultures proverbs were often used for writing practice by those training to be scribes. They would be gathered together into collections, like the Biblical book of Proverbs. The book is attributed to King Solomon, but without evidence. Some of the proverbs in the Bible may have come from Egyptian or Babylonian texts.

The proverbs were literature of the well educated and reasonably wealthy class. What kind of advice do you think they would give their children and students? They advocated hard work and criticized laziness. They warned people to think before they act and to be open to listening to criticism. (Proverbs 13:16-18) They recommended cautious speech (Proverbs 15:1 - 4) and obedience to one's parents.

Many proverbs deal with advice on what type of friends to have and how to keep friends. Avoid friends that will lead one into folly. Be aware that wealth brings friends; poverty drives them away. (Proverbs 19:4) It recommends casting lots to solve arguments for "A brother wronged is more unyielding than a fortified city; disputes are like the barred gates of a citadel." (Proverbs 18:19 NIV).

Kare Van Der Joorn, a professor of religious studies who writes about the influence of scribal culture in the making of the Bible, argues that the scribes were vulnerable to slander and being pushed out of their patron's favour. A king or high priest might stop listening to a particular scribe and that scribe's friends would abandon him. The advice given in proverbs might have helped prepare a person to survive the culture of the royal courts and scribal communities. The reader is told that "a good name is more desirable than great riches; to be esteemed is better than silver or gold." (Proverbs 22:1)

Many of the proverbs promise rewards for the person who is wise and hard working. Sometimes it is implied that wealth is a sign of goodness and wisdom. The foolish person is expected to lose their wealth and the evil to be punished by God, so if a person has wealth, it must be a sign they are neither of those. Yet, that type of thinking can lead to some problems. Does that mean the poor deserve their poverty? The wealthy are encouraged to be compassionate and generous to the poor, but there's still an implication that the poor might deserve their poverty. This is tempered a little by the suggestion that the rewards and punishments might be delayed, and a good poor person might someday be rewarded while a bad wealthy person will someday be punished.

Besides the short-pithy sayings the book of Proverbs contains a few longer pieces of literature. It is good to read these so you can recognize when they are referenced to in other literature. Read the poems about wisdom found at Proverbs 1:20 – 33 and Proverbs 8:1 – 9:6. Read the "Ode to the Capable Wife" at Proverbs 31:10 – 31.

Another important proverb to be aware of is Proverbs 13:24, because mention of it reaches into popular culture. It reads "Whoever spares the rod hates their children, but the one who loves their children is careful to discipline them." (NIV) Many people paraphrase this as "spare the rod; spoil the child." Some of the people trying to follow the Biblical practices today take it to literally mean that they should hit their children with rods as a form of discipline. Others take the saying to mean one should use discipline, but dismiss the reference to physical discipline as just a cultural thing from the time the Bible was written.

Follow-up Activities

1. Read the following proverbs. What do they each mean? Which help to promote justice for the poor? Which blame the poor for their own suffering?
    a. The blessing of the LORD brings wealth, without painful toil for it. (Proverbs 10:22 NIV)
    b. The LORD detests dishonest scales, but accurate weights find favor with him. (Proverbs 11:1 NIV)
    c. A wicked person earns deceptive wages, but the one who sows righteousness reaps a sure reward. (Proverbs 11:18 NIV)
    d. An unplowed field produces food for the poor, but injustice sweeps it away. (Proverbs 13:23 NIV)
    e. People curse the one who hoards grain, but they pray God's blessing on the one who is willing to sell. (Proverbs 11:26 NIV)
    f. Whoever disregards discipline comes to poverty and shame, but whoever heeds correction is honored. (Proverbs 13:18 NIV)
    g. Better a little with righteousness than much gain with injustice. (Proverbs 16:8 NIV)
    h. Better a dry crust with peace and quiet than a house full of feasting, with strife. (Proverbs 17:1 NI

2. In many ancient cultures, proverbs were an important way for scribes to practice writing. Go to Biblehub.com and try copying a proverb in Hebrew!

3. Compare the Biblical proverbs to the ancient Sumerian proverbs. Ancient Sumerian proverbs can be found online as part of the ETCSL project. (http://etcsl.orinst.ox.ac.uk/)

Job and the Problem of Evil

The first thing to know about the book of Job is how to pronounce it. The name Job is pronounced with a long /o/ sound. (Take the first and last sounds of the word Jello and add a /b/ to it.) Joab, not job.

The second thing to know about the book of Job is that it consists of a several parts. The bulk of it is written as poetry. It is a dialogue between a man named Job and his friends. Job faces heavy misfortune and his friends try to counsel him that the misfortune must in some way be his fault. Job argues with them before demanding to be able to present his case before God. God appears and argues back.

The poetry of Job is framed by a prose section at the beginning and end of the book of Job. It is unclear whether the prose section was written before or after the poetry. Was there originally a short prose story into which a long poem was inserted, or was there originally a poem around which a piece of prose was written?

We will look first at the poetry, imagining for the moment that it was written independent of the prose. Remember how the Psalms rely on parallel ideas instead of rhyme? The same is true in the poetry of Job. The poem begins with Job speaking:

> "May the day of my birth perish,
>   and the night that said, 'A boy is conceived!' (Job 3:3 NIV)

The lines link two opposites: day and night. That is one parallel. They also link someone being born with someone being conceived. That is a second type of parallel. Being born and conceived aren't opposites. Being conceived is what happens before one is born, when one first starts growing inside a mother. This is an intensification. Imagine two people and one says "I could eat a horse" and the other says "I could eat a whole herd of horses." That's an intensification. Job is saying "I wish I hadn't even been born!" and then following that with "I wish my mom never became pregnant with me!"

(Job is really, really unhappy. If you're ever really unhappy, make sure you talk to a trusted adult about it.)

In Job 3:1 – 10, Job speaks of darkness over and over, wishing that the day that brought him into the world did not exist. In verses 11 – 19 he describes wishes that he had died at birth. Then in verses 20 – 26 he moves onto the topic of light, asking a number or rhetorical questions.

> ²⁰ "Why is light given to those in misery,
>   and life to the bitter of soul,
> ²¹ to those who long for death that does not come,
>   who search for it more than for hidden treasure,
> ²² who are filled with gladness
>   and rejoice when they reach the grave?
> ²³ Why is life given to a man
>   whose way is hidden,
>   whom God has hedged in?
> ²⁴ For sighing has become my daily food;
>   my groans pour out like water.
> ²⁵ What I feared has come upon me;
>   what I dreaded has happened to me.
> ²⁶ I have no peace, no quietness;
>   I have no rest, but only turmoil." (Job 3:20 - 26 NIV)

Which parallels can you see? Hidden treasures are paralleled with the grave. Rejoicing and being glad are repetition. Bitterness is the opposite of rejoicing. There is a reference to seeing the way, which implies a path or a route something that he cannot see, and then the sense of limits is intensified by the reference to God having fenced him in. Does that mention of a fence remind you of anything? The advocate had said previously that God had fenced Job in with good things!

Sighing and groaning are parallels, as are bread and water, but what do the references to those things mean? Bread is the staple food. If sighing is coming like his bread, then he's sighing routinely. He's living on sighs. His groanings are poured out like water. He's not holding anything back. What other parallels can you see in the last four lines quoted above?

Job's friends come to talk to him. The first friend, Eliphaz the Temanite, starts with his reluctance to speak. "If someone ventures a word with you, will you be impatient? But who can keep from speaking?" (Job 4:2 NIV) He says that Job had once encouraged others when they were weak or discouraged but now that bad things have happened to Job he's given up all confidence. Shouldn't his beliefs and integrity sustain him even in hard times?

Turn to Job 4:7-9. See if you can understand the argument in those three verses before reading on.

In 4:7 Eliphaz says the same idea twice. He's asking the question of whether the innocent people ever perish. Or, in simpler terms, can bad things happen to good people? Take a minute or two to think about this. Can bad things happen to good people? Good people get cancer. Good people have car accidents. Bad things can definitely happen to good people. Yet Eliphaz doesn't believe that. He's accepted a belief that God rewards the good and punishes the bad, therefore what happens to you must be a sign of whether you are good or bad.

In Job 4:8 Eliphaz states that those who plow iniquity and sow trouble reap the same. "Iniquity" means bad behavior so what he's using is a harvest metaphor implying that people who plant evil, harvest evil. Presumably the same goes for those who plant good. Presumably they harvest good.

How do people who plant evil harvest evil, according to Eliphaz? Job 4:9 describes God's anger destroying people. Eliphaz' view is that God punishes the wicked and rewards the evil.

What implications does Eliphaz' view have for Job? Job has suffered evil, so according to Eliphaz' understanding, Job must have done evil. There is, for Eliphaz, no other explanation. Eliphaz tries to explain this to Job as gently as he can, starting with a story about a dream (Job 4:12 – 21).

In his dream he hears a voice that asks him if mortals can be pure before God. Verse 4:18 speaks of the imperfections of God's angels. If even God's special servants are not perfect, how much more so must humans be? Check the images used in 4:19-20. The houses of clay mentioned are the human bodies!

In other words, Eliphaz believes that Job must be guilty of some bad thing, because he's suffering. However, he also believes that the badness is a part of being human. Of course Job did something bad – all humans do! Job just needs to accept that it is his fault. Eliphaz goes on for the whole next chapter about how wonderful God is and how Job needs to trust in God.

The idea that some the disability reflects a moral failing shows up again at other points in the Bible. In the the book John 9:1-3 someone asks why someone was born blind. Was it because that person sinned or his parents? The passage in John rejects both those possibilities, but for the moment think about the implications of people believing that a disability is a sign of someone doing wrong. How would people treat those who are blind if they believe that? How might they treat someone who is ill or dying?

Wealth and poverty are also seen as signs of how good or bad a person is at times. There have been many people who have argued that God rewards those who do good and punish those who are evil, and therefore if someone is wealthy or successful it is a sign they are doing good in God's eyes. When people embrace that point of view they can end up justifying allowing some people to become very poor and others very wealthy. They don't need to worry about whether or not the systems that might prevent good people from succeeding in life, because they assume God is controlling people's fate They may believe that people should listen to the opinions of the wealthy more than those who lack wealth, because the wealth is a sign that the person's is favoured by God.

Job rejects the idea that has done something wrong. To his friends this makes it look like he's being stubborn and unreasonable. Proverbs recommends being willing to listen to criticism and admit the possibility of mistakes. This is what Eliphaz is recommending. Moreover Eliphaz is assuring Job that everyone makes mistakes and Job shouldn't have to feel bad about making a mistake, just admit his wrong and seek forgiveness. Yet Job refuses to admit he might have done wrong.

The conversation grows heated at times. Job's friends lash out at him for his foolishness and Job lashes out at them. Each of Job's friends urge him to consider the possibility that he has brought the trouble upon himself somehow. They urge him to try to reach out to God to seek forgiveness.

Job believes his suffering to be out of proportion to anything he might have done. He starts demanding that God should tell him what he's done wrong. He asks to put his case before God, to defend himself against the accusations. In chapter 21 he begins to question whether God is really just at all. He points out that the wicked are often prosperous. If God is just, why does he allow the evildoers to go unpunished? Why do good people suffer while bad people thrive?

Then God responds to that. Take a few minutes and think about the possibilities. What could God say to Job? How can you imagine a god explaining why Job is suffering or why evildoers are allowed to thrive?

In the book of Job God responds by listing all his amazing accomplishments in the form of questions, contrasting his own abilities with Job's limitedness.

> *⁴"Where were you when I laid the earth's foundation?*
> *Tell me, if you understand.*
> *⁵ Who marked off its dimensions? Surely you know!*
> *Who stretched a measuring line across it?" (Job 38:4-5 NIV)*

The poem credits God with cosmic responsibilities, such as creating the world, restraining the sea, overseeing the rain and snow and binding the constellations. Yet it also describes involvement in the lives of the animals, observing the mountain goats giving birth and making the hawk soar.

After listening to the mightiness of God, Job admits his own ignorance.

> *¹ Then Job replied to the LORD:*
> *²"I know that You can do all things*
> *and that no plan of Yours can be thwarted.*
> *³ You asked, 'Who is this*
> *who conceals My counsel without knowledge?'a*
> *Surely I spoke of things I did not understand,*
> *things too wonderful for me to know.*
> *⁴ You said, 'Listen now, and I will speak.*
> *I will question you, and you shall inform Me.'b*
> *⁵ My ears had heard of You,*
> *but now my eyes have seen You.*
> *⁶ Therefore I retract my words,*
> *and I repent in dust and ashes."(Job 42:1 - 6 NIV)*

Job admits his limited knowledge and God's greatness. He doesn't specifically admit to having done wrongs which would cause his suffering. It is like the incredible vastness of God's domain wipes aside the question of whether or not Job deserved what he got. It renders all of that irrelevant. Job is humbled. He cannot question God.

After this the book of switches from poetic dialogue back to story-mode. The story part which frames the poetry will be the topic of the next chapter.

Follow-Up Activities

1. The poetic dialogue is long and beautiful, filled with mythological references, old even at its time. Here are some of my favourite bits. Choose a few to read. Look for parallels and then try writing a paraphrase, in your own words, of what the passage says:

   a. Job 6:24 – 30 – Job accusing his friend and asking his friend to see that he does not lie.
   b. Job 7:1 – 6 – Job speaking of how miserable he is.
   c. Job 8:1 – 7 – Job's friend Bildad expressing his complete confidence that God is just.
   d. Job 11:2 – 12 – Job's friend Zophar being rather insulting and then arguing that humans cannot possibly know as much as God.
   e. Job 21:7 – 26 – Job points out that the evil people often prosper.
   f. Job 24:1 – 12 – Job speaks more of the economic injustice and theft.
   g. Job 38:1 – 11 – God answers Job.

2. In Job 40:15 – 41:34 describes two big beasts, the Leviathan and the Behemoth. Read the passage, and try drawing creatures based on the descriptions. Do the creatures sound like any animals you might recognize? People have hypothesized that the Behemoth may have been a hippopotamus, known to the poet only inaccurately through legends. Others argue that these are dinosaurs. Leviathan may be a reference to the sea monsters connected with the Canaanite god Yamm. You can look up William Blake's illustration of the Leviathan and Behemoth online.

In Chapter 23 of Job a fourth friend makes a sudden appearance. Some scholars believe the fourth friend was a late addition to the story by a different author. The friend's name is Elihu the son of Barachel the Buzite from the clan of Ram, which literally translates to "He-is-my-God the son of God-has-blessed the Scornful One from the High Clan." The name is likely intentionally outrageous. What would you expect from a character called that?

Note that the book of Job does not include any mention of a life after death. No one makes the argument that Job's suffering on Earth will be rewarded after his death. At the time it was written, the Jewish people probably did not believe in an afterlife.

Later people would turn to the idea of an afterlife to explain why good things happen to bad people. One line of thought from the early medieval period was that all good actions will be rewarded and that all bad actions will be punished, and no one is perfectly good or perfectly bad. Thus the bad people obtain good things before they die so that they have all the reward they are entitled to and their afterlife will be miserable. Meanwhile the good people suffer during their life so that their bad actions are all paid for before they die, and their afterlife will be wonderful.

Job, God, and the Advocate

The bulk of the book of Job is a poem, but the very beginning and ending of the book is written as prose. Scholars disagree on whether the prose section was written before the poem or the poem section written before the prose. The meaning of either part is transformed when merged with the other part.

So what is the story told in prose? The prose begins this way: "In the land of Uz there lived a man whose name was Job. This man was blameless and upright; he feared God and shunned evil." Job, we are told, is both good and wealthy. He has seven thousand sheep, three thousand camels, five hundred yoke of oxen and five hundred donkeys. He also has seven sons and three daughters. (Job 1:1 – 3)

In the prose section of Job there is no question of whether Job's friends may be right about him harbouring some secret guilt. He is blameless. Not only does he not do anything wrong himself, but his children were good, and just in case they might have accidentally somehow in their innermost hearts not been perfectly good, well, Job offered special sacrifices to God to seek forgiveness for them for that. (Job 1:4 – 5)

Like a fairy tale, the story of Job moves from talking about a wealthy man to talking about a royal court. Only this isn't just a king's court, but the court of God, where the heavenly beings present themselves before God. Besides God, one heavenly being stands out. He is the advocate, or the opponent. From the Hebrew word for him we get the name Satan, but forget everything you might have heard about Satan. He's not a demon dancing in fire. He's a member of God's court. He's there, talking with God. (Job 1:6 - 7)

God asks the advocate what he's been doing.

"I've been walking to and fro," the advocate answers.

"Have you considered my servant Job? There is no one on earth like him; he is blameless and upright, a man who fears God and shuns evil." (Job 1:8 NIV)

Job is so perfect even God is complimenting him, but the advocate isn't impressed. Of course Job is perfect! The advocate says that it is as though God has put a fence around Job, surrounding him with only good things. The advocate argues that if things went bad for Job, he'd be a very different person and curse God. God gives the advocate permission to test the advocate's theory. The advocate is allowed to take what he wants from Job, but not to hurt Job directly. (Job 1:9 - 12)

Note the difference between this question and the poetry of Job. The poem asks whether bad things can ever come to good people (or whether the bad situation is a sign the person was in some way bad). The prose part reverses this asking whether people are good only because of the good things surrounding them. Can a good person survive a bad event? It is not a question of whether God only gives good things to loyal people, but is Job loyal only because of the good things God gave him?

The advocate's test brings about a fateful day. A messenger comes to Job and tells him that all of his oxen and donkeys have been carried away by another tribe. A second messenger comes and reports that fire came from heaven and burnt up all of Job's sheep. A third messenger comes and tells him that raiders have come and stolen all his camels. Then one last messenger comes. This fourth and final messenger brings news that all of Job's children were eating in one house and a great wind came and collapsed the house, killing all the occupants. (Job 1:13 – 19)

Job falls to the ground. He tears off his robe and he cries out "Naked I came from my mother's womb, and naked I will depart. The Lord gave and the Lord has taken away; may the name of the Lord be praised." (Job 1:21 NIV) Just in case we are unclear as to whether this cry of Job means Job acted the way the advocate thought he would act or the way God thought he would react, the Bible spells it out for us. It says "In all this Job did not sin or charge God with wrongdoing." Job is being really patient with all these things going wrong, which is probably why people talk about "the patience of Job." If someone is really tolerant of bad things happening, you can tell them they have the patience of Job.

Back in his court, God brags to the advocate again about how great Job is. Job has passed the test! However, the advocate is still not impressed. He says that Job is still healthy, but Job will be different if his health is taken away. God agrees to let the advocate test this, but Job is not to be killed. So the advocate goes and inflicts sores all over Job.

Job's wife tells him to curse god, but he doesn't. He calls her foolish and says "Shall we accept good from God, and not trouble?" (Job 2:10b) Note that this doesn't suggest any guilt on his part or any belief that his actions have caused the trouble, only acceptance and trust in God.

Job's friends come to comfort him. They sit with him for seven days and seven nights.

After the seven days and seven nights, the poem begins and Job speaks, wishing he had not been born. Knowing all of Job's misfortunes, we can understand why he would feel so devastated! Knowing that his misfortunes are the result of a bet between God and the advocate, we know that Job is innocent and does not deserve his fate.

Knowing that Job's misfortunes are the result of a bet between the advocate and God transforms the poem. No longer is there any possibility that the friends might be right about Job having deserved his misfortune. The question becomes one of whether Job ever does what the advocate predicts and curses God. Does his pleas to present his case before God count as cursing God? Does his doubting?

God's answer to Job's cry becomes even more of a non-answer, for he does not tell Job what is going. Even if the world is too complicated for humans to understand why bad things happen, surely God could tell Job that the advocate was testing him and he has passed the test? It might be understandable that a mere mortal cannot see the whole picture why things happen, but could not this one set of events be easily explained?

The majesty of the poem about God's accomplishments hints that God could have all sorts of hidden knowledge about why he must allow Job to suffer so, but in the story we know Job is suffering because of a bet! A petty bet!

The prose story resumes after the poem. God says that he is angry at Eliphaz the Temanite and Job's two other friends for speaking wrong of him. He instructs them to give a burnt offering and to ask Job to pray for them. He accepts Job's prayers and spares them.

Job's brothers and sisters and all who knew him from before come to him to comfort him. They give him some money and gold. Then God blesses him, giving him more wealth and new children. He is blessed. It is possible that the order of these blessings matter and that the author is pointing out that God works through people.

Biblical scholar Rainer Albertz suggests that Job was written by someone in the post-exilic time period. The authors were concerned about injustice and may have been involved in efforts to help the poor, only to watch as the wealthy continue to grow wealthier.

To Rainer Albertz, the author of the prose story is making the case to be good for the sake of being good, accepting that God might give one both good and bad, but trusting that in the end one will be rewarded. Job being called upon to pray for his friends and Job's family contributing money to help him rebuild his life might have been included to demonstrate the value of people keeping helping others, despite the fact that one cannot be assured one will not, at some point, suffer.

Albertz suggested that the poet then inserted his poem into the story as a counter argument, allowing for people to feel and express grief at the misfortunes of the world. He provides an example of a God strong and mighty enough to be able to handle people lashing out.

Was Albertz right that the prose came before the poem? Perhaps. I have presented them in the opposite order because my suspicion is that the poem came first, though I acknowledge I may be wrong.

The question of why bad things happen to good people has been struggled with throughout history. While the poem and story of Job together seems to suggest that God's decisions are too complicated for us to understand, it also argues – through Job's voice and by having God angry at Job's friends at the end – that people are not the cause of all their own suffering. It also presents a remote and unconcerned God. In exchange for finding Job and others who suffer innocent, the text sacrifices the idea of a just God. Job's God is powerful, but not just, at least not in any way humans can understand.

Follow-up Activities

1. Job deals with the question of how bad things happen to good people. In a way the story of Jonah could be considered to deal with why good things happen to bad people. Jonah gets angry when people he thinks should be destroyed are spared. How do the two stories differ in their portrayal of God? How are they similar?

Two Stories of Creation

The first book of the Bible is called Genesis, which means "origin" or "beginning." It tells stories about the time from the creation of the world to the death of the patriarch Joseph. We have not discussed the creation stories yet, because it is important to start with the foundation of who the Hebrew people were and how their religious beliefs changed and grew. To focus on the creation stories first might create the sense that they appeared out of nowhere.

The Bible has two descriptions of how the world and humans were created. Stories about how the world and humans are created are one way in which groups can explore questions about why humans exist and what humans are supposed to do. When you read stories about the creation of humans – in the Bible, or in books of mythology from other cultures - ask yourself these questions:

- Does this story say that humans were created accidentally or for a purpose?

- If the story says that humans were created for a purpose, what was that purpose?

- If there is a god in the story, how does that god participate in creation?

- If there is a god in the story, how does the god interact with humans?

> In Canaanite mythology the great sea creatures are servants of Yamm, and Yamm is defeated by Baal. Genesis 1:21 proposes an alternative to that Canaanite mythology by saying that God created the great creatures of the sea. The sea creatures are not separate opposing powers.

Genesis 1 – 2:4 tells the story of God creating the world in six days and rested on the seventh. God speaks and things appear. There is a repeated phrase over and over that "God saw that it was good."

There are many theories about this six-day creation story. There are people who believe that it means the world was created in six of our twenty-four-hour days, just magically popping everything into existence. This theory is called "young Earth creationism." Other people argue that each of those days might represent millions or billions of years. Then there are others who say this story, like the rest of the Bible, is a myth. It is meant to communicate something about the world, but not meant to be taken literally.

The writers of this story were probably writing during the exile or post-exilic era. The story of creation in six days with a seventh day to rest portrays an orderly, positive universe. It shares much in common with the book of Leviticus. Among other things, the writers of both this story and Leviticus believe that humans should work six days and rest the seventh. Both texts are concerned with dividing things into categories.

The orderly nature of this creation myth can be contrasted with other mythologies, such as an ancient Babylonian story in which heaven and earth are created by dividing the dead body of a goddess. The god who speaks and things are created seems more powerful, less personified than a god that has to shape or mold things.

The story suggests humans were to imitate the creator. They were created not as servants or workers, but in the image of the god. Male and female are presented as equals in this story.

Genesis 2:2 – 9 gives a second story of creation, and you should read the text in your Bible. The order in which things were created is different in the second story of creation. Earth and heaven are created, and a spring, then man, then after that a garden – the garden of Eden - was planted. Man is created out of the dust of the ground.

If you continue reading Genesis further, you'll read about the rivers flowing out of the garden and how man was given permission to "You are free to eat from any tree in the garden; but you must not eat from the tree of the knowledge of good and evil, for when you eat from it you will certainly die." (Genesis 2:16b - 17)

God decides that the man, named Adam, should have "a helper suitable for him." (Genesis 2:18, NIV) Out of dust God created every animal and bird, and they were brought before the man to be named. The man named them but did not find a suitable partner among them. So God made the man fall asleep and took one of his ribs and made a woman out of it. Then the man said:

> *"This is now bone of my bones and flesh of my flesh; she shall be called 'woman,' for she was taken out of man."(Genesis 2:23 NIV)*

The story continues with a crafty serpent telling the woman that she will not die if she eats from the tree of good and evil but "will be like God, knowing good and evil" (Genesis 3:5b). So, she ate from the fruit and gave some to her husband. They both realized for the first time that they were naked and sewed fig leaves together into loincloths, to cover what we cover with underwear. (Genesis 3:6 – 7)

> The idea that humans were created out of clay has parallels in the ancient Sumerian creation stories. The ancient Sumerians had a number of different creation stories, but in several of them the creation of humans came from clay. In some of the stories humans were created to take over the work of the lessor gods after the lesser gods complain. How does that compare with the story in Genesis? Pay special attention to Genesis 2:5.

> The NRSV translates the description of the woman in Genesis 2:18 as "a helper as his partner." How does this change the meaning from "a helper suitable for him"?

That evening when they heard God walking in the garden, the man and woman hid. God called to them to find out where they were, and they answered that they hid because they were naked. God asked how they knew they were naked, and they admitted to eating from the tree, explaining that the woman had given the fruit to the man after the serpent told her to eat it. (Genesis 3:8 – 13)

God replies first to the serpent, telling it that it will be cursed and go on its belly in the dust forever. Then he replies to the woman saying that she will have painful childbirths. He says to the man that he will have to toil every day of his life and eat the plants of the field. Then the man and the woman were dressed in skins and they went out of the garden of Eden. At this point the woman was named Eve. (Genesis 3:14 – 24)

This story of creation and of Eve eating the fruit from the forbidden tree has been used by many, many people to claim that men should get to make decisions and women must obey them. It has been used to argue that women should feel pain in childbirth and that medication to take away that pain is wrong, because women should somehow all feel the pain as part of the punishment for Eve's eating the fruit! It is very sad when old stories get used to justify things like that.

It is possible the story originally had a different meaning. One author, Carol Meyers, argued that the story was originally about the transition to agricultural life and the work it entailed. She argues that comments about women was not that women were being punished with childbirth but rather that God was acknowledging the double duty they would do, both working alongside the man and bearing children. She attributes the pain mentioned in the Bible story not to the pain of childbirth but to the work everyone had to do!

Some studies of hunter-gatherer societies say that people who live as hunters and gatherers have to spend fewer hours a day working than those who were in ancient farming communities. Perhaps the story contains a memory of that transition. Or you can imagine the group of people that moved into the highlands and began to identify themselves as Hebrews. The land was difficult to farm. There were no springs from which to gather water, so they had to dig cisterns - a type of lined pit – so that they could gather rain water to use. They had to shape the ground with terracing so they could plant their crops. It was hard work, at least much harder work than farming in the valley. Men and women would have both worked long hours, but women would have the additional work of bearing the children. Perhaps the exile from Eden reflects those challenges.

The next Bible story, about Adam and Eve's children, also touches on the topic of agriculture. Adam and Eve had two sons. The older son, Cain, tilled the ground. The younger son, Abel, raised sheep. Each made an offering to their god. Cain offered plants, and Abel offered the fat from a lamb. God gave approval to Abel's offering, but not Cain's offering. (Genesis 4:1 – 5)

Cain becomes angry that God was displeased with his offering and goes and kills his brother Abel. After that God says he is cursed and drives him away. Cain goes away, marries and has a family. One of his descendants is described as "the father of those who live in tents and raise livestock." (Genesis 4:20b NIV) One of them is described as "the father of all who play stringed instruments and pipes" (Genesis 4:21b NIV) and another is described as making "all kinds of tools out of bronze and iron." (Genesis 4:22b NIV)

Like all Bible stories, the story is open to different interpretations. One possible explanation is that God's rejection of Cain's offering has nothing to do with what was offered and everything to do with Cain's behaviour. Cain's willingness to go ahead and murder someone afterwards seems to support the idea that he's not a great guy. Presumably some of his previous unmentioned behaviour would also be bad.

Alternatively, the fact Cain is offering wheat could be very important to the story. Is the story critical of the transition to an agrarian society? Does it suggest that the ancient people believe God favoured shepherds to farmers? What do you make of his descendants? Blacksmithing, which allows the development of deadlier weapons, is attributed to Cain but so is music. Learning to farm allowed humans to settle. Hunters had to follow their animals and shepherds had to travel in search of better pastures, but farmers could stay where they were. They could build bigger homes and support specialists like artists and blacksmiths. However, that also meant they could develop kingdoms, build armies and go to war easier.

Follow-up Activities

1.   Read the first four chapters of Genesis. Answer the questions listed at the beginning of this chapter for the two separate Biblical creation myths.

2.   Look up a different creation story, such as the ancient Greek creation myths or a North American creation myth. Ask yourself the questions listed at the beginning of this chapter.

3.   Look up the "Debate between Sheep and Grain." You can find a translation of it online at the Electronic Text Corpus of Sumerian Literature. How does it compare with the story of Cain and Abel?

4.   Look up "Dumuzid and Enkimdu. The dispute between the shepherd and the farmer." You can find it on the Electronic Text Corpus of Sumerian literature as well. How does it compare with the story of Cain and Abel?

Augustine of Hippo, who lived from 354 - 430 CE, argued that Adam eating the fruit was the "original sin" which ended up changing humans forever. There are slight hints of similar ideas in other writings from the first century CE and later, but the idea wasn't really fully formed until Augustine.

Noah to the Tower of Babel

Between the stories of creation and the stories of Abraham, we have other stories. One of these stories tells of the "sons of God" seeing humans and deciding to come down to earth to marry human women. It says their children were the heroes of old. (Genesis 6:1 – 4)

Perhaps that reminds you of ancient Greek mythology, where different gods have half-human children who perform marvelous feats. The Greek and Hebrew stories might have a common origin in Hittite myth.

> The story also refers to these sons of Gods or to their half-human children as "nephilim" which means "fallen ones." This gave rise to stories about fallen angels. Later stories elaborated on this to portray demons and devils as fallen angels with one of them, Satan or Lucifer, as their leader.

The Bible says that God didn't want his spirit mixed with humans and decided to limit people to a hundred and twenty year life-spans. (Genesis 6:3) In this way the Bible rejects the ideas within the Greek myths of celebrating the demi-gods. It presents those as a possibility only in the very beginning, but as something banned by God.

Some people see the "sons of God" as angels. This becomes interesting. Some people think that humans become angels when they die. Yet in early times, angels were portrayed as a totally different species than humans. Humans were made of flesh or clay and lived short lifespans. Angels were not made of flesh or clay. Only later (probably sometime after the exile) did people start to believe that humans themselves could become angels.

In Genesis 5, just before the story of the sons of God, there is a list of Adam's descendants. Included in that list is a man named Enoch who "walked faithfully with God; then he was no more, because God took him away." (Genesis 5:24) This was probably just a fancy way of saying that he was a good person who died, but this line also became the basis of later elaboration. Texts from the Hellenistic time that were not included in the Bible told of how Enoch became an angel. The boundary between human and angel – affirmed in Genesis 6:3 – was broken down.

Immediately after the story of these "sons of God" having children with humans comes a story that God saw the wickedness of humankind and decided to have a flood to wipe out the humans. The placement of the two stories next to each other has led some to interpret it that God decided to make the flood to wipe out the half-humans or that the fallen angels lead to the evilness of mankind. It is possible that the author intended this or simply that the author wanted to order the stories in what he felt was chronological order.

In any case, the story says that one man, Noah, was perfect and walked with God. God decided to spare him and his family. God instructed him on how to build an ark. The word "ark" comes from the Latin word for something that holds or protects, so an ark is a protective container. In this case it was a boat, and so the word "ark" has come to mean boat. (Genesis 6:9 – 22)

Noah built a boat and took his wife, his sons, his sons' wives, and a bunch of animals. According to one passage of the story he took two of every type of animal on the boat and according to another section he took seven pairs of all the animals that were suitable for eating and only two of the ones that were not suitable for eating. Someone likely edited the story after the writing of the priestly and holiness codes, so as to suggest that Noah was aware of them. (Genesis 7:1 - 16)

It rained for forty days and forty nights. The waters lifted the ark up and like a good boat, it floated. Everyone that was not on the ark died. All the animals and birds that were not on the ark died. Only the creatures in the ark survived. (Genesis 7:17 – 24)

Eventually the waters began to recede. Noah released one bird but it was unable to find anywhere to rest so it returned to him. He waited seven days, and released another bird. This one brought back an olive leaf. After another seven days he conducted the experiment again, and this time the bird did not return because it had found land. (Genesis 8:1 – 12)

The waters continued to recede and eventually Noah could open up the covering of the ark. Still later the land was dry enough they could release all the creatures and go out onto land. Noah made an altar and offered a sacrifice to God, and God promised that he would never do a flood like that again. (Genesis 8:13 – 9:17)

Then Noah planted a vineyard, got drunk and fell asleep naked. Two of his sons carefully covered him without looking at him but one of his sons saw him naked. When Noah woke up he cursed not the son who saw him naked but that son's son, Canaan. Then he blessed the descendants of Shem, one of the sons who helped cover him up. From each of the sons came different tribes. Like the stories of Abraham to Jacob with the extra relatives creating different tribes that are connected but not part of the special covenant, the story of Noah provides an explanation for the different tribes on the Earth. You'll note that Canaanites are the people who lived in the area where the Hebrews lived before them, and while the Hebrews might have been Canaanites themselves, they fully and completely reject that idea in their literature. They claimed to be descendants of Shem. (Genesis 9:18 – 10:32, 11:10 – 31))

However, the story of Noah is followed by another story of why the world is divided into different people. This story is often called the Tower of Babel. The language is a little tricky and how one tells the story will lead to interpreting it in different ways. You can read it in Genesis 11 but I'll try to retell it here.

Once upon a time the whole earth spoke one language, and everyone traveled East till they found a plains where they settled. Everyone decided to make some brick and bake, and they learned to make mortar. Then with their stone and their mortar they began to build a city with a tower that could touch heaven. To touch heaven was a common ancient way of saying the tower would be really tall, like we refer to tall buildings today as skyscrapers. However, sometimes people think that it meant people were trying to touch heaven in a competitive way – like they were trying to become more powerful than God. (Genesis 11:1 – 4)

God saw the people all working together. Was he jealous? The Bible says God said "Behold, they are one people, and they have all one language, and this is only the beginning of what they will do. And nothing that they propose to do will now be impossible for them." Does that mean he's jealous or scared of their power? Maybe. Or maybe he saw that they could do whatever they want living in that one area and he didn't want them to stay contently right there. Whatever his motivation, he mixed things up. He made them unable to speak to one another and dispersed them over the earth to populate the whole thing rather than just stay in one spot. (Genesis 11:5 – 9)

The city was called Babel, and it is thought to be Babylon. So here we have to stop and think about what Babylon would have meant to the Hebrews and other ancient people. The ancient Babylonians thought Babylon was created by the gods as a meeting place between the gods and heavens. They built big ziggurats – step pyramids – as temples or paths between themselves and their gods. Perhaps the story of the tower of Babel was a criticism of the Babylonians and their attempt to reach god through their religion and their empire.

Yet in some ways the story of the tower of Babel is like a repeat of the story of people being forced out of the garden of Eden. It tells of people working together, speaking one language. Does that sound like a paradise from which they are dispersed?

Or is working together under one language too close to being one empire? Ancient empires tried to yoke together all different kingdoms, and make them work together to support one Emperor. All those problems the Bible recognizes kings bringing would be multiplied under empires. Perhaps the splitting apart of the people was freeing them from being an empire like the Babylonian Empire, which the Hebrews experienced as evil.

The Babylonians attacked Jerusalem and destroyed the temple there. The Babylonians become known as the symbol of evil. Isaiah 13:19 – a poetic, prophetic section of the Bible - is hopeful for the destruction of Babylon. It describes "And Babylon, the glory of kingdoms, the splendor and pride of the Chaldeans, will be like Sodom and Gomorrah overthrown."

There is a frequent movement back and forth from Babylon to Canaan in the Bible. The stories of the patriarchs insist that the Jewish people came from Ur, a city that was part of Babylon and that God led them into Canaan, which they make into their kingdom of Judah. Then later the Babylonians conquer the kingdom of Judah and take people into Babylon. The Persians allow some of those exiles to go back to the kingdom of Judah. The story of the tower or Babel becomes a part of that movement back and forth. People came from Babel and spread out from there.

Later the author of the book of Acts would describe God's spirit coming upon Jesus' followers and making them all speak the same language. The scene suggests he felt Christianity was a sort of reversal of the tower of Babel, where people once spread out to speak different languages were called in to become one people again.

Try looking at the big picture of the book of Genesis. It starts with creation and Adam and Eve, with all people branching out from two people. People build the tower of Babel and everyone is dispersed from there. Then there's another bottle-neck where everyone but Noah's family dies, and all people branch out from Noah's three sons. Then from Noah's son Shem we come to the ancestors of Abraham, and to Abraham. With the story of Abraham, the book of Genesis narrows its focus from the (perceived) ancestors of all of humanity to the ancestors of just one group. As the story continues the different branches of Abraham's descendants are excluded from the covenant God makes with Abraham.

Likely the framing and the editing of the book of Genesis was done in post-exilic times when ideas about who God was were changing. People were starting to see God as not just the god of one place, one people, but a god that created everything. How could his special relationships with one group be reconciled with his creation of the whole universe? The way in which the stories in Genesis are ordered and framed portray God as the creator and ruler of everyone who chose to have a special covenant with one group of people.

The book of Genesis incorporates subtle hints at older mythologies, from the mention of the "heroes of old" and the flood story (popular in other ancient cultures too).

Follow-up Activities

1. Read Genesis 10:6 – 14. Notice the order of the people listed in the text. First it lists the descendants of Noah's son Ham and then the descendants of Ham's son Cush. Then it lists the descendants of one of Cush's children. Then, in 10:8, it jumps back to talk about Nimrod, said to be another of Cush's sons, unmentioned in the earlier list of Cush's children. The way the text jumps from Cush's sons, to Cush's grandsons, and the to another yet unknown son of Cush has made some people suspect that the story of Nimrod came from a separate source and was inserted, somewhat clumsily, into the list of Noah's descendants. Many scholars have wrestled with the question of who Nimrod is. Was he based on a historical person, such as Tukulti-Ninurta I, King of Assyria or the earlier Sargon of Akkad? Is he Gilgamesh, the mighty warrior of the Babylonian epics? Is he human or a giant? Make a guess about how a historical figure from Mesopotamia might have ended up included in this list?

2. Look up the Babylonian flood myths.

Maccabees to Herod the Great

Not every Bible has a book of Maccabees in it, and of those that do, not all of them have all four books of Maccabees. Not everyone considered them to properly belong to the Bible. Orthodox churches accepted 1, 2, and 3 with 4 Maccabees relegated to an appendix. The Catholic church accepted 1 and 2 Maccabees. Early Protestants rejected all of them because they were not written in Hebrew, but rather in Greek. However, many study Bibles will now include them all.

When Alexander the Great died, his empire was divided between his generals. Those generals and their descendants led new empires. The land around Jerusalem belonged first to the Ptolemaic kingdom (ruled from Egypt) and then the Seleucid empire (which was ruled from what is now Syria). The time after Alexander the Great, while Greek emperors ruled, is known as the Hellenistic period.

The Greeks were generally accepting of other people having different religious practices. For a while, the Jewish people were free to practice their religion as they wished. However, many Jewish people learned Greek and some adopted a Greek lifestyle. Other Jewish people were angry at this.

When the Seleucid emperor Antiochus IV appointed a high priest of his choosing to the temple in Jerusalem, people questioned whether the temple was still faithful to their god or not. Then the high priest's brother bribed the emperor to appoint him as high priest instead! What scandal! When a third person obtained the position (again, through bribery) and had his predecessor assassinated, the country moved even closer to civil war.

Antiochus IV grew impatient. He wanted Judea to be a peaceful territory so he could make his way down to Egypt and attack the Ptolemaic kingdom. So, he put forward decrees meant to get rid of the troublesome religion that was stirring up trouble. A statue of Zeus would be installed in the temple of Yahweh in Jerusalem. Jewish practices were declared crimes.

1 Maccabees avoids much of the details about infighting between different Jewish groups and frames the revolt as a war against the oppressive Seleucid Emperor Antiochus IV, who tried to force all Jewish people to adopt the Greek ways and religion. It says that a priest, Mattathias refused to worship in the Greek ways but instead fought back. He killed the Greek officer attempting to make him worship in a Greek manner and he killed the Jewish man who was willing to do so. He and his followers gathered an army and revolted. Then, after Mattathias died his son Judas Maccabee took command. Eventually the Maccabees were able to capture the temple in Jerusalem and purify it. The Jewish holiday of Hanukkah celebrates the re-dedication of the Temple and a miracle in which a small jar of oil was able to last for eight days.

The war created some theological problems for the Jewish people. They were fighting to defend their faith in the face of persecution. 2 Maccabees tells of situations of martyrdom, where people were asked to deny their god and on refusing to do so they were killed. This posed a problem. If their god rewarded devotion and good behaviour and punished bad, what happens when someone does something super amazing – like stand up for their faith – and is killed right after? What is the reward for that action? 2 Maccabees 7 tells of a whole family being killed. If whole families are killed, the martyr's sacrifice wouldn't even result in God rewarding their family! How could that be?

The Jewish people were aware that other cultures around them believed there was life after death, but they had not adopted similar beliefs. After life there was only *sheol*, the grave. (Isaiah 26:14, Job 14:12 – 13) Only God was immortal. It wasn't until the time leading up to the Maccabean war that Judaism began to adopt the idea that something must come after death. There must be some reward for the martyrs. The idea began to spread that there would be some sort of resurrection, when the dead would be brought back to life.

The mother in Maccabees who watched her children be brutally killed in front of her says:

> [22] *"I do not know how you came into being in my womb. It was not I who gave you life and breath, nor I who set in order the elements within each of you.* [23] *Therefore the Creator of the world, who shaped the beginning of humankind and devised the origin of all things, will in his mercy give life and breath back to you again, since you now forget yourselves for the sake of his laws."* (2 Maccabees 7:22 – 23 NRSV)

Not everyone accepted the idea of the resurrection. The topic of resurrection proved a point of contention between different Jewish groups. You will learn more about that soon.

Eventually the Maccabee family allied with Rome, and Rome helped John Hyrcanus, the nephew of Judas Maccabee, become both ruler and high priest. He attempted to expand to reconquer all the land he believed that King David had once ruled. He destroyed the major temple in Samaria. He crucified his enemies.

Josephus tells that once John Hyrcanus had a feast for the Pharisees and asked them to correct him. He was powerful, and they relied on his power, so most of the Pharisees just told him how wonderful he was. Only one Pharisee, a man named Eleazer, was willing to speak out against him, questioning whether John Hyrcanus was qualified to be high priest, probably believing that the king and high priest should be separate people. John Hyrcanus was furious! The other Pharisees hurried to assure him that Eleazer was speaking only for himself, and not for them. Then a Sadducee friend of Hyrcanus suggested that he test the Pharisees by asking them how Eleazer should be punished. When the Pharisees did not sentence Eleazer to death, Hyrcanus grew angry at them. He withdrew his support for them and let the Sadducees gain influence over him instead.

> 1 Maccabees 8 tells of the Maccabees forming an alliance with Rome. How does the description there, particularly 1 Maccabees 8:11 – 16 compare with the image you have of Rome?

Over the next few generations there was fighting as different family members claimed power. Brother fought brother for power. In such situations, support of the people became necessary. The rulers had to try to accommodate both the Pharisees and Sadducees, lest either use their influence to help an usurper.

Support from the Romans was also vital, and at some points tricky. When Hyrcanus II and his brother Aristobulus II were fighting over the throne the Roman general Pompey was willing to support Hyrcanus II, and Marc Anthony captured Aristobulus II. However, when Julius Caesar broke with Pompey, he had Aristobulus II released. After all, if Hyrcanus II was busy defending his position from his brother he wouldn't be able to assist Pompey, to whom he owed his assistance. However, Pompey's supporters poisoned Artistobulus II and executed one of his sons.

When Pompey died, Hyrcanus II knew he needed to find a new patron to support him. He offered his services to Caesar, sending soldiers to help fight on Caesar's side in Alexandria. As a thank you, Caesar was willing to appoint Hycranus *ethnarch* (which means ruler of one particular ethnic group, in this case the Jewish people) and he appointed Hycranus' advisor Antipater the Idumaean as Procurator. Caesar was also willing to exempt Judea from some tribute and taxes.

> The relationship between John Hyrcanus and the Pharisees would have been a patron-client relationship, until he became angry and withdrew his patronage.

A few years later Julius Caesar was murdered. Mark Antony and Gaius Octavius declared war on the two Romans they saw as most responsible for Caesar's death, Decimus Brutus and Gaius Cassius. When Brutus and Cassius were defeated, one of their generals appealed to the Parthians to invade Roman territories. The

Parthians aided Antigonus II, the surviving son of Artistobulus II, in revolting against his uncle Hyrcanus II. Antigonus II soon declared himself king and high priest.

Antipater the Idumaean's son Herod went to Rome and sought protection from the Romans. After all, he and his father had worked for Antigonus II's enemy. The Roman senate decided to support Herod and declared him "King of the Jews." Of course he then had to go back to Judea and liberate it from Antigonus II's control, but after a couple of years and with the support of Rome, he had control of Judea.

The Romans displayed their power and might in their building projects, and Herod, eventually known as Herod the Great, was eager to do the same too. He improved his palace at Masada and built a compound at Jericho. These weren't just luxuries. They were fortresses, preparation in case anyone should try to overthrow him. He had a city built that he named Caesarea Maritima, a majestic port to the Mediterranean to increase trade.

Herod the Great died in 4 BCE. After his death his kingdom was divided between three of his sons. The Romans permitted the oldest to be *ethnarch* and the other two to be *tetrachs*, but not kings.

Follow-up Activities

1. Choose one or two of the historical figures mentioned in this chapter to research.

2. Choose one of the places mentioned and look for information about it.

Daniel

The book of Daniel is a historical fiction. It was very common in ancient times for there to be stories of advisors to the king who were pushed out by jealous competitors only to eventually return to the king's favour and the book of Daniel includes a collection of these stories all set during the time of the exile. It attaches a set of prophecies to the hero of the stories.

Both stories and prophecies were likely written hundreds of years later, closer to the time of the Maccabees. As you read the summary presented here, think about how during the Hellenistic period some Jewish people were angry at others for adopting Greek ways of life instead of staying true to what they believed their religion told them to do. Watching for ways in which the story of Daniel encourages those who refuse to assimilate.

The book starts with King Nebuchadnezzar of Babylon besieging Jerusalem. Among those he is said to take away is Daniel and his three friends. The four are taken into the king's palace, given new names, and trained to take a role in the king's court. (Daniel 1:1 – 7)

Daniel refuses to eat the royal food and wine given to him at the palace. Instead he makes a deal with the man in charge of him that he and his friends be allowed to eat vegetables and water. He promises that after a trial period they'll be shown to be healthier and better than those young men who eat the royal rations. This is important because it allows Daniel and his friends to keep practicing the dietary restrictions that are a part of their faith. (Daniel 1:8 – 21)

One day King Nebuchadnezzar called all his advisors and magicians together because he wanted them to interpret a dream he has had. The advisors ask him to tell them the dream, but Nebuchadnezzar could not remember it. Still, he was determined to have an answer. He announced that unless someone told him what he dreamed and what it means, he would have all of his advisors killed. (Daniel 2:1 – 12)

Daniel and his friends were among the wise men at risk of being killed, though the story implies they weren't present when King Nebuchadnezzar gave the advisors the challenge. Daniel finds out about the problem from talking to the executioner, who has been sent to find and execute Daniel and his friends. Daniel secures a temporary reprieve during which he and his friends pray. God gives Daniel the same dream. (Daniel 2:12 – 23)

Daniel is taken before the king and he explains that while no wise men, enchanters, magicians or diviners can discover someone else's dream, his god can reveal it. The dream, he says, was of a great statue. The head of the statue was gold. Its chest and arms were silver. Its middle and thighs were bronze. Its legs were iron and its feet had clay mixed in with iron. A giant stone struck the statue on the feet and the whole statue fell and broke apart, and the wind carried the pieces away. Daniel explained that the different materials of the statue represented different kingdoms. Nebuchadnezzar's kingdom was the head of gold, but after him other kings would rule, each representing a different kingdom. Eventually there would be a divided kingdom, represented by the clay and iron feet, and then God would destroy it and set up another kingdom, represented by the stone that crashed into the statue. (Daniel 2:24 – 45)

By interpreting the dream, Daniel earned the promotion to ruler of all Babylon and chief over all the wise men. He was able to promote his three friends too. (Daniel 2:46 – 49)

Does this story sound similar at all to one of the earlier Bible stories? Do you remember a story about another young man taken away from his homeland, made into a servant, who earned a huge promotion by interpreting a ruler's dream? If it doesn't sound familiar, review the story of Joseph, told earlier! The writers of Daniel would have known the story of Joseph and are paralleling it, though the miracle God does for Daniel is greater than the one for Joseph, in that the king can't even tell Daniel the dream.

In the next of the stories, King Nebuchadnezzar built a giant gold statue that all the nobles and officials in the land were ordered to bow down before. Anyone who refused to bow was to be thrown into a fiery furnace. Daniel was not mentioned in this story, but his three friends refused to bow down. They will not worship a statue, but will stick to worshiping their god. Into the furnace they were thrown! However, the king looks into the fire and sees not three people but four, and the fourth had the appearance "of a god." (Daniel 3:1 – 25)

King Nebuchadnezzar called the three friends out of the fire, and they walk out unharmed. Not a single hair on their head was damaged by the fire. Nor was any of their clothing. The king was amazed. He ordered that if anyone criticized their god, that person would be "torn limb from limb" for the god those three friends worshiped was most powerful. Then he promoted the three friends. (Daniel 3:26 – 30)

Another story tells about King Nebuchadnezzar having a dream which Daniel interprets to mean the king had grown so great that he would be cut back and forced to live like an animal of the field for seven years. (Daniel 4:1 – 27)

The dream comes true. Nebuchadnezzar went walking on his palace roof and he thought about how magnificent all his buildings were. How great and marvelous a king he was! God became angry, saying that Nebuchadnezzar's kingdom would be taken from him and he would be driven away from human society and made to dwell with the animals and eat grass until he learned that God has sovereignty over all the kingdoms. (Daniel 4:28 – 33)

> There are parallels between the story of Daniel and the ancient story of Gilgamesh. One version of the epic begins with King Gilgamesh strutting on the walls of his palace. The people cry out to the gods for mercy because of how powerful and abusive their king is and the gods hear them. The gods create an equal for Gilgamesh – a man named Enkidu. Enkidu is a wild man, who eats grass and lets his hair and nails grow long. A woman teaches him to behave like humans do, and after that he goes and meets Gilgamesh. They wrestle, and then become the best of friends. The two go off and have many adventures together.

Without knowing what he was doing, Nebuchadnezzar went out into the fields. He ate grass like a cow. He let his hair grow long and his fingernails grow out. Eventually though, he looked up into heavens and blessed God, and then he could think clearly again. He re-established his kingdom. (Daniel 4:33 – 37)

When Nebuchadnezzar died, Daniel went on to serve the next king, and then the next king after that. A group of officials searched for a way to push Daniel out of power but they could find no faults in Daniel's behaviour. He had not been untrustworthy. He had always done his work properly. Since Daniel never broke any rule or law, they decided to pass a new law that they knew he would break. They convinced the king to make it a crime to pray to any god or man except the king for the next thirty days. Anyone caught breaking this law would be thrown into a den of lions. (Daniel 6:1 – 9)

> The story of Daniel takes a figure of speech common among the scribes and makes it literal. There are many examples where people said their enemies were like lions. One example is in proverbs: "A king's wrath strikes terror like the roar of a lion; those who anger him forfeit their lives." (Proverbs 20:2)

Sure enough, Daniel went ahead and broke the law. He prayed to his god, the same way he always did. Daniel's enemies saw him get down on his knees and pray before an open window, and they reported this to the king. The king was upset. He liked Daniel and appreciated his work, but the law had been passed and the king did not have the ability to change his own laws! Daniel was thrown into the lion's den at sunset and a stone was rolled over the mouth of the den to keep Daniel and the lions inside. (Daniel 6:10 – 18)

All night the king waited, grieving for his friend. Then morning came and he rushed to the lion's den and called inside to his friend. Daniel answered. He was safe and sound. Daniel was let out and the men who accused Daniel were thrown into the lion's den instead. (Daniel 6:19 – 28)

No one knows for sure how old the stories about Daniel and his friends are, but there are hints in the language used that they come from around 200 BCE. This is long after the exilic period and would explain why the author of the story had details of the exilic period wrong. The stories might reflect the concerns people had at the time of Antiochus IV. Antiochus IV tried to make it a crime to follow Jewish religious practices. Perhaps the stories of Daniel and his friends were meant as encouragement and guidance for people at that time. If properly butchered meat was unavailable, they could turn to vegetables as Daniel does. If they must face martyrdom, they should do so trusting in their god.

> The image of a younger god taking authority from an older God was common. In Greek mythology Uranus is defeated by his son Chronos, who in turn is defeated by his son Zeus. In Babylon the younger god Marduk replaced the older god Enlil as head of the Pantheon. In the Canaanite pantheon Baal, who rode on a chariot of clouds, became more powerful than his father El! The myths all vary, and some may reflect questions of succession and inheritances while others might reflect a slow shift whereby people feel less attached to one god and more to another younger deity, until that newer god is seen to be more powerful.

After the stories of Daniel, the book of Daniel tells about Daniel having several visions. One of them involved four great beasts coming up. Likely the beasts represented different empires. The first was like a lion with the wings of an eagle. That might have represented the Babylonian empire. Daniel watched as the beast's wings were torn off and it became human. Then the second beast was like a bear, holding three fleshy bones in its mouth. The third beast was like a leopard with four wings and four heads. The fourth beast was large with iron teeth and ten horns. Some people believe that the kingdoms were the Babylonian, Persian, Greek and Roman kingdoms. Others believe that they were the Babylonian, Medean, Persian and Greek kingdoms.

After the four beasts, Daniel saw a great fiery throne upon which an old man in white clothes with white hair sat. He was called the Ancient of Days, and he had thousands of beings attending him. Then one "like the son of man" came riding on clouds, and Daniel saw him as given total authority over all people in a kingdom that would not pass away.

In many ways Daniel's vision about the four great beasts, the Ancient of Days and the Son of Man were very similar to the King Nebuchadnezzar's dream about a statue made of different materials, that were destroyed by a rock. Both visions speak of a hope that the different human empires would be replaced by something greater and longer-lasting. People wanted hope.

Later, people would read the visions of Daniel and say that Jesus was the Son of Man, the being to whom authority would be given to rule over all the world.

> Throughout the centuries, the book of Daniel has inspired people to hope for God's intervention in world affairs. One group of Englishmen in the mid 17th century called themselves the 5th Monarchy. They believed that Jesus, coming as the Son of Man after the four beasts' monarchies, would arrive in the year 1666.

Follow-up Activities

1. Think about the ways in which Daniel and his friends maintained their religious practices when they were under pressure not to do so.

2. Read Daniel Chapter 7. Summarize it in your own words or try to draw a picture of any part of it.

3. The musical *Fiddler on the Roof* contains a song, "Wonder of Wonders," which references to a number of Biblical stories. Look the song and its lyrics up online and see if you can recognize all the references.

Entering the "Common Era"

There are two major events in what we call the first century of the Common Era relevant to the study of the Bible. One of these we have no independent confirmation for, yet it is the major focus of the New Testament. The other event we have much evidence for having taken place, and yet it is only ever hinted about in the Bible. I am speaking of course about the life of Jesus of Nazareth and the destruction of the second temple in Jerusalem.

We do not have historical evidence that Jesus of Nazareth, the figure of whom the New Testament of the Bible focuses, existed, though a lack of evidence is not proof that he did not exist. What we do know is that a group of people declared him the *Christos* - a Greek term that means "the anointed one" comparable to the Hebrew term *Messiah*. His earliest followers were Jewish. They would have offered sacrifices at the temple in Jerusalem and followed the Jewish teachings. Over time, Gentiles (non-Jewish people) started following Jesus too, and a decision was made that the newcomers did not have to convert to Judaism in order to be part of the new religious movement. From this, Christianity was born.

Christians do not always agree on what type of Messiah Jesus was. Would he bring about the general resurrection that people had been hoping for since the time of the Maccabees? Early Christians may have hoped he would be a king to overthrow Roman rule and create a new kingdom on Earth, but if that was all they believed about him his death would have surely put an end to the religion. They had other ways of understanding him as their Messiah.

The second event we have historical evidence for. During Emperor Nero's reign, a bit less than forty years after Jesus' death, a revolt started in the Roman province of Judea. The revolt lasted for about seven years. The Romans invaded Jerusalem and destroyed the Jewish temple there. Many Jewish people were taken away as slaves. The Jewish religious council, called the Sanhedrin, was dissolved.

Adult Jewish men throughout the Roman Empire had paid a tax to the temple in Jerusalem. After the destruction of the temple, this was abolished and the Romans instituted a "Fiscus Judaicus" or "Jewish Tax" on men, women and children age three to sixty years old with money from the tax going to rebuilding the temple to Jupiter in Rome. It was an unimaginable insult to be

---

Now in many ancient times people dated years by how far into a king's reign it was. You've seen that in the two Biblical books of Kings. Then during the Roman rule, the years were identified by the consuls that held office that year. But, a monk writing over five hundred years after Jesus was born started describing the year based on the number of years since Jesus birth. This was described as "Anno Domini" meaning "year of our lord." When the system of dating caught on, everything before Jesus' presumed date of birth was labeled "before Christ" or BC.

Dating all of history according to the presumed date of Jesus' birth has come into question. Does it constitute a statement of faith for a person to say a date with the phrase "Anno Domini" in it? Why should that event be seen as the defining feature of world history? Why should Christianity be embedded within our system of dating events?

The solution for this has been to shift from speaking of the Common Era (CE) and Before the Common Era (BCE). The Common Era starts at the same time Anno Domini did. The year 2020 CE is the same year as 2020 AD. The year 571 BCE is the same as 571 BC.

Historians have realized that the 6th century monks calculations for Jesus' presumed birth do not work. The Bible tells us Jesus was born during the reign of Herod the Great, but Herod the Great died in 4 BCE. This means that if Jesus was born at the latest time he could have according to the events described in the Bible, then the year 1066 AD, for example, would not actually be the thousand and sixty-sixth year since Jesus was born. It would be at least 1070 years!

forced to financially support a pagan temple, symbol of the empire that was trying to destroy them.

Two more Jewish revolts followed. One was from 115 - 117 CE, the other from 132 - 135 CE. The Romans forbade the practice of Jewish religious customs.

Yet Jewish practices continued. A new form of Judaism slowly developed, known as Rabbinic Judaism. Rabbinic Judaism embraced two sets of scripture, called the Torah, which means law or instructions. The written Torah roughly corresponds to the Old Testament of the Christian Bible, though there are some differences, particularly in the order in which the different books are arranged. The oral Torah were eventually written down as the Mishnah.

> Some of those who had begun to follow Jesus interpreted the destruction of the temple in the light of their beliefs about Jesus. They said that Jesus had predicted the destruction of the temple. Some would have seen the changes as signs of the end-time coming. To other people, the destruction of the temple would have been a sign that the Messiah had not yet arrived.

Meanwhile the people who had begun to follow Jesus were faced with new questions. Were they still Jewish? Should they pay the Jewish tax? For years before, being Jewish had allowed a person to avoid offering sacrifice to the Roman emperor, so many Christians were likely content to be seen as Jewish as well, but now Christians had a reason to pull away and to identify themselves differently.

Christianity continued to grow, and over time the Roman Empire itself became Christian. The stories of Jesus and letters by early Christians were eventually collected and in the fourth century the Council of Rome codified which books they believed belonged in the scriptures.

Throughout Christian history, Christians have often interpreted their religion as an improvement upon Judaism, viewing Judaism as being replaced by Christianity. You will see in the next chapters passages that are often seen as agreeing to this interpretation. Some of these passages were written at a time when most Christians understood themselves to be Jewish and were arguing with their fellow Jews. Some passages were written as the early Christians were defining themselves as separate, possibly partly a hope to distinguish themselves as different than Judaism, during periods when Judaism faced persecution. In any case, these passages have caused a great deal of suffering over the centuries.

Even the titles of the sections in the Bible become problematic. The Christian Bible is divided into the Old Testament and the New Testament, but the terms "old" and "new" can imply that one is a replacement for the other. Many Christians have adopted the terms "Hebrew Scriptures" for the Old Testament and "Christian Scriptures" for the New Testament. In this book I have kept the older, common terms to avoid confusion, trusting that the reader can recognize that I do not see the earlier texts as less important than the later ones.

Follow-up Activities

1. Read Mark 13:1 - 8. How does it deal with the destruction of the temple in Jerusalem? More specifically, what hope does it encourage its first or second century readers to have.

2. Find pictures and information online about the Arch of Titus, built by the Romans to celebrate their victory over Judea.

The New Testament & Jesus' Birth

The New Testament starts with four versions of the stories of Jesus. These are called the gospels. The gospels are followed by a book about the early Christian community. After that, the New Testament has letters written by early Christians. The most prolific of those Christian writers was a man named Paul. Paul wrote his letters before the gospels were written, so even though in the Bible they appear after the gospels, they preserve an earlier record of Christian beliefs.

Between the birth and death of Jesus and the writing of the gospels, something really big happened. The Jewish-Roman War started. Before it ended, the Romans recaptured Jerusalem from the Jewish rebels. They destroyed the city walls and the temple. This huge traumatic incident might have been in the back of the minds of the writers of the gospels.

> The Gospels are called the Gospels of Matthew, Mark, Luke and John. People used to assume they were written by people with those names. Now scholars are more cautious and will talk about "the author of Matthew" or "the author of Luke" instead of "Matthew" or "Luke." However, we're going to call the authors by these presumed names, even knowing that they weren't necessarily the author's names.

The first three gospels are called Matthew, Mark, and Luke. They are called the synoptic gospels because they are quite similar to one another. Most scholars believed that the gospel of Mark was written first. Matthew and Luke probably had copies of the gospel of Mark, because they borrowed quite a bit from it. There are other things that are the same in both Matthew and Luke that didn't come from Mark. This has led people to guess that Matthew and Luke might both have had access to a different source. People call this hypothetical source the Q gospel, after the German word for "source." No one knows for sure if it ever existed.

Some people read through the different stories and assume the differences don't matter much. They assume the differences are just different people's perspectives of the same events, sort of like how you and your friends might all tell a different story about the same event. They assume the true story involves bits from everyone's different descriptions of it.

Other people focus on the differences, as clues to tell us what the gospel writers believed. If two people tell the same story with just a few changes, we can ask "what message does the change convey?" Looking at the differences we can get a clearer view of the specific writers and their theologies.

Two of the Gospels have stories about Jesus' birth. The Gospel of Matthew tells of his mother Mary becoming pregnant when she was engaged to marry a man named Joseph, but before they lived together. It says her husband wanted to quietly break off the agreement to marry, but an angel of the Lord appeared to him and told him to marry her anyway. (Matthew 1:18 – 25)

Some wise men or astrologers saw a star they believed meant a "King of the Jews" had been born and went to pay homage. They went to Herod the Great, whom the Romans had declared "King of the Jews," and they asked him where the baby was. He didn't want any other king to replace him, but he didn't know what they were talking about, so he called his advisors. They told him the baby would be born in Bethlehem, so he passed that message on to the wise men. Then he asked them to return and tell him where the child was. (Matthew 2:1 – 9)

The wise men delivered gifts to the baby and his mother Mary. A dream told them not to return to Herod, so they went home without telling him any more about the baby. (Matthew 2:10 – 12)

Then Joseph had a dream warning him to take Mary and Jesus and to flee to Egypt. They went to Egypt, and while they were there Herod realized that the wise men where not going to return to tell him about the baby, and he got angry. He sent soldiers to kill all the little children in Egypt. (Matthew 2:13 – 18)

After King Herod died, an angel appeared in a dream and told Joseph to return to the land of Israel. He took Mary and Jesus and they went back to Israel, but they went to live in the town of Nazareth instead of Bethlehem. (Matthew 2:19 – 23)

Does this story sound familiar to you? It might, as the story is told and retold at Christmas time. The wise men are sometimes called Magi or kings. Sometimes people think there were three of them. The Bible doesn't specify the number, but it does mention three gifts.

The story of Jesus' birth might sound familiar in a different way. Can you remember the story of Moses, the little baby put into a basket on the Nile because the pharaoh wanted all baby boys killed? (Exodus 1:15 – 2:9) Matthew's story of Jesus' birth has several little clues in it to remind the reader of Moses. Both stories include mention of Egypt. Both have one baby being spared among many. Even the story of an angel telling Joseph to go ahead with a marriage he was thinking of canceling parallels a (non-Biblical but quite ancient) legend about Moses' father having a dream. Matthew would have wanted people reading the story to think about Moses, because he wanted to portray Jesus as a new Moses!

Notice how in Matthew's story Mary and Joseph started out in Bethlehem but eventually end up living in Nazareth. Bethlehem was known as the city of David. It is where Ruth, David's great-grandmother was supposed to have lived with Boaz and Naomi. Yet at the same time, Jesus was associated with Nazareth. How could he be from both? According to Matthew it was because he was born in one but moved to the other after living for a while as a refugee in Egypt.

The Gospel of Luke has a different story about Jesus' birth, and it intersperses the story of Jesus' birth with that of another baby, John, being born. John's birth was a miracle come to a woman too old to have children, but according to Luke Jesus' birth was an even greater one! (Luke 1:5 – 24, 39 – 80) John would be portrayed as a great man, but Jesus an even greater one.

Luke says that Joseph and Mary lived in Nazareth but had to go to Bethlehem so they could register for a census. When they got there, the guest room was filled, so Mary laid her baby in the manger. (Luke 2:1 – 7) Many people read the Bible passages and picture Mary going to an inn – like an ancient sort of hotel or a motel – and being told that there wasn't room so they could stay in the stable instead. However, Luke was probably picturing a small house with one or two rooms for sleeping in and then a room where the animals could stay during the night. It would have been that extra front room of a peasant's house that Luke would have pictured Mary and Joseph staying, probably in the house of a relative.

Luke doesn't mention any wise men, but he does tell of shepherds being told to go and see the miracle baby. (Luke 2: 8 – 20)

You may have seen Christmas books, movies, or pictures that combine the stories told by Luke and Matthew. This is one way that people deal with the differences between the stories. They imagine that the two authors recorded different things but that everything they recorded happened. It isn't the only way to deal with the two different stories. We can also read them as stories and see the two authors having different creative ways of solving the problem of how Jesus could be connected to both Nazareth and Bethlehem. We can see them as trying to make different points about Jesus' birth.

The John that Luke spoke of grew up to be known as John the Baptist. He baptized people in the Jordan river. (Luke 3:1 – 3:17) Have you heard of baptism? In some modern churches babies are baptized soon after they are born in a ritual that involves sprinkling a bit of water over the baby's head while saying special words. In other churches people are not baptized as babies but as older children, teenagers or adults, able to make the choice to undergo the ritual themselves. Some churches do baptism by sprinkling water and others do it by having the person step into a lake, river or pool. Many people read about John the Baptist and assume he was the one who started baptisms, or perhaps that baptisms were common at the time and picture him as a popular preacher. No one is certain about the truth though. Scholars disagree on whether John's baptism was related to Jewish rituals of purity or whether they were an attempt to ritually re-enact the crossing of the Red Sea in the hopes that doing so would bring about a new kingdom. John preached that something special was going to happen. All four gospel writers agree that Jesus was baptized by John the Baptist, so there is a pretty good chance that if there was a real Jesus and a real John, then Jesus was baptized by John.

John the Baptist was executed by Herod – not King Herod the Great whom Matthew said killed all the baby boys near Bethlehem, but his son Herod Antipas. John the Baptist had been very critical of Herod Antipas. (Luke 3:19 – 20, Mark 6:17 - 29)

After John the Baptist died, all the crowds that gathered to follow him drifted away. Some people might have thought that John had been wrong about a great thing going to happen soon, but the gospel writers make it clear they believe the great thing was Jesus and that John was preparing the way for Jesus. (Luke 3:16 – 37)

Matthew declares that "'The virgin will conceive and give birth to a son, and they will call him Immanuel' (which means 'God with us')" (Matthew 1:23 NIV) This is a paraphrase of a verse from Isaiah.

In the original passage Isaiah was speaking to Ahaz of Judah, when he was facing attack from King Pekah of Israel and King Rezin of the Arameans because he wouldn't unite with them against Assyria. Here is the passage and some of its context:

Therefore the Lord himself will give you a sign: The virgin will conceive and give birth to a son, and will call him Immanuel. 15 He will be eating curds and honey when he knows enough to reject the wrong and choose the right, 16 for before the boy knows enough to reject the wrong and choose the right, the land of the two kings you dread will be laid waste. 17 The Lord will bring on you and on your people and on the house of your father a time unlike any since Ephraim broke away from Judah—he will bring the king of Assyria." (Isaiah 7:13 – 17 NIV)

It is important to note that the word "virgin" in the Isaiah text can also mean "young woman." In the original context, the prophecy was not predicting any sort of miraculous birth but assuring Ahaz that before a baby not yet born grows to know what is right or wrong, Ahaz's kingdom will be secure and prosperous.

Matthew and Luke both give genealogies for Jesus. The genealogies are different from one another. Some people attempt to explain the difference by saying that they are tracing different branches of Jesus' family tree. More likely, the ancient readers would understand the genealogies are not meant to be taken literally but speak to a different sort of truth about who a person is.

Matthew divides the genealogy into three eras. The first goes from Abraham to king David, the second from King David to the time of the deportation to Babylon, and the third from the deportation to Jesus. In doing so, Matthew establishes his timeline of how he understands the history of this people. Matthew says each era lasts fourteen generations. The era of the Babylonian exile didn't end with Cyrus and the establishment of the second temple. Instead the next era will begin with Jesus, a descendant of David and the other rulers of Judah.

Matthew's genealogy has another interesting detail. There are four women mentioned in it. These women are Tamar, Rehab, Ruth, and the wife of Uriah. What do all these women have in common? Rehab assisted the spies in Jericho. Ruth was the Moabite woman who snuck into the field at night to lie next to Boaz before asking him to care for her. The wife of Uriah was Bathsheba, who became pregnant with King David's child while still married to Uriah. Tamar has an equally unorthodox history. Why do you think the author would include these four women? How does it contribute to the story of Jesus' birth?

Mark

The Gospel of Mark is the shortest gospel. People used to think that it was an abridged version of the gospel of Matthew. Now, people think Matthew and Luke borrowed from it. The gospel doesn't have any story of Jesus' birth, but mentions John the Baptist. John promises that "After me comes the one more powerful than I, the straps of whose sandals I am not worthy to stoop down and untie. I baptize you with water, but he will baptize you with the Holy Spirit." (Mark 1:7 – 8 NIV) It says that when Jesus was baptized, "he saw heaven being torn open and the Spirit descending on him like a dove. And a voice came from heaven: 'You are my Son, whom I love; with you I am well pleased' " (Mark 1:10 – 11 NIV)

Mark then moves quickly through little stories about Jesus. Jesus was tempted by Satan in the desert for forty days. He went into Galilee and traveled teaching and healing. He gathered followers – called disciples. He answered questions people asked him. For example, some people asked why Jesus' disciples didn't fast when John's disciples did. Jesus' response was that "How can the guests of the bridegroom fast while he is with them? They cannot, so long as they have him with them." (Mark 2:19) Then when people asked why his disciples plucked grain on the Sabbath – a religious day when no one was supposed to work – he replied telling them about how when King David and his friends were in need of food they ate bread that only priests were allowed to eat. (Mark 2:23 – 28, 1 Samuel 21:3 – 6) The implication is that he was like King David, able to let his followers do things others were not allowed. It is worth noting that when early Christians were debating whether new converts should have to follow Hebrew dietary laws, they did not reference to this story, suggesting they either were unfamiliar with it or did not take it as a sign that Jesus had negated all dietary restrictions.

> Can you remember other Biblical references to the number forty?

Jesus told parables. Parables were little teaching stories and many of his parables were about something he called the Kingdom of God. No one knows for sure what he meant by the Kingdom of God. Some people believe he was speaking of an afterlife. Others believe it would be a kingdom that would be created on Earth. Was he speaking of the same kingdom that the book of Daniel predicted, and if so, was it supposed to be an empire similar yet different to the empires of the Babylonians, Greeks and Persians?

Jesus said the Kingdom of God is like a man scattering seeds on the ground. Day and night, while the man is doing other things, the seeds are growing and then suddenly the harvest is there. (Mark 4:26 – 29) In another parable he said the kingdom of God was like a mustard seed. He said it was the smallest of seeds but that it grows to become the so large that birds can perch in its shade. (Mark 4:30 – 32)

> The Bible uses a couple of special terms for Jesus. One of these is "The Son of God." To some this means that Jesus is God's son, adopted by Joseph but part-divine. Other people argue that the term Son of God is a term used by the Roman Emperor to refer to himself, and that Jesus' followers applied the term to him to say he's a king.
>
> Another term the Bible uses for Jesus is "Son of Man." Some people say this refers to Jesus being human, not just divine. However, this term is the one used in the book of Daniel for the god-like figure that was given control of the Earth, so it might be a reference to Jesus being divine.

Ever since the parables were written people have struggled to make sense of them. Is the main point of the parable of the mustard seed that the Kingdom of God would grow really quickly from small to large? But what type of plant were they talking about? Most mustard plants are herbs or bushes, not trees in which a bird can perch. Perhaps the parable is using the example of a common weed to show that the kingdom would be started in a decentralized, weedy manner.

Jesus gathered twelve people as his disciples and then he sent them out in pairs, giving them authority to cast evil spirits out of people and to anoint the sick with oil and heal them. He told them to take nothing except a staff with them. Imagine traveling with nothing but a single set of clothing and staff that you could use for protection. You would need other people to provide you with food and lodgings. Furthermore, he told them that when they go into a town and stay at someone's home, they were to remain at that home until they leave the town. This might have been so that as they got to know the different people in the community, the people wouldn't be competing to get them to come and stay at their houses. (Mark 6:7 – 13)

> Why would there be twelve disciples, not ten or another number? Can you remember other references to the number twelve?

In one story there were so many people coming to talk to Jesus that he and his disciples took a boat out into a solitary area. The crowds watched and walked on land around the lake to get to Jesus. Jesus taught them, but since it was late in the day, his disciples urged him to send everyone away to get food. Jesus said that they should give the people food. The disciples expressed surprise. The crowd was so big it would take a man eight months wages to feed everyone! All they had was five loaves of bread and two fish. But Jesus divided up the food into small bits and gave them to the disciples to pass out. Everyone ate and ate until they were full, and when all the leftovers were gathered up there were twelve baskets full of pieces of bread and fish. It was a miracle! (Mark 6:30 – 44)

In a novel written in 1942 titled *The Robe*, Lloyd C. Douglas has a character suggest that perhaps many people had food with them but were unwilling to pull the food out and eat in front of others who might be hungry until after they saw the disciples start passing food around. Perhaps then everyone who had food pulled their food out and started sharing it too. Douglas' character proposes that as a potential explanation for how the miracle could take place, but then rejects the idea of trying to find explanations for individual miracles. I will suggest that imagining explanations for the different miracles ignores the points the authors were trying to make. The authors don't try to say Jesus inspired everyone to pull out their food and share. The authors either believed that Jesus could literally make an abundance of food appear out of nowhere or they believed that a story about that would in some way illustrate some sort of truth about Jesus. The writers portrayed Jesus as having tremendous power.

The gospel writers also portray the miracles as teaching about Jesus. In Mark 8:1 – 10 there is another story of Jesus feeding the crowds of people. In this story the disciples had seven loaves of bread and some small fish, but when this little bit of food had been distributed to four thousand people, they had seven baskets full of food left over. Afterwards, the Pharisees ask Jesus for a sign, and he says he will not give one. He and his disciples go off in a boat, where the disciples start discussing their own shortage of bread. Jesus replies for them to be careful and to "watch out for the yeast of the Pharisees and that of Herod." (Mark 8:15b) The disciples are understandably confused. What does Jesus mean, speaking about yeast? They say, "It is because we have no bread." (Mark 8:16b) and Jesus responds "Why are you talking about having no bread? Do you still not see or understand? Are your hearts hardened? Do you have eyes but fail to see, and ears but fail to hear? And don't you remember?" (Mark 8:17b – 8:18) He then reminds them of the crowds he had fed and the baskets full of food gathered later, and asks them, "do you still not understand?" (Mark 8:21b) While the meaning of the text is unclear and open to interpretation, it is clear the miracles are a message to his disciples. Perhaps the message is about trusting God to provide for their needs. Perhaps the message is about Jesus' ability to meet people's needs being greater than that of the other groups competing for people's loyalties. Or perhaps the story is to show how no matter how many miracles Jesus did, people would still misunderstand.

In between the two stories of Jesus feeding the five thousand and Jesus feeding the four thousand is a story about a time when Jesus had gone up a mountain to pray and his disciples went out onto the lake in their boat. Jesus walked out towards the boat, walking on the water! He was about to pass by them, but then they saw him and cried out to him, thinking he must be a ghost. He told them not to be afraid, and he came onto their boat. "They were completely amazed, for they had not understood about the loaves; their hearts were hardened." Why would Jesus walk on water? Why would he almost pass by his disciples? What does him walking on water have to do with the loaves?

A Biblical scholar named Dane Ortlund suggested that the Biblical writers were trying to allude to Moses. She suggests early readers of the texts would recognize the feeding of the crowds as being a reference to manna – bread from heaven – being given to Moses and his followers in the wilderness. (Exodus 16) Jesus goes up a mountainside, as Moses did at Sinai. (Exodus 33:18 – 23, 34:29 – 32) Walking across the water could be similar to Moses splitting the Red Sea for the Hebrew people to walk through. (Exodus 14)

Jesus almost passing by the disciples could be a reference to how God 'passed by' Moses to reveal himself to Moses. Moses asked to see God, and God said that no one could see his face, but that he would put Moses in a little cave and he would pass by and Moses would only be able to see his backside. God was revealed to Moses but also hidden from Moses.

In Mark, Jesus attempts repeatedly both to reveal and yet to hide himself. Throughout the book of Mark, Jesus frequently tells people not to tell others about him. He brings a dead child back to life (Mark 5:37 – 43) and tells her family not to tell anyone about it. He heals a deaf man (Mark 7:31 – 36) and tells him not to tell anyone about it. People did not obey his injunction to not tell.

At the very end of the story of Mark, when Jesus was dead and gone, a young man – likely an angel - gave some women visiting Jesus' tomb the opposite instructions. He told them to go and tell others what they have seen, but in that case the women said nothing to anyone, they were too afraid. (Mark 16:1 - 8)

It is almost as if the writer of Mark is trying to hint at whom he believes Jesus to be, but he's also trying to hint that people can only really understand it retrospectively. There's something too mysterious and powerful to be said straight out, so he has to tell a lot of tales to try to make it clear. Or perhaps the author felt that God could only reveal a small part of himself through Jesus.

The heart of the book of Mark is probably found in Mark 8:27 – 9:2. In this section Jesus is talking with his disciples. He asks them "who do other people say I am?"

The disciples say that other people think he is John the Baptist, Elijah, or one of the prophets.

Then Jesus asks, "who do you think I am?"

Peter, one of Jesus' disciples, replies that he is the anointed one. The term for anointed one is *Christ* in Greek and it is *Messiah* in Hebrew. This is another title frequently used for Jesus. It carries in it implications of being a king, as kings were anointed with oil, but it also carries implications of being more than just a normal king.

In the story, Jesus hears Peter's answer and tells Peter not to tell other people about him. Then he tells them that the Son of Man (himself, under that title that refers to a great heavenly being like in Daniel's dream), will undergo great suffering and be killed, but that after three days he'll rise again.

Peter tries to tell Jesus not to say all this, but Jesus rebukes him. "You are setting your mind not on divine things but on human things."

Jesus had been speaking just with his disciples, but then he calls the crowd over to join them and he tells everyone that if they want to be his disciples they have to "take up their cross and follow me. For those who want to save their life will lose it, and those who lose their life for my sake and the sake of the gospel will save it." He also says that "Truly, I tell you, there are some standing here today that will not taste death until they come to see the kingdom of God has come with power."

The writer of these lines had a clear expectation that something tremendous was going to happen right away. He expected that the new kingdom – God's kingdom – was at hand. He may have been writing before the Romans had crushed the Jewish revolt or just after, when there was still hope that the revolt was just the beginning of the end times, when a kingdom ruled by God would be firmly established.

The Pharisees and Sadducees

Josephus, a 1st century Jewish historian, described several different Jewish groups as though they were equivalent to Greek schools of philosophy. Josephus was trying to appeal to a non-Jewish audience to convince them that they should give Jewish people more rights than Jewish people had at the time. We can't take his descriptions as 100% accurate. The different Jewish groups weren't exactly like the Greek schools of philosophy. However, it is clear from the sources available that two of these groups, the Pharisees and Sadducees, had both attempting to influence society through their interpretations of the Jewish scriptures. At times the kings that ruled after the Maccabees' revolt would give support to one group or the other in exchange for political support.

In the Bible the Pharisees confront Jesus about how to interpret scriptures. In chapter seven of Mark, a group of Pharisees and some scribes complain that Jesus' disciples had eaten without washing their hands. The issue was not just general cleanliness and common sense, which says washing hands before eating can help us avoid getting sick. The Pharisees were likely arguing that all Jewish people everywhere should follow certain rules that had may have originally applied only to people eating special meals inside the temple. In the Bible passage Jesus rejects that interpretation.

Likely someone later went through and added their own commentary. Mark 7:3 says the Jewish people washed their hands before eating and in Mark 7:19 it says that Jesus declared all foods to be clean, meaning that Jesus' followers could eat even food forbidden by the Jewish texts. Those little details are likely late additions to the gospel of Mark, or, at the very least, don't reflect what other earlier Christian writers believed. After Jesus died but before the gospels were written there was a big argument within the early Christian community as to whether non-Jewish people joining the Christian community had to follow Jewish dietary laws. The texts that describe this big argument never reference to Jesus saying what Mark has him say. If Jesus had so clearly permitted his disciples to break all Jewish laws anytime then the early Christians would have known that and referenced to it. They don't! They come up with other reasons for people being able to eat food forbidden by Kosher laws, including one of Jesus' disciples having a vision from God. We'll talk about that later. The point now is that the gospel of Mark contains a small disagreement about one detail of how to interpret Jewish laws that later people took as a sign that Jesus meant for people to not follow any Jewish laws.

When many Christians read the passages that have Jesus arguing with the Pharisees, they think "oh, this is a sign that the Pharisees were evil." Yet the Biblical writers weren't concerned with the places where the Pharisees and Jesus agreed. They were concerned with pointing out the differences between Jesus and a group that were probably his closest competitors.

At another point in the gospel of Mark a group of Sadducees came up to Jesus to argue with him about resurrection. The Sadducees didn't believe in resurrection, so they tried to pose a tough question about resurrection to Jesus, to point out how silly they thought resurrection was. They asked him to imagine a woman who marries a man and has no children with him. He dies, and then she marries another man. Again, she has no children, but the man dies and she marries another man. This happens over and over until she has had seven husbands. Then she dies. If there is a resurrection, to whom will she be married ?

Jesus answers that their question shows they do not understand either the scriptures nor the power of God. He says in the resurrection no one will be married but everyone will be like angels, but then he adds that "as for the dead being raised, have you not read in the book of Moses, in the story about the bush, how God said to him, 'I am the God of Abraham, the God of Isaac, and the God of Jacob?' He is the God not of the dead, but of the living; you are quite wrong." What do you make of that? The logic being applied in that quote is that for God to be the god of Abraham, Isaac and Jacob and the God of the living, then those three patriarchs must be living. They could not be dead, even though their story was set many generations before.

Matthew's Sermon on the Mount

Probably one of the most famous parts of the Gospel of Matthew is a section commonly known as the Sermon on the Mount.

The Sermon on the Mount begins with the Beatitudes. The Beatitudes consist of a series of statements about groups of people who are, the text says, blessed. You can find them in Matthew 5:2 – 12. Open your Bible to this section and read them. What do these groups have in common?

After the Beatitudes, the sermon continues with a number of exhortations about how to live. In the midst of these instructions is an example prayer that is known today as the Lord's Prayer. (Matthew 6:9 – 15)

Like any section of the Bible, the Sermon on the Mount is open to vastly different interpretations. However, the sermon is focused on directing the listener / readers thoughts and behaviour, so the differing interpretations will seem more personal to most than differing interpretations over, for example, why there are three stories of Saul being crowned. Most people, even those to whom the Bible means a great deal, will not worry too much about the details of the history of different kings, but for those to whom the Bible is a religious text the meaning of the passages on how to live become very important. The effect the text has on people depends greatly on their context. Let's look at how some of the passages could sound from different contexts.

The Beatitudes praise the meek, the powerless, and those who attempt to make peace or do good despite everything. To a community that is oppressed or impoverished, these words could bring great comfort. They provide a contrast to the idea that wealth and power denote goodness. The Roman Emperor and his followers build their villas to signify their might and power, but the Beatitudes say it is not them who are blessed, but the weak and the hungry.

Yet the Beatitudes can be heard in a completely different way. They can be heard not as encouragement for a marginalized community to believe in themselves, but as a way of keeping people in oppression. The poor who hear these words and take them to heart may believe it is wrong for them to fight to improve their lives. A young woman who takes the words to heart may believe that she should peacefully accept others mistreating her. Those who hold the power to make things better for people might thing it unimportant to do so, because poverty and suffering are blessed. The same text can have different meaning for different people.

Matthew 5:17 – 48 urges people to be inwardly perfect. It says, for example, that it is not enough to just not murder, but that one is not to be angry. Matthew 5:33-36 talks about swearing oaths. An oath is a very serious statement that one pledges to be true. The passage says that it is not enough to simply be true to one's oath, but rather that one should not have to swear any oaths: one should be honest all the time, so that every word one speaks is like an oath. Matthew 5:38 – 52 says that it is not enough to just limit your revenge to equal to the damage done to you, but instead you should not resist evildoers at all! And give to anyone who asks of you. And love your enemies, not just your friends! Each part builds upon the last to say: be better but not just better; be perfect. It ends with "be perfect; therefore, as your heavenly Father is perfect." (Matthew 5: 48 NIV)

How does this sound to you? Are you one who always strives to do better? Do you like encouragement to always try to be better? Does perfection seem like a beautiful dream to strive towards?

Or does the pressure to try to be better scare you? Does perfection seem like an impossible task?

Again, these passages could help encourage people. They are very spiritually meaningful to many people.

The advice to not seek revenge could also be very practical in situations where seeking revenge – or even justice – could result in drawing punishment down on the community. For early Christians trying to live within Roman society, this might have been very important advice. Don't draw the Roman's attention. Don't fight back. Don't give them cause to be angry. The text was likely written after the Roman empire had destroyed the temple in Jerusalem and kicked all Jewish people out of the city as punishment for attempts to create a new Jewish nation. Both Jews and Christians in Egypt and Antioch may have also faced persecution at times and in those cases any attempt to respond to the persecution with anything but acceptance and grief might have fueled more persecution.

So again, these passages can be meaningful and useful. They can also be dangerous. If a person tries to be perfectly loving and never angry, they will likely fail. In some communities these passages are likely read with acceptance for that inevitable failure. A good attempt will be enough for some. But what if the community does not encourage such acceptance of failure? People could end up feeling very guilty about human emotions like anger or dislike.

Matthew 5:31 – 32 speaks about divorce. Like the other passages mentioned above it mentions a good, but not good enough, way of doing things, before criticizing it. In this case the good but not good enough way is to give a woman a certificate of divorce. In Biblical law it would be the man who gets to decide to divorce the woman. Giving her the certificate of divorce would allow her to remarry, which would be more compassionate than just throwing her out of the house without it or mistreating her inside. The text implies that way isn't good enough and that a man should just not get divorced. This – and other Bible passages against divorce – have been used to justify people staying in very unhappy and even abusive marriages. Yet it is possible to see that in its context, the passage was probably about protecting a woman's right to home, family, and care. It was probably about not casting her out helpless, and that just expecting some other man to help her was not good enough. A man had a duty towards his wife.

The escalating advice of Matthew 5:17 – 48 focuses largely on people's relationships to other people. The next section focuses on the believer's relationship to God. It mentions three ways in which people serve their God – through charity, prayer and fasting – and it urges that all of these be done in secret so that God "who sees in secret" will reward them. No one else is supposed to see. People are not to be rewarded by others for their show of piety.

> *"Do not lay up for yourselves treasures on earth, where moth and rust consume and where thieves break in and steal, ^{20} but lay up for yourselves treasures in heaven, where neither moth nor rust consumes and where thieves do not break in and steal. ^{21} For where your treasure is, there will your heart be also." (Matthew 6:19 – 21 NIV)*

How does this passage support the message of the Beatitudes? What does it say about wealth?

The sermon continues:

> *"No one can serve two masters; for either he will hate the one and love the other, or he will be devoted to the one and despise the other. You cannot serve God and wealth." (Matthew 6:24 NIV)*

This is followed by a section about not worrying.

> *"Look at the birds of the air: they neither sow nor reap nor gather into barns, and yet your heavenly Father feeds them. Are you not of more value than they? ^{27} And which of you by being anxious can add one cubit to his span of life? ^{28} And why are you anxious about clothing? Consider the lilies of the field, how they grow; they neither toil nor spin; ^{29} yet I tell you, even Solomon in all his glory was not arrayed like one of these. ^{30} But if God so clothes the grass of the field, which today is alive and tomorrow is thrown into the oven, will he not much more clothe you, O men of little faith? ^{31} Therefore do not be anxious, saying, 'What shall we eat?' or 'What shall we drink?' or 'What shall*

we wear?' ³² For the Gentiles seek all these things; and your heavenly Father knows that you need them all. ³³ But seek first his kingdom and his righteousness, and all these things shall be yours as well." Matthew 6:26 – 33 NIV)

There is truth that worrying does not help. However, this text would sound very different to one who has food, compared to one who was watching those they love starve. If you remember the story of Job, you might notice similarities between this and the story of Job. There is an expectation that bad things – like starving to death – will not happen to good people. How then, does one explain, when it does happen? For some the hope is in the image of a heavenly kingdom, and a belief that the bad things on earth do not matter, because at least there will be that heavenly kingdom.

Follow-up Activity

1. Read the Sermon on the Mount and choose one section of it to write a paragraph about. In your paragraph argue for how following the advice could be helpful or why it could be harmful.

Parables from Luke

The gospel of Luke is the first part in a two book set. We've already looked at how it portrays the births of John the Baptist and Jesus and in a few chapters we'll look at the second book connected with Luke, that of the Acts of the Apostles. Right now, we will look at a couple of parables found within the gospel of Luke but not within any other gospels. These parables have become so well known they are often referred to in literature, television and even laws.

The parable of the good Samaritan is found in Luke 10:25 - 37. Remember that Samaria was the capital of the northern kingdom, Israel, which fell to the Assyrians. Later, the southern kingdom fell to the Babylonians and then the Babylonians fell to the Persians. The Persians allowed the different areas of their empire to be ruled as provinces with their own traditional law. One province was established out of Samaria, another out of Jerusalem. Those who ruled in Jerusalem rejected the help of the northerners in rebuilding the temple, seeing them as not quite Jewish enough. The exact details of how the Samaritan identity was created is still debated, but what is known is that they formed a group of outsiders within Judaism, at times seen as Jewish and at times seen as not-quite-Jewish. They accepted the first five books of the scriptures as true, but rejected the other texts as non-canonical. They were not alone in doing so, as the canon had not quite been established yet. Geographically, they were centered to the south of Galilee, between Galilee and Jerusalem, though a large number of them lived in the Roman city of Caesarea and others were scattered throughout the Roman Empire.

The Samaritans feature fairly regularly in the Gospels. In Luke 9:51 - 56 we have an enigmatic little story about Jesus preparing to go to Jerusalem. He sends messengers ahead of him to a Samaritan village, but the Samaritans reject him because he's heading towards Jerusalem. Two of his disciples urge that he call down fire from heaven to consume the village, but Jesus rebukes them instead. The text illustrates the hostility the Samaritans had towards Jerusalem. They rejected the city as a religious authority. The story also draws a connection between Jesus and Elijah. Remember the story of Elijah being summoned by King Ahaziah of Israel (the northern kingdom ruled from Samaria), when the fire of heaven burns up the groups of fifty soldiers? Here Jesus has the opportunity to do the same, but rejects the idea. Jesus is like Elijah, but different.

Not many verses after Jesus rejects summoning fire from heaven, Jesus is talking to a lawyer and tells the lawyer a story. In the story a man was on the road from Jericho to Jerusalem. Along the way he is beaten, robbed and left for dead. A priest traveled down the road, saw the man and went past. A Levite - another type of religious leader - came along the road, saw the man and likewise moved to the side to pass without interacting with the man.

Now first century Jewish listeners would have likely been familiar with a number of texts referring to the whole people of Israel by reference to "the priests, the Levites and the Israelites." They might have been familiar enough with that phrase that when they heard the story of a priest passing by, and then a Levite, they would have expected the next person to pass by to be an Israelite. But that is not how the story goes.

According to the story, the next person was a Samaritan. The Samaritan saw the injured man and rushed to help him. The Samaritan loads the man onto his animal and takes him to an inn, where he pays for the man to be cared for.

What does the story mean? Some interpreters have argued that the priest and the Levite failed to help the man because they assumed he was dead, and their purity codes would prohibit them from touching a dead body before going to serve at the temple. Some Christian interpreters have taken that story as evidence that Judaism was more focused with laws and ritual purity than compassion, and have used the story to justify antisemitism. It is unlikely that was the original message and is not one that should be taken from it. By substituting "the Samaritan" into the expected triad of "the priests, the Levites and the Israelites" the text is broadening the accepted community, not rejecting part of it.

Luke places the story of the good Samaritan within a conversation between Jesus and a lawyer. The lawyer tests Jesus by asking him what he must do to inherit eternal life. Jesus responds by asking the lawyer what the law says he must do. The lawyer responds saying the law says he must love God with all his heart, his soul, his strength and mind, and that he must love his neighbour as himself. Jesus says that is the right answer. Then the lawyer asks who his neighbour is, and Jesus responds with the story of the Good Samaritan. After telling the story of the man, Jesus asks, who was the man's neighbour? The lawyer answers it was the one who showed mercy. It was the good Samaritan.

> Even some scholars who believe that Jesus himself told a story of the good Samaritan believe that the conversation with the lawyer might not have been part of the original tradition associated with the story. The author of the book of Luke could have taken a parable that others had told him and then written the story of the lawyer's conversation with Jesus himself. There are many possibilities. For this story, and any other story of what Jesus said, it may be that:
>
> 1) Jesus said something and it was directly quoted.
>
> 2) Jesus said something, it was recorded and passed down, and then fit into a new framework by the author of the a gospel.
>
> 3) The gospel authors received text they believed was from Jesus, that wasn't, and they fit it into their books.
>
> 4) The gospel authors wrote their own stories about what they think Jesus might have said.
>
> A group of scholars known as the Jesus Seminar have attempted to discern the statements spoken by the historical from the statements attributed to him by later writers. You may wish to look up the criteria by which they attempted to judge the different statements. Their work is controversial and some Christians argue that which words were spoken by the historical Jesus is irrelevant compared to the messages given by the gospel writers and church fathers.

Probably the second most famous parable from Luke is the parable of the prodigal son, found in Luke 15:11 - 32. The word prodigal originally meant extravagant or recklessly wasteful, but because of the parable it has come to mean a wayward person who returns home.

In the story a man has two sons. The younger son asks for his portion of his father's wealth - his inheritance - and then goes and squanders it. Later, in desperation, he takes a job as a swineherd, eating the same food as the pigs. Then he thinks about how his father's servants are better off than him, and he decides to return to his father and ask to be accepted as a servant. When he returns home his father greets him joyfully, embraces him and sends that a calf be slaughtered for a feast to celebrate the return of the prodigal son.

The older son is annoyed, for he has worked unendingly for the father with no reward The father assures him that everything the father owns will someday go to the older son, "But we had to celebrate and be glad, because this brother of yours was dead and is alive again; he was lost and is found." (NIV Luke 15:32)

At times the two sons have been imagined to be the Jewish people and the Gentiles. In this interpretation the Gentiles are the extravagant ones welcomed back into the fold, while the Jewish people are the grumpy older brother annoyed at his father's acceptance of the younger son. The New Testament does record tension between the Jewish-Christians and the Gentile-Christians. But it is worth noting that in the parable of the prodigal son the father does not supplant the older son with the younger son. The father maintains that everything he owns will go to the older son, even while they welcome the younger son back into the family. At times in the New Testament and in Christian writings since, people have portrayed the Gentile world as inheriting the role as followers of God after the Jewish population rejects Jesus. This dangerous belief has contributed to the persecution of Jewish people.

Others have interpreted the story of the prodigal son as a story of God's forgiveness for individuals who stray from worshiping him. According to this view the story acts as assurance that everyone is welcome back into the faith community.

The story of the prodigal son and the idea of welcoming people back into the faith community may have been particularly relevant at times when the early Christians faced persecution from the Romans. Roman governor Pliny the Younger wrote to Emperor Trajan around 112 CE for advice on what to do with those accused of being Christian. One of his questions was whether to pardon those who deny being a Christian and offer proof through worshiping the Roman gods, offering sacrifice to the Emperor, and cursing Christ. Emperor Trajan responded that Christians were not to be sought out for persecution and yes, if they are accused but prove themselves the should be released. Assuming similar procedures took place at any or most of the places where Christians were, at times, being persecuted it would means people were being spared by denying their faith. Then the Christian communities would have had to decide whether to accept those deniers back into the fold or reject them in honour of the sacrifice made by those who stood true to their faith.

> While once historians believed that the Romans regularly persecuted Christians, recent scholarship suggests in the early centuries it was occasional and localized, taking place in specific communities rather than being consistently practiced across the Empire. Still, at specific times in specific communities it would have been devastating.

Follow-up Activities

1. Look up Good Samaritan laws. Do any apply to your community?

2. Look up the Jesus Seminar led by Robert Funk. What criteria did they use to try to evaluate the historicity of the statements of Jesus?

> The term "Good Samaritan" has become a term for anyone who does good that is not required of him. Some governments pass Good Samaritan Laws which are meant to protect those who try to help others from being sued, if, in the process of trying to help they make a mistake and harm the person they are trying to help.

Crucifixion

The different gospel writers included different stories about Jesus, but all four gospel writers told that Jesus went to Jerusalem, and that when he entered Jerusalem he did so in a special procession. Instead of walking into the city, he rode into it on a colt or a donkey. The crowds gathered around to watch. People spread out their cloaks and waved leafy branches.

At the time only kings or conquerors normally rode into cities with crowds waving at them, but they rode big splendid horses not lowly donkeys. So what did it mean that Jesus entered the city on a donkey? Was it simply to fulfill a prophecy? Was it a way of saying that he is a king? Maybe it was a way of saying Jesus was a king or maybe it was a way of saying that his ideas were more important than those of the Empire. Or perhaps it was like street theatre, a way of protesting the ideas of kingship.

Claiming to be a king was dangerous. Herod the Great had been declared King of Judea in 37BCE with the consent of the Romans, but his sons were granted the titles *tetrarch* or *ethnarch* instead. (The former is a type of governor and the latter refers to a governor of a particular ethnic group – in this case the Jewish people.) Claiming to be king would not only anger people like Herod Antipas, the *tetrarch* of Galilee, but would also be an affront to the Romans.

The most important building in Jerusalem was the temple. According to the gospel of Matthew Jesus had been to it as a child, but naturally he had to return to it again as an adult.

Inside the temple people offered animals for sacrifice. Some might have brought their own animals but others would have bought an animal there. The Roman coins had pictures of the Roman Emperor on them and were not considered acceptable for use in the temple, so money-changers traded the Roman currency for special temple currency.

When Jesus entered the temple he became angry, and he overturned the tables of the money changers. He yelled, "Is it not written, 'My house shall be called a house of prayer for all the nations? But you have made it a den of robbers!" (Mark 11:15 - 19, Luke 19:45-47, Matthew 21:12-14, John 2:13-22)

> The prophet Jeremiah had complained that the leaders of Jerusalem had made the temple into a den of thieves. You can review the context of his complaint in Jeremiah 7. Jesus' use of the same phrase might have been meant to remind people of Jeremiah's complaint.

Imagine how the authorities in Jerusalem would have felt hearing the news of what Jesus did in the temple. Some might have been angry at the chaos he caused. Some might have been scared that he would stir the crowds into violent protest. Some might have been angry because he cost them money by overturning the tables. Some might have worried that the Romans would hear about the chaos in the temple, and that the Romans would intervene. Roman intervention could be dangerous to everyone.

The gospels describe Jesus being arrested and then crucified. Crucifixion is a punishment the Romans used on rebels. They crucified large numbers of people and tended to throw the bodies of the victims into pits to decay quickly. It was a painful way of killing people. There was also lots of public shame.

Normally in history when a group of people believe someone is the king who will bring about a wonderful new kingdom freeing them from an oppressive post, the person's death will put an end to that dream. From the Roman point of view, that should have happened as soon as they crucified Jesus. His followers should have fled back to their home for fear of also being crucified, with a good dose of shame for having followed him in the first place. Jesus' body would have likely been thrown into a pit of quicklime to decay.

Now read Mark 16:1 – 16:8a The "a" after 16:8 means the first half of verse 8, and not the entirety. 16:8a is believed to be where the original gospel of Mark ended. The last words would be "Trembling and bewildered, the women went out and fled from the tomb. They said nothing to anyone, because they were afraid." (Mark 16:8 NIV) Someone felt that was not a very satisfactory ending and added the rest of that verses.

The original ending suggests that the followers of Jesus were scared and did go home afraid, but it isn't totally without hope either. It promises people that they will see Jesus in Galilee. Since most of the gospel takes place in Galilee, this might be a message to the reader to go back to the beginning. It might also be a message to the early Christians arguing that they should leave Jerusalem and the Jerusalem community and go to Galilee. (You'll read about the early Jerusalem community soon.) Or it might be a message to leave the city for other reasons too.

> As Christianity expanded becoming a religion of the Romans and not as much a branch of Christianity, it became expedient to place the blame for Jesus' death on the Jewish leadership. This has had unfortunate effects throughout history, as Jewish people have been blamed for being "Christ-killers." This has had horrible consequences. It is important to recognize that crucifixion was a Roman method of punishment against traitors, and not how the Jewish community dealt with those who had different beliefs.

Now we have to think about the time in which the gospel of Mark was being written. It was likely being written between 66 – 70 AD, during a revolt against Rome. Mark 13:1 – 8 has Jesus predicting war and destruction in Jerusalem. The other later gospels specify that Jesus was talking about the temple itself (See Matthew 24:1 – 2) but in Mark it is unclear exactly which buildings are being spoken of, suggesting that Mark was written when the war had begun but before the temple itself was destroyed. During the war many people fled from Jerusalem to the countryside, and the suggestion to leave the city might have been related to that. That seems like a very mundane message for a religious text like the Bible, but there's another reason to suspect that the gospel writer of Mark wasn't in favour of the rebellion against Rome.

Mark 15:6 - 12 tells that during the festival of the Passover the Roman in charge of Jerusalem, Pontius Pilate, would release a Jewish prisoner. It says that he offered to release either Jesus or a rebel named Barabbas and that the crowd chose to have Barabbas released.

There is no historical record of any tradition of releasing a prisoner over the festival period. The custom of releasing a prison is invented in the gospel of Mark to serve a literary purpose. It presents two options for the people: rebellion (represented by Barabbas) or salvation through Jesus. The gospel writer believed the Jewish people of his time had chosen the wrong one. In modern times some argue that the division is between a physical kingdom or a heavenly kingdom, but Mark probably didn't make that distinction. The issue was likely more a question of whether one attempts to bring about the kingdom by fighting violently with Rome or through following Jesus.

According to Mark, salvation comes from the Son of God. His death wasn't the end of the story, and everyone was to wait for him and his return.

Someone didn't like the gospel of Mark ending with people being afraid. Someone added that Jesus sent people out to proclaim salvation. However, that little line wasn't considered a satisfying enough ending. Another longer end was added. Read Mark 16:9 – 19. In this longer ending Jesus appears before the disciples.

Follow-up Activity

1. Read Mark 14 and 15 and make a list of the events it describes. Note the ways in which the gospel attempts to put the blame on the Jewish population. What are the signs the Romans were actually in control?

Implications of a Crucified Messiah

Early dreamers of a Messiah were hoping for a human king. They wanted someone who would re-establish their kingdom as an independent nation. Over time this image changed to a belief that there would be a divine Messiah, a human-like god that would bring about that independent kingdom or perhaps even a whole new world.

Christianity formed around the image of a crucified man, though the crucifixion of a leader is a sign that the rebellion has failed and no new empire will be established. What happened that Christianity didn't just die out? How did his followers justify believing that he was a Messiah if he didn't overthrow the Romans and become king of Israel? Obviously, he must have been a different type of Messiah.

One possibility some Christians embrace, both historically and today, is that Jesus' kingdom is something that will come, at some point in the future. The prophecies, they argue, are not wrong. They just haven't taken place yet. They envision this as coming some time in the future still, and they try to follow Jesus' teachings in order to secure them a good place in God's kingdom when it does come through divine means.

Some people envision God's kingdom as being what the world would look like if everyone lived out those teachings. They are inspired to follow Jesus' teachings about loving their enemies because they believe that this helps bring God's kingdom here on Earth.

Different Biblical writers gave hints as to what they think will happen before God's kingdom comes. Some writers predicted great violence and suffering. Would wars or plagues feel different if one believed that the suffering was just a precursor for a great miracle? It might make a person accept wars and suffering as okay or inevitable. This belief could cause more suffering if those who had the ability to try to stop wars, plagues or other problems instead accepted the destruction as the first steps to Jesus' kingdom coming.

Not all Christians expect God's kingdom to take place here on Earth. Perhaps the prophecies were not predicting an Earthly kingdom, but a heavenly one, which humans will enter through the afterlife. Within this view, Jesus' mission can be seen as accomplished. He came, taught people, was killed, and by doing all that made it possible for people to enter the heavenly afterlife. The idea of a general resurrection where everyone comes back from the dead was shifted so Jesus was the only one to be resurrected on Earth and others would be resurrected in heaven.

Christians don't just disagree on what or where Jesus' kingdom was. They also disagree on what Jesus was doing. Was he here predominantly to teach people how to be good people? Or to teach people about God? Was his death a necessary part of his story? If he hadn't died on the cross, would his mission have failed? If he had to die on the cross, why did he have to? Was it to show people they didn't need to fear death by assuring them that death isn't the end of life? Was it to be a sacrifice, and if so, why?

Some people believe that Jesus' death was required and inevitable. Sometimes they portray it as a necessary sacrifice, the animals that were offered as a sacrifice in the temple yet greater than all the animals so that no more sacrifices are necessary. This idea was probably helped by the destruction of the temple, which put an end to the sacrificial rituals. His death is portrayed as the magic act that wipes sin away.

Other people reject the idea that Jesus' death was necessary, arguing that a loving god would not require such thing. To some Christians, Jesus death was the consequences of the unjust world, and his life and teachings are seen as more significant than his death.

Different Christians came up with different answers for who Jesus is and what his kingdom was. Certain answers gained more popularity than others. Certain answers were accepted by the earlier churches – the

Catholic and Orthodox churches – and then rejected during the Protestant Reformation. One of the major differences between Catholicism and Protestantism is where they look for the answers. Catholicism embraces a long tradition of different theologians and suggests looking at the collected church doctrines for answers. Protestantism embraced the idea that Christians had, over the years, gotten the answers wrong and that they should look at the Biblical texts themselves to find the right answers.

Of course, if the church got it wrong over the years then one must ask, could the Biblical writers have gotten things wrong? For some Christians – both Catholic, Orthodox and Protestant – that question makes no sense. They believe the Bible was written by God and that it could not have anything wrong. However, other Christians accept that the Bible wasn't written by God. Some say it was inspired by God instead. In that case there is the possibility that some Biblical writers got things right, and others made mistakes. Maybe some writers got some things right and other things wrong.

Some scholars try to search for the earliest traces of Jesus and Christianity, hoping to find out what it was like before Christians made mistakes about who Jesus was. This is sometimes called searching for "the historical Jesus."

Others argue that it doesn't matter who Jesus was historically, because what matters is the Jesus of faith. They argue that rather than burying the real Jesus under doctrine, the doctrine is the important thing. They say the early Christian writers were inspired, and it's their faith-filled stories people should listen to.

Follow-up Activities

1. The Gospel of John was likely the last of the four canonical gospels. Read chapter 1:1 - 14 and chapter 3:1 - 8. What images of Jesus do these passages promote? Does it portray a collective salvation where the Messiah saves the whole kingdom or the whole world, or does it portray an individual salvation where some can be saved and others not?

2. Read John 11. The name Lazarus is one you should learn to recognize, as it appears in many literary contexts. Then look up the Life of Apollonius of Tyana, specifically section 4.45, which tells of Apollonius performing a miracle similar to that attributed to Jesus. Does it change your perception of the stories of Jesus to know that there were other similar stories told of Greek philosophers?

Jerusalem Community

The book of Acts begins with a dedication, the same as the gospel of Luke does, leading people to assume that the two were written by the same author. While the gospel of Luke tells of the life of Jesus, the book of Acts tells of the "Acts of the Apostles" after Jesus died. We'll call the author of the two works Luke.

Read Acts 1:1 – 12 to find out how the book describes Jesus leaving. There are three important points made in that passage. Can you guess what they might be? Read the text and write down your answers before reading further.

Did you guess? They are:

- The promise of baptism of the Holy Spirit

- The unpredictability of when the kingdom of Israel would be restored

- The call to witness to Jerusalem, to Judea and Samaria, and to all the ends of the Earth

Why are these details important? The earliest Christians probably believed that Jesus' return was imminent. Paul, whom you'll read about shortly, believed that it would happen within his lifetime. However, by the time the books of Luke and Acts were written, people were starting to wonder if that was true. Likely people saw the revolt against Rome as a sign that God was re-establishing his kingdom. They could have seen that as one of the events Jesus was bringing about. Then when Rome reconquered Jerusalem and destroyed the temple, people were devastated. The author of Luke argues that the end times will still come, but the timing is unpredictable. He believed it could be a long time before Jesus' return.

The book of Acts also attempts to explain how and why the gospel was spread outside of the Jewish community. Picture three circles, one inside the other. The smallest circle is Jerusalem. The apostles believed they were called to witness – that is, to testify to the truth of their beliefs – to the people of Jerusalem. The next circle is Judea and Samaria, the lands the Hebrews once had as their kingdoms of Judah and Israel. This circle probably represents all the Jewish people, and not just those in the land. The larger circle stretches all the ways to the ends of the Earth. This includes non-Jews, called Gentiles. Watch how the book of Acts argues that Gentiles need to be included.

The baptism of the Holy Spirit becomes proof of God's presence in the time of waiting as well as proof that God wants Gentiles to join the Christian community.

Keeping with the concentric circles, the spirit of God descends first within Jerusalem. The author moves back and forth between stories of how the Jerusalem community lived and grew with stories of their persecution. Miracles permeate both story lines. The apostles heal people. They are arrested but released from prison by an angel of the Lord.

Read Acts 5:17 – 42, about the apostles being before the council, but pay special attention to Gamaliel's speech. What would Gamaliel's speech imply about the failed revolts against Rome? How might it offer hope to those who were disappointed in that revolution?

> The apostles in Jerusalem invite people to sell their possessions and give the money to the community, which then held everything in common. Read Acts 4:32 – 5:11 for a description of the community living in common and one couple's breaking failure. What does Peter accuse the couple of?

The persecution grows. One of the apostles – a man named Stephen – is accused of saying that Jesus will destroy Jerusalem and change the customs given to the Jewish people. Stephen responds with a long speech, given in full. Read it in Acts 7:1 – 53. The speech recounts the stories of Abraham, Joseph, and Moses. It tells that the Hebrew people were hesitant to follow Moses and turned to false gods. It recounts the building of the temple but says that God does not live in buildings made of human hands.

Think though of the context of this story. It is set before the war with Rome but written after. The Jewish people have been kicked out of their homeland, yet again and their temple is destroyed. Within this context the author of Luke is trying to suggest that all is not lost. God has led them back to their homeland before. People have followed false gods. They have hesitated in following true leaders. Yet still, God has led them back. The temple is destroyed, but God does not live there.

Yet the passage ends with accusations that his listeners are "stiff-necked people" that killed the prophets. The accusation is an awful one that has helped lead to horrible persecution of Jewish people through time.

Throughout the New Testament, different writers struggle with the question of why all Jewish people did not follow Jesus. To the writers Jesus was the fulfillment of the promises made to the Jewish people. The logical response that many Jewish people would have made would be "well, he can't be the Son of Man, the Messiah we've been waiting for, because he hasn't actually brought about God's kingdom, has he?" The New Testament writers would either respond "it's coming, it's coming… be patient" or "his kingdom is a different type of kingdom…. see, we're enacting his kingdom by caring for the poor."

Now we see Christianity and Judaism as totally separate religions, but that division was a slow process. Modern Judaism and Christianity are like siblings, born from a common faith community. Both reinterpreted the early texts in their own ways, but both claimed to be the true interpretation. The early Christian writers tried to argue that they were the rightful inheritors of the early faith. Sometimes the argument is nasty and judgmental towards the Jewish people, but even in the places where it is worded the gentlest, it implies a nasty idea that somehow Judaism is wrong and Christianity right.

After Stephen's speech, he is stoned to death and the persecution against the church in Jerusalem increases. Many believers scatter into Judea and Samaria. With the believers scattering, the story moves to the second of the concentric circles – the larger Jewish community.

One of the men to have been involved in stoning Stephen was a man named Saul. Acts tells us that he was sent by the high priest with letters to deliver to the synagogue in Damascus, to aid in the persecution of Jesus' followers. Along the way a light flashed, he fell to the ground. Though he opened his eyes, he could not see. He could only hear a strange voice. The voice was Jesus, asking why Saul was persecuting him. Before Saul could try to explain, Jesus told Saul to get up and go into the city. The men who were traveling with Saul could not see anything strange, but they helped him into Damascus.

In Damascus, a follower of Jesus had a vision telling him to seek out the man named Saul and heal him. The man protested at first. Saul had done much evil! In the end though, he was persuaded to go. He healed Saul and baptized him. Saul changed his name to Paul.

Paul joined the community of believers in Damascus and preached there about Jesus. After a bit he heard rumour that someone from the Jewish community was going to murder him, so his friends lowered him over the city wall in a basket so he could escape. From Damascus he went to Jerusalem.

Mission to the Gentiles

A certain Roman centurion, Cornelius, had received a message from God that he should send people to fetch the man named Peter. Cornelius was what the people of his time would have called a god-fearer. He worshiped the Jewish god, yet he was not Jewish. He would have been like a bridge between the Jewish community and the Roman community. He likely supported the Jewish community financially and with whatever political power he had, but because he had not converted he could still participate fully in Roman society.

Meanwhile, Peter had a dream that helped prepare him for the summons from Cornelius. He saw heaven open and something like a large cloth being lowered to the ground by its four corners. Inside the cloth were four footed animals, reptiles and birds. A voice told Peter to get up and eat.

Peter said no, he had never eaten any food that was considered unclean. This doesn't mean food that was physically dirty, but food that the religious texts said was taboo.

A voice answered that "what God had made clean must not be called unclean."

After some repetition, the dream ended. Peter awoke and was confronted by Cornelius' messengers. The Holy Spirit told him to go with them, and he did.

When Peter arrived at Cornelius' house the house was crowded with people. Cornelius had brought his relatives and friends to meet Peter. Peter told them all about Jesus and while he was speaking the Holy Spirit fell upon everyone. Peter was surprised but said that if God had baptized them with the Holy Spirit how could he possibly refuse to baptize them with water.

Afterwards Peter went back to Jerusalem and told the leaders that had gathered there about his vision and about the Holy Spirit descending on Gentiles.

Saul, whom you met in the last chapter, changed his name to Paul. He journeyed with another disciple, Barnabas, to Antioch, in what is now Turkey. They preached first in a synagogue amongst the Jewish community. Then they preached the next sabbath to "the whole city" and many Gentiles believed them. (Note the concentric circles here: first to the Jewish community, then to the whole city including the Gentiles). Acts 13:49 says that the Jews of high standing got upset and had Paul and Barnabas chased out of the city. Can you imagine possible reasons why they might have done that?

Here are a few possible reasons why early Christians might have faced hostility from the Jewish community:

- They seemed to be preaching a false Judaism.

- The Jewish leaders might have feared that they were taking some of the God-fearers away from the Jewish community. If these men supported the Christian community instead, it might leave the Jewish community more vulnerable to persecution.

- They might have feared that the Christians were going to stir up trouble that would attract either local or Roman persecution of Jewish people.

Paul and Barnabas travel on. In one place they are believed to be Zeus and Hermes, and people attempt to worship them. Eventually they return to Jerusalem.

In Jerusalem a large debate is held. The question is whether Gentiles must become Jewish before they can become Christian. Peter speaks out against it. Paul and Barnabas testify about their experience preaching to Gentiles. Eventually it is agreed to that the Gentiles wishing to become Christian must only follow a few simple rules including abstaining from eating food that had been offered to idols, eating blood or what has been strangled.

A second debate takes place in Antioch over the question of food. When the new communities of believers eat together, should everyone obey the Jewish rules about food – Kosher laws, as they are called – or should they not? Paul alone argues that they should not follow the Kosher laws.

After the disagreement in Antioch, Paul traveled separately from Barnabas, pursing his mission in his own way. He worked as an awning-maker, staying with other awning makers during his time in Corinth. The book of Acts says he goes to the synagogues in the cities he visits, but his own letters emphasize his mission being to the Gentiles, so it is likely that he was working on converting the gentiles who were involved with the synagogues – the god-fearers, like Cornelius to whom Peter was said to have preached.

As he traveled Paul collected money to take back to Jerusalem to give to the Jerusalem community. This might have been partly a way of showing respect and deference to the Jerusalem community, but it might have also been because Paul believed that doing so would help bring about the end times.

Paul believed that the end times were coming within his lifetime. He saw Jesus as the first to be resurrected, but he believed others would follow soon and there would be a great transition in the world. The end times would arrive.

It is possible that Paul believed a tribute from nations "to the ends of the earth" sent back to Jerusalem was required as part of bringing about the end-times, based on some of the prophecies that predicted that Judah would head an empire. Paul traveled around the Mediterranean and spoke about wanting to go all the way to Spain, which at the time was understood to be "the ends of the earth." Perhaps he thought that if he sent tribute back to Jerusalem from churches in all those locations, the prophecy would be fulfilled and the end-times would begin.

> We have two main sources of information about Paul. One is the collection of letters he wrote. Another is the book of Acts, written by the same author as the Gospel of Luke. This book was probably written quite a while after Paul's death. In some places it contradicts things said in Paul's letters. The book of Acts was written after Paul's death by someone who believed that the end-times would be a long time in coming.

Letters from Paul

We have several sources of information about Paul. Paul wrote a number of letters. Most of these were written to churches he had visited or established. One is written to an individual. However, not all the books attributed to Paul were written by Paul. Remember how later law-makers would attribute their laws to Moses? So too did later writers attribute their letters to Paul. The later letters, written by other people, are sometimes called pseudo-Pauline letters. Often their theology is different than those written by Paul.

Like everything in the Bible, Paul's letters sound different depending on how you approach them. Some people view them as being filled with timeless wisdom, important for all believers. Others see them as written for specific people in specific times. In this chapter we'll go through 1 Corinthians. You should open your Bible to Corinthians and read the parts mentioned.

Pauline letters start with introducing who is writing and then who the letter is addressed too. Then there is a blessing. Turn to Corinthians 1: 1 – 9 and identify the role of each verse.

Paul had traveled to Corinth and established the church there. The church was a community of people who met regularly, probably in someone's home. The members of the community would not always have agreed with one another, and Paul wrote to try to sort out problems among them. Read Corinthians 1:10 – 16. What is the first problem that Paul is writing about?

Paul is concerned about the divisions within the church. He mentions Apollos, a fellow Christian. Do you recognize the name of the Greek god this man is named after? The church in Corinth had probably spoken of inviting Apollos to come and guide them, and Paul dislikes this idea. For three and a half chapters of the book he writes to assure them they do not need Apollos' guidance.

Apollos was likely quite skilled in the art of rhetoric, which is the art of persuasive speaking. This might have been why the Corinthians had wanted him to come to them. There may have even been complaints relayed to Paul that he (Paul) didn't speak with as much skill and beauty. Paul responds with a criticism of "eloquent wisdom." Read Corinthians 1:17 - 4 and try to summarize one of his arguments in your own words.

> Shakespeare has one of his characters, Bottom, misquote Corinthians 2:9 in Mid Summer's Night Dream Act 4, Scene 1, lines 205 – 214.

In Corinthians 4:6 we have a curious example of what might have been an addition to the text. The original likely said: "I have applied all this to Apollos and myself for your benefit, brothers and sisters, so that you may learn through us, so that none of you will be puffed up in favour of one against another." Then someone scribbled in the margin "nothing" and the next person copying it tried to note that the word was included there but not part of what was written and in doing so the phrase "nothing beyond what is written" was added to the text. This didn't make sense to a later writer, who then added "the meaning of the saying" to the text. The end result is the text saying "I have applied all this to Apollos and myself for your benefit, brothers and sisters, so that you may learn through us the meaning of the saying 'nothing beyond what is written' so that none of you will be puffed up in favour of one against another." All this is hypothetical, of course. The text may have originally been written as it is within the text. However, the passage itself makes more sense without the additions.

After Paul's argument against those who claim themselves to be followers of Apollos, he deals with other issues that have arisen in the church in Corinth. Some of his advice is about keeping a respectable reputation in the city. Believers are not to be drunkards or robbers. If they have trouble with one another, they are to deal with it within the church rather than involve the authorities.

Paul believed that the end times were coming soon, so he had advised against marriage and praised those who devote themselves to their church work. However, his praise for the unmarried state led to believers abandoning their spouses. That was causing problems within their community, so Paul advised against that, saying people were not supposed to divorce except in the case where an unbeliever leaves a believing spouse, in which case they were to accept that.

> What could be good things about keeping the church problems inside the church rather than going through the authorities? What could be bad things that happen when churches do this?

Another issue was food. In the ancient world much of the meat available for purchase would have been from animals butchered in offerings to the various gods. That meat was forbidden to Jewish people, but what about the Gentile believers? Should they have to reject such food? Paul's first argument is that their belief in one god makes it safe for them to eat food offered to useless idols, but that they should not eat the food if it would cause problems for other believers. Read 1 Corinthians 8:7 – 13 and identify how Paul says the eating of the food might be dangerous to some. Paul continues his argument against eating the food by saying that he has the right as an apostle to ask the community to financially support him, but he chooses not to for their benefit. So too, they are supposed to choose not to do things they can, for the sake of others within their group.

> The Lord's Supper is the basis for one of the most common rituals in the Christian church, the sharing of bread and wine or juice. In most churches participants do not eat a full meal, but simply a small piece. The terms Mass, Eucharist, and Holy Communion all refer to this ritual.
>
> Some people believe that during the ritual the bread itself becomes the body of Christ and the wine his blood. This belief is called Transubstantiation. It was a point of contention during the Protestant Revolution, with the Catholics defending the belief and the Protestants rejecting it.

The church in Corinth had both poor and wealthy members. Paul had introduced a shared supper, where they would bring their food to eat together, but in his absence the unity of their meal began to fall apart. The wealthy would arrive early and share their expensive food amongst themselves with the poor arriving later and eating poorly. Paul urged against that. Read 1 Corinthians 11:17 – 33 and take note of how Paul describes the shared meal.

Another point of contention within Corinthians was some people claiming the power to speak in tongues – that is, in the language of angels. Others were claiming the ability to interpret the tongues, and some to prophesize. Given what Paul wrote to them, we can presume that this was causing some dispute within the church. Paul shares a metaphor with them. He says the community members are all parts of one body, and no part is more important or less important than the other. Everyone's gifts are valuable to the community, but they are to strive to use them for love. He says when people talk in tongues – that is, in the language of angels – they are talking to God alone, but when they are prophesying they are communicating to other people, and that this is more useful than talking in tongues. Read 1 Corinthians 14:26 – 33a. If Paul felt these instructions were necessary, what do you think was happening at the worship services?

> Within Paul's discussion of prophecy and speaking in tongues, he speaks about love being the most important thing. Read 1 Corinthians 13. Many people have this passage, or a portion of it, read at their wedding.

The last point of contention is the question of whether there was going to be a general resurrection and if so, what would it be like. Paul was firm in his belief that there would be one. In Paul's mind Jesus was the first person to be resurrected, but everyone else was going to be resurrected too. Without that general resurrection, he said, Jesus' resurrection would be meaningless. When people asked what kind of body people would have in the resurrection, he said it would be one different from our current ones, as the plant is different than the seed. You can read this discussion in 1 Corinthians 15.

Finally, Paul deals with practical matters. He tells people to set aside money to be given to Jerusalem and he deals with his travel plans. Then he passes on to those in Corinth the greetings from believers elsewhere. Read 1 Corinthians 16:21 – 24. What does 16:21 imply about the writing of the letter?

If you were skimming over the parts of Corinthians not mentioned in this chapter, you may have noticed that we've skipped some very interesting passages. We'll discuss those passages in the next chapter.

Paul and the Problems He Helped Cause

Some parts of Paul's letters deal with theological questions such as the nature of Jesus and the issue of the resurrection. Other parts of his letters deal with how his followers should act. This advice has been followed (more or less) by Christians for a long time and because of that it has influenced how our world is today. Certain passages in his letters have been used to support the idea that women should obey men all the time. Other passages have been used to encourage obedience to unjust governments. His writing has also been used to encourage people to judge homosexuality. In this chapter we will explore a few of these issues.

Many modern Christians dislike the social ideas attributed to Paul. Some ignore those sections of the Bible, focusing on the parts they prefer. Some ask whether Paul might have meant something very different than people commonly attribute to him. Some point to the women Paul lists in his letters as signs that he respected female leadership.

Now some people may read this and think that any effort to soften Paul and make him less objectionable is just rewriting history. It may be that Paul really did promote women being inferior to men, homosexuality being wrong and that people should obey all authority. The point of this chapter is not to convince you that Paul was a nice guy. He might have been, but he might not have been. The point of this chapter is to help you see some of the breadth of interpretation available. The same passages mean very different things to different people.

Paul & the Question of Women

Paul's first letter to Corinth has a few passages, not dealt with in the preceding chapter, regarding the issue of how women should behave. One of those passages says that women should not speak in church. This has been taken within the Catholic church to mean that women should not be priests. Another passage seems to say that women should cover their heads. Some Christian communities still follow that, insisting that married women keep their hair covered. Other parts imply that women are lesser than men and should obey their man.

Read Corinthians 2:2 – 16 and then consider the following options.

Interpretation one: Paul was urges women to cover their heads and obey their husbands.

Interpretation two: There is a possibility that married women in the community kept their hair covered, single women let their hair show. If this was the case, perhaps the passage is dealing with the issue again of women abandoning their spouses. Women are uncovering their heads, proclaiming their independence from their spouses, and Paul is saying not to do so.

Interpretation three: Others in the community of Corinth have been saying that women must have their heads covered, and Paul is saying that women already have their heads covered with hair, and don't need additional coverings. For this interpretation to work we have to consider the possibility that some of the lines in the text are Paul quoting the Corinthians back to themselves.

If the line "Every man who prays or prophesies with his head covered dishonors his head. But every woman who prays or prophesies with her head uncovered dishonors his head—" is something the Corinthians have been saying to Paul, then Paul's response "It is the same as having her head shaved" would mean that the only time the woman has her head really uncovered is when she's shaved, and yes, that's a shame. It would imply that not having cloth on a woman's head was fine, because she still had her head covered with hair.

The lines about man being the image of God and women coming from man could also be something that Paul is quoting back to the Corinthians, with his rebuttal of it being that men and women are interdependent and that men are born from women.

Consider the three interpretations. Which seems most likely to you? What type of information would help to confirm whether any of these interpretations were true?

Whether Paul wanted women to have their heads covered or not, the passage in Corinthians 2:2 – 16 seems to have accept that women are praying and prophesying during worship. In other places he commends the good work of women in the church. Yet in 1 Corinthians 14:33b – 36, the text tells us that women should stay silent in church and let their husbands do their talking for them. How can we explain this?

Read 1 Corinthians 14:33b – 36, as well as a few paragraphs above and below it.

One explanation could be that this paragraph was a late addition added by someone other than Paul. However, there has to be a reason to dismiss it other than just not liking the content. As noted above, it seems to be contradicted by the early passage on women covering their heads. That makes it seem suspicious. The text before and after it both talk about the issue of prophesying, and the text works better without that paragraph. That helps to add to the sense that the paragraph might be a late addition. A third detail supporting it being a late addition is that in some early manuscripts this paragraph appears in a different location, as though the people copying the text were not sure where it belonged.

Others have argued that Paul did want women to stay quiet during worship. He may have wanted to keep the church orderly by having less interruptions. He may have been giving in to societal expectations of the time or he may have genuinely believed that women are inferior.

Read Ephesians 5:21 – 33. Ephesians is a very short letter that might not have been written by Paul. It is at times quoted by those who want to advocate for women obeying their husbands in everything they do. Other people point out that a larger portion of the passage is devoted to telling husbands to love their wives. Could the lines about obedience to one's husband be Paul quoting the belief he is arguing against? Could his point be that while people say women should obey their husbands, really husbands need to love their wives and, as he says at the very end, a wife should respect her husband?

Paul & Obedience to Government

Paul wrote a letter to the Christians in Rome. In it, he counsels the Christians not to fight against the government or to resist the authorities. Read this section in Romans 13:1 - 7. These line has posed challenges for Christians. Does it mean that people should never resist their rulers, no matter how unjust the rulers are? Are all rulers appointed by God?

This passage has influenced political and theological writing into modern times. Christians have struggled over whether they were to fight unjust governments or obey unjust laws.

Sometimes people attempt to dismiss it by saying that it may have been a later addition to the letter. Some say Paul wanted to advise the Roman Christians to not get themselves martyred over small issues like taxes. Others say that Paul's advice was premised on his belief that the end-times were right at hand and there was no need to resist the government, and that his advice to them at that time is not relevant to people later.

John Dominic Crossan and Marcus J Borg argue that verses Romans 12:14 - 13:10 are Paul's summary of Jesus' Sermon on the Mount (Matthew 5:39 - 48) advocating for loving one's enemy and not fighting. Can you read both texts and pick out parallels between them?

Paul & Homosexuality

Many people believe that the Bible condemns homosexuality. Others argue that the Bible does not.

There are two passages in the book of Leviticus which speak of not "men lying with a man as one would with a woman" (Leviticus 18:22 and Leviticus 20:13). The way Leviticus is structured it has a series of prohibitions leading up to the heart of the text (Leviticus 19) and then it reverses direction and goes back through similar prohibitions in the opposite order. In both Leviticus 18 and 20 there are a long list of sexual taboos. Many of the other situations described in the list include situations where one person has power over other people, so this passage again might be more about abuse than the physical act. Or the taboos might originate from concerns about keeping clean boundaries between things. Leviticus also forbids mixing two types of materials together when making clothing and it forbids eating the types of food that seem to cross boundaries, such as food like fish without fins or insects that fly. In that case, the taboo might be about keeping men's roles different from women's roles. In any case, those who wish to argue that the rule is still relevant today must explain why it would remain relevant but not the surrounding texts, such as the one which advocates for adulterers to be killed. For this reason, those trying to justify homophobia on the basis of the Bible tend to turn to Paul's writings.

In 1 Corinthians 5:9 – 6:9 Paul wrote about believers not associating with immoral people. He lists those who are greedy, idolaters, robbers, drunkards, revilers, male prostitutes and also men who have sex with other men. In Paul's letter to Romans, 1:26 – 32, he talks about humans failing to worship God and falling into all sorts of evilness instead. Among this he says women became sexually involved with other women and therefore men became sexually involved with other men, and people fell into everything bad imaginable: envy, murder, strife, gossip, slander, rebellion against parents, foolishness, etc. These two passages, as well as the passages in Leviticus, are often taken to mean that homosexuality is a sin.

One important thing to note though, is that none of these passages is really about homosexuality. Homosexuality is when men love and desire other men, or women love and desire other women. Paul would not be confronted with either of those. In ancient Rome, male-on-male sexual activity was something that someone in power does to someone with less power. In ancient Greece, it was something to be done between the older and younger person of a similar social rank. In ancient Hebrew texts, it was primarily something of abuse, done to shame or humiliate the other person.

Earlier in this book you read about Abraham's nephew, Lot, moved to a city called Sodom. Before God destroyed the city (according to the story), he sent angels to rescue Lot. While they were being rescued they were told not to look back at the city. Lot's wife did, and she was turned to a pillar of salt. The other part of that story, not discussed earlier, is what happened when the angels came. They appeared as normal men. Lot was sitting at the city gate at the time, like the elders and judges of the city did, even though he was a newcomer to the city. He rose and addressed the angels in disguise very politely and invited them to stay at his house.

That night the men of the city came to Lot's house and angrily demanded that Lot's two guests be sent out to them so they could abuse them. Lot refused, suggesting that his two daughters could be abused instead, as the men were under the protection of his house. The men rejected that offer and their response reveals a bit of why they were angry at Lot hosting the guests at his house. They said "This fellow came here as an alien, and he would play the judge! Now we will deal worse with you than with them." They were not homosexual men. They were looking to abuse the guests to assert their authority over Lot, for daring to act like an elder of the city. The angels pull Lot inside the house and blind the men outside. (The daughters were still safe inside.)

From the Biblical story of Sodom, we get the word "sodomy" which is used for man-on-man sexual activity. Many Bibles translate the word in 1 Corinthians with the word "sodomy." They are not talking about homosexuality. They are not talking about loving relationships between two men. They are talking about men using another man as a way of marking that man as his inferior.

Whatever the original intent of the passages was, the Bible has been used by many to justify the condemnation of homosexuality. Sometimes this condemnation leads to people being killed for being gay. Sometimes it means people being denied the ability to marry. Sometimes it means social rejection or people trying to change another person's sexual orientation.

Some Christians have spoken out against the Bible being used to oppress homosexuality. Some argue that the Bible passages used to criticize homosexuality are misunderstood passages about abuse, as argued here. Others argue that the condemnation of homosexuality was a mistake on the part of the Biblical writers, where they reflected the errors of their time period and that the Biblical passages calling on people to love their neighbour, not judge others, and for only the innocent to cast the first stone override these.

Revelations

The last book of the Bible may perhaps be one of the most challenging texts. It is called Revelations and claims in the first verse to have been written by someone known as John. At times people have assumed that this John was one of Jesus' disciples. A few people have said it was John the Baptist. Neither of those are likely candidates, as the text itself was likely written after both of those were believed to have died.

Revelations is written as a letter to seven churches. It is possible John was an itinerary preacher, as Paul was, and had traveled to the seven churches he names. He criticizes some of the churches for following false leaders (Revelations 2:14 – 15, 2:20) and compliments others for not. (Revelations 2:2 – 6) He criticizes one church for being "lukewarm" and not faithful enough. (Revelations 3:15 – 18)

Revelations describes a series of visions that John had. Many of the visions focus on the number seven. There is a scroll with seven seals to be broken, with a new event taking place as soon as each seal is broken. There are seven trumpets, and after each is blown something new happens. There are earthquakes. The sea becomes blood. Stars fall out of the heavens. Everything is monumental.

A pregnant woman wears a crown of twelve stars. As she prepares to give birth to someone who will rule the world, a red dragon waits to snatch the baby away. God intervenes and the woman and baby are saved. (Revelations 12:1 – 6)

Revelations tells of dragons, beasts and plagues. The world is destroyed. A rider on a white horse is labeled the "King of kings and Lord of lords." (Revelations 19:16b) The power of empire is personified as a woman of Babylon drunk on the blood of the martyrs. (Revelations 17:4 - 7)

The violence within Revelations has led many people to suggest that John would have written it while suffering from trauma. Perhaps he had lived through a time of persecution. In the book *A History of the End of the World* Jonathan Kirsch argues the opposite is true. He argues that John did not suffer through a time of persecution but was instead angry with the way in which the Christians of his time could fit in with pagan society.

The book of Revelations is not easy reading. Even those who believe the book to describe the future disagree on how to interpret it. There are several main divisions in thought, mainly divided on their interpretation of Revelations 20.

Revelations 20 describes four visions. In the first vision Satan is locked in a pit for a thousand years, after which temporarily released. In the second vision those who were martyred come to life and reign with Christ for a thousand years. In the third vision Satan is released and there is war. In the fourth vision all the dead are raised and judged.

Postmillennialism is the view that Jesus doesn't return until after Satan has been set free. In this world view Christians are responsible for creating the thousand year peaceful paradise. The Social Gospel Movement of the late 19th century and early 20th century was influenced by postmillennialism. Members of the Social Gospel movement wanted to eliminate the problems of their day, including crime, poverty, and alcoholism.

Premillennialism is the view that Jesus will return himself create a thousand years of peaceful paradise. This belief does not require people to try to create a paradise on earth themselves, but instead to be loyal enough to Jesus to be found worthy of living in that paradise he creates.

The time in which Satan was to be released has been called the Great Tribulation. In the 19th century many American Christians began to doubt that God would allow his devote believers to endure the Great

Tribulation, and a belief began to develop that God would take his followers safely to heaven to wait out the Great Tribulation. Only after Satan was banished at the end would these followers return to the new Earth in order to live with those of the dead judged worthy. This miraculous rescuing of the believers was called the Rapture.

Believers in the rapture took inspiration from a paragraph Paul wrote:

[13] Brothers and sisters, we do not want you to be uninformed about those who sleep in death, so that you do not grieve like the rest of mankind, who have no hope. [14] For we believe that Jesus died and rose again, and so we believe that God will bring with Jesus those who have fallen asleep in him. [15] According to the Lord's word, we tell you that we who are still alive, who are left until the coming of the Lord, will certainly not precede those who have fallen asleep. [16] For the Lord himself will come down from heaven, with a loud command, with the voice of the archangel and with the trumpet call of God, and the dead in Christ will rise first. [17] After that, we who are still alive and are left will be caught up together with them in the clouds to meet the Lord in the air. And so we will be with the Lord forever. [18] Therefore encourage one another with these words. (1 Thessalonians 4:13–18 NIV)

Remember that Paul had believed the general resurrection would come within his lifetime and he encouraged his followers to believe that too. As the time slipped on, the question arose. What happens to those who died before the general resurrection? Paul was writing to comfort his followers. He might have been inspired by the image of a royal triumph. An emperor visiting one of his cities would be greeted with trumpets sounding. Before the emperor reached the city he would pass the graveyards. The dead would "meet him." It wasn't until the 19th century that this began to be interpreted literally as a promise that the dead and the faithful would rise into the air.

Ever since Revelations was written people have watched for signs that its predictions were being carried out. Plagues and climate changes have been taken as warning signs. So have wars. Napoleon and Hitler were both seen as possible anti-Christs, in their day, as have some popes. Revelation 13:3-8 describe an evil beast "given authority over every tribe, people, language and nation." While the text can be interpreted that the beast is conflict or evil personified, others take the passage more literally. They believe that it refers to there being a single government ruling over the world. Some people, assuming the end times are coming soon, have even cast the United Nations in the role of this great beast!

Revelations 21:9 – 14 describes a new Jerusalem with a gates inscribed with the names of the twelve tribes of Israel. Ever since the exile, Jewish people had hoped God to restore their nation to its earlier glory. People had been optimistic when the Persians had allowed some exiles to return to set up the province of Judea and rebuild the temple, but that had been a limited restoration. Hope was reborn again under the Maccabees and again when the Jews had revolted against the Romans. Yet none of these had restored the Davidic kingdom in its glory and the Roman destruction of the temple in 70 CE had confirmed that none of those were the promised restoration.

Many Christians have seen their religion as the rightful heir to the promises they believe God made to the Abraham, David, and the kingdoms of Judah and Israel. To them Jesus was the fulfillment of many of the prophecies and his return would bring the promises' completion. This meant that some Christians interpreted the promise of a new Jerusalem as a promise to them of a new city of God. Over the years many saw it separate from the historic Jerusalem. Some expected it to appear in other parts of the world. When Europeans found their way over to the continents now known as America, some interpreted this as the new world God had promised and expected their cities there to be the new Jerusalem.

Other Christians believed that Revelations 21:9 – 14 refers to the city of Jerusalem becoming a Jewish city again. In the 19th century an American named William Eugene Blackstone became convinced that a Jewish

Israel was a necessary precursor for the second coming of Jesus. He worked to make that part of America's foreign policy and hopes of bringing about the end times have continued to influence American foreign policy ever since.

Follow-up Activity

1. Read the full book of Revelations. Then watch the television miniseries *Good Omens* and count the Biblical references you can find in it.

The visions of Revelations are tantalizing. Many assume that John was hinting at things that had already happened, historical figures, and things he thought were yet to come. The visions contain just enough detail to allow people to formulate their theories about what they mean, but not quite enough detail to allow confirmation of any of the theories. Revelations 13:18 mentions the "number of the beast" which is either 666 or 616, depending on which version of the Bible one believes. Various theories have been proposed for what this means, with many people arguing for a code that would link it with the Roman Emperor Nero. Attempts to match the seven kings mentioned in Revelations 17:9 – 10 with Roman emperors have also created mixed results with different people guessing which emperors should or shouldn't be included.

For those who believe that Revelations accurate describes the future, there are many more avenues of speculation. Some speculate as to what Revelations 13:17 means when it says that unless someone has the mark of the beast one would not be able to buy and sell. Likely this originated as a reference to coins, as the Greek word used for "mark" can mean engraving or coin, but some believers today suggest it could be a reference to microchips implanted into the human to allow bank account access without needing a bank card.

A Few Last Thoughts

The Bible stories have been interpreted over and over again, with new arguments and disagreements at each step of the way. Many modern concepts about angels, heaven, hell, and salvation were created in the years after the Bible was written. In the late fourth century the Bishop Augustine of Hippo wrote his thoughts about the Bible and God. His thoughts became so well respected that people hundreds of years later would read Bible stories trusting that the stories were supposed to be interpreted as he did. An early fourteenth century Italian author Dante helped shape people's images of heaven and hell with his book *Divine Comedy*. The fifteenth century religious reformer Martin Luther provided yet another way of understanding the Bible. Seventeenth century poet John Milton helped shape people's notion of the devil with his literary work *Paradise Lost*. Those are but a few of the many influential writers that stand between us and the ancient understandings of the Bible.

In this book I have tried to step back from the later theologians and approached the Bible as an ancient text. A group of people conceived of being in a covenantal relationship with their god, similar to the way smaller kingdoms would pledge loyalty to a more powerful king, crediting that powerful king with granting them their land. They claimed their god gave them their land and would protect them. When the northern kingdom fell, they said it was the punishment because the northern kingdom had not put its trust properly in their god. Under King Hezekiah and again under King Josiah, the southern kingdom attempted to reform its religious practices to be able to withstand the pressure of foreign empires. When the southern kingdom fell, they rewrote their history to support them as a people united in their faith traditions and in their temple. Their religious beliefs were shaped by the contact they had with other ancient kingdoms, and while their god likely originated as a warrior god not unlike their neighbours' gods, they eventually pictured him as the creator of the whole universe. Visionaries dreamed of him restoring Jerusalem to glory and putting back on the throne someone of their royal family.

Centuries past, and during the reign of the Roman Emperor Tiberius, a group of Jewish people declared that the promises made by their prophets had come true in the form of a poor carpenter. The carpenter's name was Jesus and he traveled through Galilee teaching with parables and interpreting the religious law before traveling to Jerusalem where he was put to death in the manner of traitors and rebels. His followers argued that he was the first to return to life in what they thought would be general resurrection of the dead. The war between the Jewish people and the Romans in the late 60s was probably interpreted by at least some of his followers as a sign that the end times were quickly coming, but the failure of the revolt and the destruction of Jerusalem did not break their faith. New scriptures were written declaring that Jesus' kingdom would still come. Over the years this kingdom of Jesus has been interpreted in many ways, so that some people are still waiting with expectation.

This is only one way of telling the story. I believe that everything before the monarchical period must be considered myth and legend. I believe that monotheism may have been a late edition to the Hebrew religion, and that at the times when the early kings worshiped multiple gods their community would not have seen this as a problem or foreign influence, as the Biblical writers want to portray it. I believe much of the Old Testament was written during the exilic and post-exilic time periods. I believe that Jesus' early followers envisioned their god creating a kingdom here on this Earth, during their lifetime, and not in heaven or thousands of years later.

I come to these beliefs from reading many academic articles written by Biblical scholars, but there is still much more to be learned. I encourage you to continue reading and studying. Archaeological discoveries, new translations of ancient text, and further debate will likely lead to new theories and new models being proposed in the coming years, as people continue to search for the origins of the Biblical texts.

Index

5th Monarchy 94
Abel 85
Abraham 9, 21, 65, 118, 129
Absalom 34–35, 37
Acts of the Apostles 117
Adad-Nirari III of Assyria 50, 51
Adam 84–85
Advocate (Satan) 80–82
Ahab 41
Ahaz 53, 100
Ahaziah 45
Ahaziah of Judah 48
Albertz, Rainer 59, 81–82
Alexander the Great 66, 89
Ammonites 9, 28
Amnon 34
Anderson, James S. 20
Anthony, Marc 90
Antiochus IV 89
Antipater the Idumaean 90
antisemitism 97, 110–112, 114
Apollonius of Tyana 116
Apollos 121
Arameans 9, 42, 43–44, 51, 100
Aristobulus II 90–91
ark of the covenant 17, 25
Asherah 21, 22, 27, 41
Aššur 20, 51, 55
Augustine of Hippo 85
Azazel 70
Baal 20–21, 22, 27, 41–42, 45, 49, 50, 58, 83
Baal-zebub 45
Babel 87
baptism 99–100, 102, 117
Barnabas 120
Bathsheba 34, 101
Beatitudes 107
Behemoth 79
Ben-Hadad 42
Ben-Hadad, son of Hazael 50
Benjamin 28, 63
Bethel 27, 40, 45, 58
Bethlehem 67, 99
Blackstone, William Eugene 129
Blake, William 79
Boaz 67–68
Boney M. (music group) 60
Caesar, Julius 90
Cain 85
Cambyses II 62
Chronicles 36, 66
Cornelius 119
covenant 19, 57–58, 69
Cush 88
Cyrus the Great 62, 66
Dagon 20, 25
Dan 40, 49
Daniel 92–95
Darius I 62
David 29–37, 65, 67, 102, 129
Deborah 22, 65
Deuteronomic historians 6, 28, 31, 41, 50, 52, 56, 57, 69
Deuteronomy 57, 65, 67
dietary laws 69, 92, 106, 120, 122

Douglas, Lloyd C. 103
Eden 83–85
Edomites 11
Egypt 9, 14–16, 16, 39, 59
Elamites 55, 70
Eleazer 90
Eli 25–136, 33
Elijah 45–47, 104
Elisha 45–47, 48–50
Esau 10
Eucharist 122
Eve 84–85
Exodus 14–136, 65
Ezekiel 60
Ezra 62–64, 67
fasting 29, 44, 72, 102, 108
Fiddler on the Roof 95
Funk, Robert 112
Gamaliel 117
Gath 32
Gedaliah 60
Genesis 83, 88
Gideon 22, 65
Gilgal 18, 27, 45
God-fearer 119–120
Goliath 31
Gomorrah 88
Habriu 17–19
Hadad 20
Hagar 10
Ham 88
Hannah 26
Hazael 48–50
Herod Antipas 100
Herod the Great 91, 96, 98–100, 113
Hezekiah 58, 131
Hilkiah 57
Hittite 19
holiness code 70
Hoshea 52
Hyrcanus II 90
Hyrcanus, John 90
Isaac 10
Isaiah 100
Ishbaal 33
Ishmael 10–11
Jacob 10–136, 12–13, 64
Jael 22
Jehoahaz 59
Jehoshaphat 43–44
Jehu 50
Jeremiah 59–61
Jericho 17, 46
Jeroboam 39
Jesus 96
Jesus Seminar 112
Jezebel 41–42, 49
Job 76–79, 80–82
John the Baptist 99–100, 102
Johoash of Judah (also Joash) 49–50
Jonah 72–73
Jonathan 31, 33
Joseph, husband of Mary 98–100
Joseph, son of Jacob 12–13, 92, 118
Josephus 106
Joshua 17

Josiah 57–58, 59, 131
Judah 13
Kirsch, Jonathan 128
Laban 10
Lachish 61
Lamentations 60
Leah 11–136
Leviathan 79
Leviticus 15, 65, 69–70, 83, 126
Lot 9, 126
lots, method of divination 28, 29, 72
loving one's enemy 70, 107–109, 111, 125
Lucifer 52
Luke 98–100
Maccabees 89–91, 92
Manasseh 56
Marduk 1, 55
Mark 98, 102–105
mark of the beast 130
Mary, mother of Jesus 98–100
Mattathias 89
Matthew 98–100
Menahem 51
Mephibosheth 33, 35
Meyers, Carol 84–85
Micaiah 43–44, 48
Midianites 14, 22
Moabites 9, 46–47, 67
monarchy 28, 31, 37, 38
monolatrists 54
monolatry 1, 21
Moses 14–136, 39, 57, 99, 104, 118
Mot 41
Mount Sinai 15
Na'aman, Nadav 18
Naboth 43–44
Naomi 67
Nathan 34
Nazirite 23
Nebuchadnezzar 59, 92–95
Necho II of Egypt 59
Nehemiah 62–64, 67
nephilim 86
Nero 96, 130
Nimrod 88
Nineveh 72–73
Noah 86–88
Numbers 15, 65, 70
Omri 41, 50
Ortlund, Dane 104
parables 34, 102, 110–112
Paul 118, 119–120, 121–123, 124–125, 129
Pekah 51, 53, 100
Peter 104
Pharisees 106
Philistines 23, 25, 31
Pliny the Younger 112
Pompey 90–91
Priestly Code 69–70
prophecy 44, 47, 48, 73, 94
Proverbs 74–75
Ptolemy II Philadelphus 66

Q Gospel 98
Rachel 10–136
Ramoth-Gilead 43–44, 48–50
Rebecca 10
Rehab 17, 101
Rehoboam 15, 39
resurrection 106, 120, 122–123, 129
Ruth 67–68, 101
Sadducees 106
Samaria 41, 62, 62–64, 64, 110–112
Samson 23–24, 65
Samuel 28, 33
Sarah 10, 64
Sargon II 52
Satan 102, 128
Saul 28–33, 65
scapegoat 70
Seleucid Emperor 89
Sermon on the Mount 107–109, 125
Shakespeare, William 121
Shalmaneser III 50
Shalmaneser V 52
Shaphan 57
Shem 87
sheol 89
Shiloh 25, 27
Sisera 22
Sodom 88, 126–127
Solomon 15, 39, 65
Son of Man 94
Stephen 117–118
Tiberius 131
Tiglath-Pileser III 51, 53
Trajan 112
transubstantiation 122
Tukulti-Ninurta I 88
Ur 10, 20, 88
Van Der Joorn, Kare 74
Wilson, Stephen M. 24
Yamm 20, 79, 83
Zarephath 41
Zeus 2, 16, 20, 89, 94, 119

Selective Bibliography

Albertz, Rainer. *A History of Israelite Religion in the Old Testament Period: From the Beginnings to the End of the Monarchy. Vol. 1*. Westminster John Knox Press, 1994.

Albertz, Rainer. *A History of Israelite Religion in the Old Testament Period, volume II: from the Exile to the Maccabees.* Westminster John Knox Press, 1994.

Armstrong, Karen. *The Great Transformation: The Beginning of our Religious Traditions.* Anchor, 2006.

Balentine, Samuel Eugene. *The Torah's Vision of Worship.* Fortress Press, 1999.

Borg, Marcus J., and John Dominic Crossan. *The first Paul: Reclaiming the Radical Visionary Behind the Church's Conservative Icon.* Harper Collins, 2009.

Boyarin, Daniel. *The Jewish Gospels: The Story of the Jewish Christ.* New Press/ORIM, 2012.

Crossan, John Dominic. *How to read the Bible and still be a Christian: Struggling with Divine Violence from Genesis through Revelation.* Harper Collins, 2015.

Crossan, John Dominic. *God and empire: Jesus against Rome, then and now.* Harper Collins, 2007.

Crossan, John Dominic, and Jonathan L. Reed. *In search of Paul: How Jesus's Apostle opposed Rome's Empire with God's Kingdom: a New Vision of Paul's words & world.* London: SPCK, 2005.

Crossan, John Dominic. *The First Paul.* London:SPCK 2009.

Douglas, Mary. *Leviticus as Literature.* OUP Oxford, 1999.

Douglas, Mary. *Jacob's Tears: the Priestly Work of Reconciliation.* Oxford University Press, USA, 2004.

Gabel, John B., ed. *The Bible as Literature: an introduction.* Oxford University Press, USA, 2006.

Gottwald, Norman Karol, and Barbara J. MacHaffie. *The Hebrew Bible: A Socio-literary Introduction.* Vol. 205. Philadelphia: Fortress Press, 1985.

Kirsch, Jonathan. *A History of the End of the World: How the most controversial book in the Bible changed the course of western civilization.* HarperSanFrancisco, 2006.

Meyers, Carol L. *Discovering Eve: ancient Israelite women in context.* Oxford University Press on Demand, 1991.

Na'aman, Nadav. *Canaan in the Second Millennium BCE. Vol. 2.* Eisenbrauns, 2005.

Na'aman, Nadav. *Ancient Israel's History and Historiography: the First Temple Period: Collected Essays. Vol. 3.* Eisenbrauns, 2006.

Saldarini, Anthony J. *Pharisees, Scribes and Sadducees in Palestinian Society: A Sociological Approach.* Wm. B. Eerdmans Publishing, 2001.

Tadmor, Hayim, Benno Landserber and Simo Parpola. "The Sin of Sargon and Sennacherib's Last Will."

Wilson, Stephen M. "Samson the man-child: failing to come of age in the Deuteronomistic History." *Journal of Biblical Literature* 133.1 (2014): 43-60.

Bible Translations

Alter, Robert. *The Hebrew Bible: A Translation with Commentary. 3 Volumes.* WW Norton, 2019.

Attridge, Harold W., Wayne A. Meeks, and Jouette M. Bassler. *The HarperCollins Study Bible: New Revised Standard Version, Including the Apocryphal/Deuterocanonical Books.* HarperOne, 2006.

The Holy Bible, New International Version. ®NIV® Copyright © 1973, 1978, 1984 by International Bible Society

Vocabulary Review

Match the following terms with their descriptions.

1. Proverbs
2. Psalms
3. Exodus
4. Deuteronomy
5. manna
6. fasting
7. ark of the covenant
8. second temple
9. kosher / kashrut
10. parables
11. drawing lots
12. scapegoat
13. leviathan
14. monotheism
15. monolatry
16. polytheism
17. Samaria
18. Jerusalem
19. Nazirite

a. a sea monster
b. capital city of Israel, the northern kingdom
c. someone whose dedication to God was expressed partially through not cutting his hair and not drinking alcohol
d. a gold covered wooden box believed to contain two tablets given to Moses
e. built in the Persian period and destroyed in 70 CE
f. a goat sent out into the desert as part of a ritual, now a term for anyone upon whom collective guilt is dumped
g. the belief that only one god exists
h. pertaining to the dietary laws
i. hymns or poems, also the name of a book of the Bible.
j. a belief in many gods
k. food given by God while the Israelites wandered in the desert.
l. name of a book in the Bible, and a reference to the Israelites leaving Egypt under Moses
m. fifth book in the Bible, part of which was likely the book found during Josiah's temple reconstruction
n. a belief that many gods exist but only one should be worshiped
o. short pithy bits of wisdom, but also the name of a Bible book
p. a method of divination
q. capital city of David's kingdom, this became the capital of the Judah, southern kingdom.
r. short teaching stories
s. purposely going without food

Memory Match Cards

Abraham	Patriarch who left Ur with the promise that his descendants would inherit Canaan.	Isaac	Son of Abraham.
Jacob	Second son of Isaac. He stole his older brother's birthright.	Joseph	Favourite son of Jacob. Sold as a slave but became second in command in Egypt.
Samuel	Prophet who heard the voice of God while serving in the shrine at Bethel.	Saul	First king anointed by Samuel after the twelve tribes ask for a king.
David	Man who kills the giant Goliath and becomes king, expanding the kingdom and capturing Jerusalem.	Bathsheba	Wife of Uriah, she became wife to David after her husband was sent to die. Mother to Solomon.
Solomon	Son of David who becomes king after David's death and has a temple built.	Jeroboam	King of the Israel, the northern kingdom, he had golden calves set up in Bethel and Dan..
Ahab	King whose wife had a man killed so that he could purchase a vineyard he wanted. He died in a war against the Arameans..	Jezebel	Princess of Sidion, she married Ahab and helped him secure a vineyard he wanted. After her sons' deaths she was thrown from a window.
Elijah	Prophet who challenged the prophets of Baal to a competition. Instead of dying, he disappeared into the sky on a chariot of fire.	Elisha	Prophet teased for being bald, he inherited the mantle of Elijah.
Josiah	King put on the throne as a child. During his reign a book was found in the temple. Reforms were made to try to follow the book.	Jeremiah	Prophet who urged that the people not resist the Babylonians but accept Babylonian rule.

www.ingramcontent.com/pod-product-compliance
Lightning Source LLC
Chambersburg PA
CBHW081415080526
44589CB00016B/2546